Preface

This book is mainly targeted for the exam of Society & Stratification for all Universities. It has been introduced in market after seeing the huge demand of ready to grasp material for exams with high level of quality, and its un-availability in market. We the GullyBaba Publishing House took a step ahead to publish the quality material focusing on exams at the same time giving you indepth knowledge about the subject.

GPH Book is the pioneer effort that provides a unique methodology so as to perform better in exams. If your goal is to attain higher grade use this powerful study tool independently or along with your text.

*On the Web : **www.gullybaba.com** is the vital resource for your exams acting as catalyst to boost up your preparation. Now you can access us on the net through **www.doeacconline.com**, **www.ignouonline.com**, **and** **www.astrologyeverywhere.com.***

We gratefully acknowledges the significant contributions of Mr. S.K. Goel, Mr. Dinesh Verma, Mr. Mahesh Chand, Mrs. Bimla Devi, Mrs. Bhawna Verma and our experts in bringing out this publication.

New Delhi

Dear Reader, You are welcome in the world of GullyBaba Publishing House.

By long, in deep study & Research, we assure / guarantee you the most reliable, latest & accurate information on the subject.

We still believe that there is always a scope for improvement.

You a reader can be our best guide in making this book more interesting & user friendly.

We welcome your valuable suggestions.

Feedback about the book can be sent at **feedback@gullybaba.com.**

Publisher.

TOPICS COVERED

Society & Stratification

ESO-14

For

Bachelor of Arts [BA]

By

Neetu Sharma

Useful For

IGNOU, KSOU (Karnataka), Bihar University (Muzaffarpur), Nalanda University, Jamia Millia Islamia, Vardhman Mahaveer Open University (Kota), Uttarakhand Open University, Kurukshetra University, Seva Sadan's College of Education (Maharashtra), Lalit Narayan Mithila University, Andhra University, Pt. Sunderlal Sharma (Open) University (Bilaspur), Annamalai University, Bangalore University, Bharathiar University, Bharathidasan University, HP University, Centre for distance and open learning, Kakatiya University (Andhra Pradesh), KOU (Rajasthan), MPBOU (MP), MDU (Haryana), Punjab University, Tamilnadu Open University, Sri Padmavati Mahila Visvavidyalayam (Andhra Pradesh), Sri Venkateswara University (Andhra Pradesh), UCSDE (Kerala), University of Jammu, YCMOU, Rajasthan University, UPRTOU, Kalyani University, Banaras Hindu University (BHU) and all other Indian Universities.

GULLYBABA PUBLISHING HOUSE (P) LTD.

ISO 9001 & ISO 14001 CERTIFIED CO.

Published by:

GullyBaba Publishing House Pvt. Ltd.

Regd. Office:
2525/193, 1st Floor, Onkar Nagar-A,
Tri Nagar, Delhi-110035
(From Kanhaiya Nagar Metro Station Towards Old Bus Stand)
Ph. 011-27387998, 27384836, 27385249
+919350849407

Branch Office:
1A/2A, 20, Hari Sadan,
Ansari Road, Daryaganj,
New Delhi-110002
Ph. 011-23289034
011-45794768

E-mail: hello@gullybaba.com, **Website**:GullyBaba.com, GPHbook.com

New Edition

Price:

ISBN: 978-93-81690-26-0

Contents

Question Papers

Introducing Social Stratification

Q1. Describe caste as a system of social stratification. **[June 07, Q. 1]**

Ans. The Indian caste system describes the social stratification and social boundaries in the Indian subcontinent, in which social classes are defined by thousands of endogamous genetic groups, often termed as *Jaties* or castes. Within a jâti, there exist exogamous groups known as gotras, the lineage or clan of an individual, although in a handful of sub-castes like Shakadvipi, endogamy within a gotra is permitted and alternative mechanisms of restricting endogamy are used (e.g. banning endogamy within a surname). Although generally identified with Hinduism, the caste system was also observed among followers of other religions in the Indian subcontinent, including some groups of Muslims and Christians. The Indian Constitution has outlawed caste based discrimination, in keeping with the socialist, secular, democratic principles that founded the nation. Caste barriers have mostly broken down in large cities, though they persist in rural areas of the country, where 72% of India's population resides. Nevertheless, the caste system, in various forms, continues to survive in modern India strengthened by a combination of social perceptions and divisive politics.

Social mobility: Social mobility is the degree to which an individual's family or group's of social status can change throughout the course of their life through a system of social hierarchy or stratification. Subsequently, it is also the degree to which an individual's or group's descendants move up and down the class system. The individual or family can move up or down the social classes based on achievements or factors beyond their control. It is a sociological concept.

Principles of hierarchy: A hierarchy is an arrangement of items (objects, names, values, categories, etc.), in which the items are represented as being "above," "below," or "at the same level as" one another. The word derives from the Greek president of "sacred rites, high-priest" and that from "sacred to lead, to rule" . The word can also refer to a series of such items so arranged. The first use of the word "hierarchy" cited by the Oxford English Dictionary was in 1880, when it was used in reference to the three orders of three angels as depicted by Pseudo-Dionysius the Areopagite. Pseudo-Dionysius used the word both in reference to the celestial hierarchy and the ecclesiastical hierarchy Caste and class point towards inequality and hierarchy. In both the cases, the principle of organisation differs. The core features of caste are: endogamy or marriage within caste, occupational differentiation and hereditary specialisation of occupations, notion of pollution and a ritual hierarchy in which Brahmins are generally at the top. Classes, on the other hand, broadly refer to economic basis of ownership or non-ownership relation to the means of production. Classes are sub-divided in terms of types of ownership and control of economic resources and the type of services contributed to the process of production. The Brahmanical ritual hierarchy of the caste is also not universally applicable and upheld by all. In many cases, ritual hierarchy is only contextual. The prosperous Jats in North India enjoy social and political dominance without equivalent ritual status. In most popular renditions of caste, hierarchy alone is emphasized and that too from Brahmanical point of view. Sometimes, caste works as a discrete community, without hierarchical relationship to other segments of society. Our conceptual categories do not always recapture the existing social reality. For instance, a conceptual distinction is often made between sharecroppers and agricultural laborers. In actual life, there is a high degree of overlap and they do not constitute discrete entities. Similar overlap is found in the rentier-landlord and cultivator-owner categories. The picture becomes hazier when we turn to caste-class configuration. Caste and class resemble each other in certain respects and differ in others. Castes constitute the status groups or communities that can be defined in terms of ownership of property, occupation and style of life. Social honour is closely linked to ritual values in this closed system. Class positions also tend to be associated with social honour however they are defined more in terms of ownership or non-ownership of means of production. The classes are much more open and fluid and have scope of individual upward social mobility. In caste system, only an entire segment can move upward, and hence, the mobility is much slower. Although there is considerable divergence between the hierarchy of caste and that of class, the top and bottom segments of the class system are largely subsumed under the caste structure. The upper castes own means of production (land in rural areas). The landless agrarian proletarian coincides with the lower castes or dalits who provide labour services for the entire upper caste people as well as rich prosperous farmers of intermediate level. At the intermediate level, articulation of class-identities is more complex. The process of differentiation of communities dislocates class-relations from the caste-structure. If caste and class show a fair degree of overlap at the top and bottom level and in some cases appears almost co-terminus, the picture is quite ambiguous at the intermediate level of caste hierarchy. Similarly, the processes of modernisation especially urbanisation, acquisition of education and new skills act as the forces of dislocation that puncture the forces of social inertia and modify caste-rigidity.

Demographic features of caste: The demography of caste or jati in India has remained extremely diversified over millennia. Studies shows that beyond a radius of 20 to 200 miles, a jati is not recognized as social group It is only recognizable with reference to the varna model. Hence, the significance of the varna as a sociological frame of reference. Also, jatis have always existed as regional or sub-regional groups numbering into thousands. The recent survey by the Anthropological Survey of Indian reports the existence of 4635 communities or caste-like groups in India. It also finds that almost all religious groups are divided into various communities which have jati-traits. Jatis also bear local and regional cultural markers based on the ecology, local history or mythology. Traditionally, castes both in villages and the urban centers were bound into systemic relationship of reciprocities or work and economic exchange or exchange of services etc. In this sense, caste system functioned on the basis of mutual cooperation and interdependence. If formed an organic system. Both in villages and cities, castes had their panchayat organisations. Even though these had nucleus in a particular village or urban centre, such panchayats or guilds (in the cities) had a network of organisation beyond a village or urban centre. If an inter-caste conflict emerged for any reason which violated the caste norms of reciprocity and if dispute could not be settle in the council of the village or the city (comprising elders from various castes) the matter was taken up in the caste panchayats. It functioned both as a body to protect rights and privileges of the caste as well as served as a mechanism for resolution of conflicts.

The stability of the caste as a system of social stratification was based on the economy which remained agrarian mercantile for a very long time. This was coupled with the stable population which due to high rate of mortality continued to remain at the level of about hundred millions for several centuries. This spell of stable population was only broken after the industrial revolution which made more advanced life-saving medical aids available to control the death rate rampant though epidemics and natural disasters of the past. The British rule in India on the one hand, destroyed the traditional base of the economy and its integrative relationship with the social structure, particularly the caste system, and on the other, new technologies of medical care were available which brought down the death rate. Thus, population of India began to go up as the Census records from 1931 onwards reveal. The British colonial policy made India a dependent economy and destroyed the foundation of its traditional manufacturing economy and trade.

Massive de-urbanisation and de-industrialisation followed and pressure on land in villages increased. The traditional balance of economy and social structure which existed between the rural and urban centers and between agriculture and manufacture and trade was vitally destabilized. At the same time, the British policy was also geared to continue the use of caste and religion as a frame of reference in the implementation of social and political policies. Caste based Census operations conducted by the British made people for the first time conscious of caste as a political phenomenon throughout the country and it led to the growth of public demand by various castes placed lower in caste ranking for being placed into higher caste hierarchy. This triggered the process of not only Sanskritisation, that is adopting the style of life, food habits, dress and ways of worship etc. of the upper castes by lower castes and then demanding that they be recognized as a higher caste status, but it also contributed to, as described by M.N. Srinivas, to the process of Westernisation (adopting the western style dress, way of living and modes of cultural expression etc.)

Q2. Describe the conceptual and theoretical issues of social stratification.

Or

Discuss about Max Weber's concept of class?

[June 07, Q. 9(b)]

Ans. In sociology and anthropology, **social stratification** is the hierarchical arrangement of individuals into social classes, castes, and divisions within a society. These hierarchies are not present in all societies, but are quite common in state-level societies (as distinguished from hunter-gatherer or other social arrangements). According to Peter Robert Saunders, in modern Western societies, stratification depends on social and economic classes comprising three main layers: upper class, middle class, and lower class. Each class is further subdivided into smaller classes related, in part, to occupation. The term *stratification* derives from the geological concept of *strata,* or rock layers created by natural processes.

Views of Karl Marx

Karl Marx made a seminal contribution to the concept of social stratification. For him, stratification divides the society into two mutually opposed or contrary social categories where one exploits the other. In his view, there are two main social groups society. First, there are those who own and control resources, technology, and valued goods. These things are collectively called *means of production*. The second group is of those who do not have any ownership or control over these things. They work for the members of the first category, who own and control resources and thus survive on the wages they receive from their employers for rendering their labour. For both the social categories, Marx used the word 'class', which is defined in terms of the *ownership* and *non-ownership* of the means of production. Thus, class is a social group whose members share a similar relationship to the means of production.

Marx also believes that those who own the means of production also exercise political power. Economic power leads to political and legal power, because of which they are able to consolidate their control over economic resources. Therefore, Marx uses the concept of 'ruling class' for the class that owns the means of production, because this ownership gives them political and legal power. The class that does not own but works on the means of production owned by the first class, is called the 'service class'. It remains in a subordinate position because it lacks the political power. It has to abide by the laws that the ruling class creates to protect its interests. For Marx, law is an instrument of exploitation because the ruling class creates and controls it.

Marx believed that not all societies were divided into classes. The first stage in the evolution of human societies was one where classes did not exist. In this society, there was neither law nor state. Nor was there any private property. Complete equality prevailed in this society, and this society was defined as having primitive communism.

After this stage, human societies were always marked by a division into classes, the ruling class and the service class. According to Marx, the last stage of a class-divided society would be capitalism, where conflict would take place between the ruling class and the service class. This conflict that Marx called class conflict would culminate in a society where there would be no classes. This would be a state of classlessness. This society is called the **communist society.** Thus, for Marx, stratification would not be a characteristic of human society for all times to come. Human society began with classlessness and would return to it after spending thousands of years in a class-divided system.

Views of Max Weber

After Marx, Max Weber made an important contribution to the ideas on stratification. While Marx thinks that the principle form of stratification is *class,* Weber believes that besides class, there are two other forms, namely *status* and power.

Like Marx, Weber also sees class in economic terms. But he moves ahead of Marx because he says that classes develop in market economies. Thus, class is a characteristic of capitalist societies because these societies have market economies. In capitalism, family is not the unit of production. The market takes over the processes of production and distribution of produce. People depend upon the market for virtually all types of goods and services.

People sell their skills in the market and derive their livelihood from the income they get. Certain skills (like of engineering, technology, medicine) fetch a higher price in the market than certain others. Those who have such skills, which may be called marketable skills, have better chances to survive and make use of the facilities than those who are unskilled or semi-skilled, or have those skills that are not a priority in the market.

The same principle also applies to property. The returns from property vary with respect to its location, even the part of the city or village where it is located. The market also determines the prices of property. Form this, it follows that the chances of survival of an individual, which are called life chances, depend upon the market situation. The individual's skills determine his class, which is dependent upon the market. People who have no ownership of property but have skills that are much needed by the market have good chances to survive. Thus, they are not 'have-nots', as the Marxian theory would call them. Weber also rejected the idea of the ruling class.

· According to Marx, class that owns the means of production also controls political power.

· According to Weber, ownership of the means of production may not always lead to a control over political power.

· Individuals get political power not because of economic power but because of their political skills, like their ability to communicate as effectively as possible, their ideology, their manifesto, their organisational skills and commitment to goals, etc.

· Thus, economic power and political power may not go hand in hand in modern societies.

· There will be two hierarchies, the economic, which has people that own the means of production, and the political, which has people who exercise political power.

The functional theory of Talcott Parson: Talcott Parsons believe that order, stability and cooperation in society are based on value consensus that is a general agreement by members of society concerning what is good and worthwhile. Stratification system derives from common values it follows from the existence of values that individuals will be evaluated and therefore placed in some form of rank order. Stratification is the ranking of units in a social system in accordance with the common value system. Those who perform successfully in terms of society's values will be ranked highly and they will be likely to receive a variety of rewards and will be accorded high prestige since they exemplify and personify common values. According to Kingsley Davis and Moore stratification exists in every known human society.

All social system shares certain functional prerequisites which must be met if the system is to survive and operate efficiently. One such prerequisite is role allocation and performance. This means that all roles must be filled. They will be filled by those best able to perform them. The necessary training for them is undertaken and that the roles are performed conscientiously. Davis and

Moore, argue that all societies need some mechanism for insuring effective role allocation and performance. This mechanism is social stratification which they see as a system which attaches unequal rewards and privileges to the positions in society. They concluded that social stratification is a device by which societies insure that the most important positions are conscientiously filled by the most qualified persons.

The Rice of Capitalism: The rise of capitalism ushered a new period in social evolution. The dialectical process of historical change both through the innovation of new technologies and social institutions made feudalism obsolescent and it was replaced by the institution of capitalism. Class structure emerges in full measure by this time by the industrial revolution. The growth in the factory mode of production of commodities, massive migration of peasants and worker from the rural areas to the urban centres and accumulation of capital by expanded use of the market made possible by the new technology of transport and colonial expansion of the European powers changed the system of social stratification. The main classes which emerged in the new scheme of social stratification were, the capitalist entrepreneurs and the working classes. A new form of acute antagonistic relationship now emerges between these two classes. This relates to demand of reasonable working hours, reasonable wages, better conditions of employment and work etc. These forces of conflict, according to Marx should have culminated into the replacement of capitalism by its obsolescence like in the case of feudalism by a socialist system, it would be, according to Marx based on collective mode of production without private ownership of capital and pursuit of profit. In many countries, socialist did come into existence by revolution of the peasants and working classes For example, former USSR, China, Vietnam etc. but as envisaged by Marx, capitalism has not been rendered obsolete as yet. On the contrary it has shown new resilience where as many socialist economies have either been weakened or have been replaced by capitalist institutions.

The essence of Marxist theory, however, does not depend upon the process of the formation of social strata or its structural composition as much as upon its basic premise on the nature of social order. Marx treats social order as a product of historical-materialistic conditions; these are defined by the modes of production and relations of production, and are continually undergoing change due to technological innovations and attempts within the society to resolve various social conflicts which are universal. Social order is thus based on the relationship among various groups which are inherently antagonistic, and cannot be resolved without basically altering the social order or system itself. The process by which this takes place, and in which the exploited classes such as the industrial workers and peasants are partners in class struggle against the capitalist classes in termed as revolution. The new social order, the socialist society which emerges through revolution does not have a place for strata based on inequalities which generate antagonism, but has social differentiation of work without class or social stratification. Such strata are called 'nonantagonistic'.

Darhendorf and Coser: In addition to the Marxist formulation, there are other theoretical perspectives in sociology of social stratification which treat conflict as the universal feature in form of social gradations in society. Ralph Daharendorf and Lewis Coser are for example, a few among many such western sociologists who accept the universality of conflict in all form of stratification but locate these conflicts in the institutional anomalies within the system rather than linking it with the theory of class struggle and revolution. Conflict according to these sociologists arises out of antagonism of interests and exercise of power by one stratum over the other which seeks upward social mobility. It represents, therefore, internal dynamics of the stratification system rather than a movement towards its total replacement or change or social order itself by revolutionary means as Marx envisaged. Such theories of social stratification, which are known as conflict theories do not accept the Marxist position of historical materialism which postulates invariable stages of social evolution through series of revolutionary movements. The nation of social order in the conflict theory is closer to functional viewpoint rather than dialectical materialist interpretation.

Q3. Briefly describe the caste and class system in India.

[June 09, Q. 15]

Ans. While a caste is hereditary, a class is non-hereditary in nature. A class system allows both exogamy and endogamy, permits mobility either up or down the system, and also allows an individual to remain in the status to which he was born. Thus, a class is primarily based on socio-economic criteria. There are three major classes found: Upper, Middle, and Lower. Each class is divided into two sub-divisions. They are upper-upper, and lower upper; upper-middle and lower-middle; and upper-lower and lower-lower. A class is more open than the caste in the sense that mobility is allowed in the class system. It is not allowed that openly in the caste system. Further, caste system is based on ritual criterion whereas, class is based on secular criterion. Ritual criterion means it is based on religious myths, secular means non-religious criterion like economic, political and social criterion. However, in changing circumstances caste is also adapting to secular criteria. Consciousness is found in the class but not necessarily in the caste. However, today caste are also changing into classes in urban areas particularly in terms of economic criterion.

Q4. Examine the dialectical approach to the study of social stratification.

Or

What are the basic features and appraisal of dialectical approach?

[Dec 07, Q. 1]

Ans. Dialectic (also called *dialectics* or *the dialectical method*) is a method of argument, which has been central to both Eastern and Western philosophy since ancient times. The word "dialectic" originates in Ancient Greece, and was made popular by Plato's Socratic dialogues. Dialectic is rooted in the ordinary practice of a dialogue between two people who hold different ideas and wish to persuade each other. The presupposition of a dialectical argument is that the participants, even if they do not agree, share at least some meanings and principles of inference. Different forms of dialectical reason have emerged in the East and in the West, as well as during different eras of history. Among the major forms of dialectic reason are Socratic, Hindu, Buddhist, Medieval, Hegelian, Marxist, and Talmudic.

Bourgeoisie and Proletariat: Bourgeoisie is a classification used in analyzing human societies to describe a social class of people. Historically, the bourgeoisie comes from the middle or merchant classes of the Middle Ages, whose status or power came from employment, education, and wealth, as distinguished from those whose power came from being born into an aristocratic family of land owners. In modern times, it is the class owning the means for producing wealth.

The **proletariat** (from Latin *proles*, "offspring") is a term used to identify a lower social class; a member of such a class is **proletarian**. Originally it was identified as those people who had no wealth other than their sons. The term was initially used in a derogatory sense, until Karl Marx used it as a sociological term to refer to the working class. The bourgeoisie is defined by Engels as the class of capitalists, who own the means of social production and are the employers of wage labour. In this sense the bourgeoisie does not include the intermediate middle class, whose labour is supervisory and intellectual. The proletariat or working class is in Marxism the political force that will destroy capitalism and effect the transition to socialism. Marxists associated with the Frankfurt school came to deplore the non revolutionary conservatism of western working classes and their gradual absorption into a growing middle class, and to put faith in other sources of revolution. The terms in their Marxist senses may appear somewhat dated, as society has changed so that the means of production are no longer generally owned by individuals, but by corporations, pension funds, and so forth, with a wider dispersion of shares. However, the extent to which this change disguises a concentration of real power in the hands of a few owners is also debated.

Dahrendorf's critical appraisal: Ralf Gustav Dahrendorf's, Baron Dahrendorf's, KBE, FBA (May 1, 1929 – June 17, 2009) was a German-British sociologist, philosopher, political scientist and liberal politician. During his political career, he was a Member of the German Parliament, Parliamentary Secretary of State in the German Ministry of Foreign Affairs, European Commissioner for External Relations and Trade, European Commissioner for Research, Science and Education and Member of the British House of Lords, after he was created a life peer in 1993.

Dahrendorf's: He was since known in the United Kingdom as Lord Dahrendorf's. Dahrendorf's was a leading expert on class divisions in modern society, and has been described as "one of the most influential thinkers of his generation". He served as director of the London School of Economics and Warden of St Antony's College at the University of Oxford. He also served as a Professor of Sociology at a number of universities in Germany and the United Kingdom, and was most recently a Research Professor at the Berlin Social Science Research Center.

The basic features of dialectical approach are the following:

i) Economic interests are the basic of all other types of relationship-social, cultural, political, etc.

ii) There are two main classes: **(a)** owners of the means of production (bourgeoisie), and **(b)** wage-earners (proletariat). Marx refers to these classes also as Haves and Have-Nots.

iii) The interests of these two classes clash with each other, as the bourgeoisie exploit the proletariat, hence a class struggle.

iv) The bourgeoisie gets more than its due share, hence appropriate surplus, and this accelerates class struggle, which finally leads to revolution and radical transformation of the stratification system of society.

Classes to Marx are basic features of society; they are the product of the process of the productive system which is in effect a system of power relations. To own means of production tantamount to domination and power and to render services, and to supply the human labour amounts to subordination and dependence. In this sense, class is social reality, a real group of people with a developed consciousness of its existence, its position, goals and capabilities. Class is like a looking glass of society by which one can see its social fabric and internal dynamics.

Appraisal of dialectical: Marx's theory of society is not materialistic and dialectical, hence also scientific. But there is also persisting shared reality in human life. Discontinuities along don't characterize history and human society. Hence Marx's eternal assertion becomes relevant: "the history of all hitherto existing society in the history of class struggles". But both Marx and Engels realised that class itself was a uniquely prominent feature of capitalist society, and hence bourgeoisie and proletariat constituted the entire social advice of modern capitalist era. However, the main question relates to social ranking or stratification in relation to these basic classes. Engels and also to certain extent Marx realised that there were intermediate and transitional strata. These would disregard the two-classes theory, and it would be quite consistent with the development of capitalism and modern state system.

Today, the newly emancipated developing states have a vibrant structure of middle classes, operating a sort of control mechanism on both the bourgeoisie and the proletariat. The non-capitalist formation having peripheral capitalism signifying crystallisation of class structure in terms of bourgeoisie and proletariat has yet to emerge as a social reality. The controllers of the status apparatus in country like India are not the capitalist but the mandarins of political parties, bobbies and intellectuals. A new dominant class/elite drawn from the these categories of people has come to power. Bureaucracy plays significant role of controlling the state. Income, education and access to cultural goods have become in some societies the main basis of status and power. Economic standing along in terms of dichotomy of the bourgeoisie and the proletariat has yet to emerge as a social reality.

Q5. Describe functionalist approach to social stratification.

[Dec 08, Q. 1]

Ans. Social stratification: In a classic article outlining 'Some Principles of Stratification' (American Sociological Review, 1945), Kingsley Davis and Wilbert Moore argued that unequal social and economic rewards were an 'unconsciously evolved device' by which societies ensured that talented individuals were supplied with the motivation to undertake training which would guarantee that important social roles were properly fulfilled. In this way, the most important functions would be performed by the most talented persons, and the greatest rewards go to those positions which required most training and were most important for maintenance of the social system. The theory was (and remains) highly influential but has generated enormous controversy. (M. Tumin's Readings on Social Stratification, 1970 ,offers a good selection of the classic contributions to the debate.) Davis and Moore's argument is based on the functionalist premises that social order rests on consensual values which define collective goals that are in the general interest. In order to encourage those who are best able to realise these goals it is necessary to offer unequal rewards. Both of these propositions have allegedly been found empirically wanting. Critics have also suggested that the theory is simply an apologia for inequality. Some also maintain that it is tautological (circular), since it proposes that the occupations and other social roles which are most highly rewarded are most important to social stability, and then cites the high levels of reward as evidence of their social importance. What was lacking throughout the lengthy debate, and has yet to be found, is a criterion of 'social importance' that is conceptually independent of the rewards being allocated. Nevertheless, the theory continues to inform important topics of sociological discussion, including for example the literatures on social mobility and social justice.

Davis and Moore: Sociologists **Kingsley Davis** and **Wilbert Moore** believed that stratification serves an important function in society. In any society, a number of tasks must be accomplished. Some tasks, such as cleaning streets or serving coffee in a restaurant, are relatively simple. Other tasks, such as performing brain surgery or designing skyscrapers, are complicated and require more intelligence and training than the simple tasks. Those who perform the difficult tasks are therefore entitled to more power, prestige, and money. Davis and Moore believed that an unequal distribution of society's rewards is necessary to encourage people to take on the more complicated and important work that required many years of training. They believed that the rewards attached to a particular job reflect its importance to society.

Melvin Tumin: Sociologist Melvin Tumin took issue with Davis and Moore's theory. He disagreed with their assumption that the relative importance of a particular job can always be measured by how much money or prestige is given to the people who performed those jobs. That assumption made identifying important jobs difficult. Were the jobs inherently important, or were they important because people received great rewards to perform them. If society worked the way Davis and Moore had envisioned, Tumin argued, all societies would be meritocracies, systems of stratification in which positions are given according to individual merit. Ability would determine who goes to college and what jobs someone holds. Instead, Tumin found that gender and the income of an individual's family were more important predictors than ability or what type of work an individual would do. Men are typically placed in a higher social stratification than women, regardless of ability. A family with more money can afford to send its children to college. As college graduates, these children are more likely to assume high-paying, prestigious jobs. Conversely, people born into poverty are more likely to drop out of school and work low-paying jobs in order to survive, thereby shutting them off from the kinds of positions that are associated with wealth, power, and prestige.

Q6. Discuss caste with reference to hierarchy and conflict.

Ans. The word *caste* derives from the Portuguese *casta* , meaning breed, race, or kind. Among the Indian terms that are sometimes translated, as caste are *varna, jati, jat* , *biradri* , and *samaj*. All of these terms refer to ranked groups of various sizes and breadth. *Varna* , or color, actually refers to large divisions that include various castes; the other terms include castes and subdivisions of castes sometimes called subcastes. Many castes are traditionally associated with an occupation, such as high-ranking Brahmans; middle-ranking farmer and artisan groups, such as potters, barbers, and carpenters; and very low-ranking "Untouchable" leatherworkers, butchers, launderers, and latrine cleaners. There is some correlation between ritual rank on the caste hierarchy and economic prosperity. Members of higher-ranking castes tend, on the whole, to be more prosperous than members of lower-ranking castes. Many lower-caste people live in conditions of great poverty and social disadvantage. According to the Rig Veda, sacred texts that date back to oral traditions of more than 3,000 years ago, progenitors of the four ranked *varna* groups sprang from various parts of the body of the primordial man, which Brahma created from clay. Each group had a function in sustaining the life of society—the social body. Brahmans, or priests, were created from the mouth. They were to provide for the intellectual and spiritual needs of the community. Kshatriyas-warriors and rulers, were derived from the arms. Their role was to rule and to protect others. Vaishyas—landowners and merchants, sprang from the thighs, and were entrusted with the care of commerce and agriculture. Shudras—artisans and servants, came from the feet. Their task was to perform all manual labor. Later conceptualized was a fifth category, "Untouchable" menials, relegated to carrying out very menial and polluting work related to bodily decay and dirt. Since 1935 "Untouchables" have been known as Scheduled Castes, referring to their listing on government rosters, or schedules. They are also often called by Mohandas Karamchand (Mahatma) Gandhi's term Harijans, or "Children of God." Although the term *Untouchable* appears in literature produced by these low-ranking castes, in the 1990s, many politically conscious members of these groups prefer to refer to themselves as Dalit (see Glossary), a Hindi word meaning oppressed or downtrodden. According to the 1991 census, there were 138 million Scheduled Caste members in India, approximately 16 percent of the total population. The first four *varnas* apparently existed in the ancient Aryan society of northern India. Some historians say that these categories were originally somewhat fluid functional groups, not castes. A greater degree of fixity gradually developed, resulting in the complex ranking systems of medieval India that essentially continue in the late twentieth century. Although a *varna* is not a caste, when directly asked for their caste affiliation, particularly when the questioner is a Westerner, many Indians will reply with a *varna* name. Pressed further, they may respond with a much more specific name of a caste, or *jati* , which falls within that *varna* . For example, a Brahman may specify that he is a member of a named caste group, such as a Jijotiya Brahman, or a Smartha Brahman, and so on. Within such castes, people may further belong to smaller subcaste categories and to specific clans and lineages. These finer designations are particularly relevant when marriages are being arranged and often appear in newspaper matrimonial advertisements. Members of a caste are typically spread out over a region, with representatives living in hundreds of settlements. In any small village, there may be representatives of a few or even a score or more castes. Numerous groups usually called tribes (often referred to as Scheduled Tribes) are also integrated into the caste system to varying degrees. Some tribes live separately from others particularly in the far northeast and in the forested center of the country, where tribes are more like ethnic groups than castes. Some tribes are themselves divided into groups similar to subcastes. In regions where members of tribes live in peasant villages with nontribal peoples, they are usually considered members of separate castes ranking low on the hierarchical scale.

Q7. Explain the relationship between caste and class. [June 09, Q. 12]

Or

Describe the approaches to the study of caste in India. [Dec 06, Q. 1]

Ans. Earlier caste was characterized by inter-caste differentiation of roles as well as differentiation within particular castes. Thus, differentiation is not necessarily related to the reduction of caste inequalities. Differentiation of roles may bring about certain new inequalities which might strengthen the existing ones, and in such a situation, differentiation becomes a double-edged weapon for the lowest groups in a caste system or for that matter in any type of system. We have a few "proletarian Zamindars" or landlords on the one hand, and also neo-rich neo-influential" neo zamindars on the other, as a result of the emergence of new structures in the village community.

Synchronic Analysis: Studies on caste have paved the way to a certain fieldwork tradition, which produced 'synchronic' analysis. The emphasis had been on presenting caste as an equilibrating, harmonic, stable and consensual system. Change was often presented as a shifted in relations from organic to segmentary, closed to open, harmonic to disharmonic. Yet, empirical evidence seems to suggest that change in the caste system has been adaptive-evolutionary. Changes in the caste system can be analysed from one structure of inequality and hierarchy to another structure of inequality. To understand this problem of change in the caste system, we should analyse the "composite status" of people of a given society, either taking 'family' or individual' as the unit of analysis of or both. Such an approach calls for the consideration of caste as a dynamic process hence we need methodology for the understanding of the process of transformation.

Both caste and class have been debated from narrow ideological standpoints. According to the 'caste model' perspective, caste is viewed as an overarching ideological system, encompassing all aspects of social life, of Hindus in particular and of other communities in general. One of the implications of such a view is that caste is basically a part of the infrastructure of Indian society. Thus, occupation, division of labour, rules of marriage, interpersonal relations are elements of superstructure, expressing the reproduction of the ideology of caste.

Caste as a Normative System: Following from this we ask the question: In what way is caste a normative system? Why in certain spheres caste adheres to its normative sanctions whereas in other domains, caste groups and their members have taken up activities which depart from traditional sanctions of the caste system? I may be noted that members of a caste compete with each other, but they also co-operate with one another. Class-based distinctions within the caste have always been found in a pronounced form. Members of a caste in a given village can sometimes be representatives of Indian class divisions for while observing all the pertinent rules of marriage, they may actually define pertinent negotiations along the axes of class conditions.

Caste refers to inequality both in theory and practice. Dumont, in his classic work-Homo Hierarchicus considers inequality based on the caste system as a special type of inequality. For him the idea of the pure and the impure is basic to the understanding of caste; it is the very basic framework of hierarchy in India. He analysed the "ideal type" of the caste system based on ethnographic and ideological descriptions.

T.N. Madan upholds Dumont's view regarding hierarchy as a universal necessity. He points that society in India has remained largely static, change in society has taken place, but there has been no radical transformation.

Caste as an Empirical Reality: The basic of the understanding the caste system as an empirical reality is to locate caste groups such as jatis in a specific rural/urban context. It is a source of placement and of identity in society. At the latter level, identity is not a function necessarily of informal day to day relations. Caste, for instance, does not usually become a basic of marriage between a Tamil Brahmin and a Kanyakubja Brahmin of Uttar Pradesh. Yet, they may have a sense of belonging to what they perceive as the same stock, and may even co-operate in situations of crises and challenges. Therefore, one may ask: Is caste an interest group? Can common interests bring together more smoothly men of different castes from various regions than those of the same caste? Caste is certainly a resource, but the nature of this resource varies from caste to caste depending upon the status of a given caste in a given area. Caste identity/membership has become a liability for the members of the upper and middle castes because a certain percentage of jobs, seats in parliament and state legislatures, as well as admissions into institutions of higher learning have been reserved for the other backward castes, scheduled castes and scheduled tribes.

The view that caste and class are ideological opposites is not correct. The assumption that class can emerge as a social reality when caste has been destroyed in an erroneous conception of the relationship between the two. Both have been inseparable parts of India's social formation, and hence the study of their nexus, continuity and change.

Caste is a very complex system, for it is not simply a system of power relations and economic activities in a nominal sense. If it gets weakened in one aspect, it also gets strengthened in another, no doubt with certain alternations, additions and accretions. We need to seriously analyse the dynamics of the system. There is after all a class basis to rituals, pollution-purity and other non-material aspects of social life. For example, an organisation like Jat Sabha is not a simple caste association, but in effect, it is an organisation of peasants. Similarly, the Kisan Sabha is not a simple organisation of peasants, it is very much an association of castes engaged in agriculture, particularly of Jats in northern Indian, and their counterparts in other states.

Q8. Explain the relationship between Gender and ethnicity.

Ans. Minority is a sociological group that does not constitute a politically dominant voting majority of the total population of a given society. A sociological minority is not necessarily a numerical minority. It may include any group that is subnormal with respect to a dominant group in terms of social status, education, employment, wealth and political power. To avoid confusion, some writers prefer the terms "subordinate group" and "dominant group" rather than "minority" and "majority", respectively. In socioeconomics, the term "minority" typically refers to a socially subordination ethnic group (understood in terms of language, nationality, religion and/or culture). Other minority groups include people with disabilities, "economic minorities" (working poor or unemployed), "age minorities" (who are younger or older than a typical working age) and sexual minorities. The term "minority group" often occurs alongside a discourse of civil rights and collective rights which gained prominence in the 20th century. Members of minority groups are prone to different treatment in the countries and societies in which they live. This discrimination may be directly based on an individual's perceived membership of a minority group, without consideration of that individual's personal achievement. It may also occur indirectly, due to social structures that are not equally accessible to all. Activists campaigning on a range of issues may use the language of minority rights, including student rights, consumer rights and animal rights. In recent years, some members of social groups traditionally perceived as dominant have attempted to present themselves as an oppressed minority, such as white, middle-class heterosexual males.

Ethnic minorities: Every large society contains ethnic minorities. They may be migrant, indigenous or landless nomadic communities. In some places, subordinate ethnic groups may constitute a numerical majority, such as blacks in South Africa under apartheid. International criminal law can protect the rights of racial or ethnic minorities in a number of ways. The right to self-determination is a key issue.

Inequality and Difference: There has been a tendency to assume in stratification studies that stratification implies hierarchy and inequality. Dipankar Gupta has sought to clarity that the common textbook analogy of stratas to geological layers within the earth's crust is misleading. It is misleading because in Guptas' words:

Gupta argues not all systems of stratification are hierarchical. Some are, but many are not.

Differences rather than hierarchy are dominant in some stratificatory systems. In other words, the constitutive elements of these differences are such that any attempt to see them hierarchically would do offence to the logical property of these very elements. The layers in this case are not arranged vertically or hierarchically, but horizontally or even separately.

As an illustration of such a form of stratification where differences hold supreme Gupta writes:

Such an arrangement can be easily illustrated in the case of language, religion or nationalities. It would be futile, and indeed capricious, if any attempt was made to hierarchise languages or religions or nationalities… India again is an appropriate place to demonstrate this variety of social stratification. The various languages that are spoken in India speak eloquently of an horizontal system of social stratification where differences are paramount. Secular India again provides an example of religious stratification where religions are not hierarchised or unequally privileged in law, but have the freedom to exist separately in full knowledge of their intrinsic difference.

Hierarchy and Difference: The importance of logical distinctions notwithstanding differences is hierarchised. Both ethnic minorities and women face a great deal of antagonism, prejudices and discrimination. Prejudice operates mainly through the use of stereotypical thinking. All thought involves categories by means of which we classify experience. Sometimes, however, these categories are both ill-informed and rigid. And where stereotypes are associated with fear and anxiety, the situation is difficult. A white person may feel that all blacks are lazy and stupid. A man may believe all women are foolish and hysterical. An uppercaste Hindu, may feel that the minority is pampered. Sociologists have used the concept of displacement for such exercises of scapegoating.

Stereotyping is often closely linked to the psychological mechanism of displacement. In displacement, feelings of hostility or anger become directed against objects that are not the real origin of these anxieties. In other words what it means is that in times of acute unemployment, other ethnic groups or women may be blamed, scapegoated, for taking up jobs that should have been otherwise theirs.

To return to our most point, even though differences are not necessarily unequal or hierarchical, in practice both gender and ethnicity is attributed with features of both hierarchy and inequality.

Q9. Define the relationship between ethnicity and stratification.

Ans. Most modern societies include numerous different ethnic groups. In Britain, Irish, Asian (many within Asian), West Indian, Italian and Greek immigrants live. The question that arises however is when we refer to a society, are we necessarily referring to a state? Most often yes, we do. Hence we refer to an Indian society, A Pakistani society, an American society and so on. What we are essentially referring to are plural entities with many 'societies and cultures' and one state. Many argue that the different cultural groups are 'nations'. Others call them 'ethnic groups'.

Anthony Smith thinks nationalism emerged from common bonds or religion, language, customs, shared history and common myths of origin; in a later work he refers to modern ethnic revivals taking the from of nationalism and defines "ethnic" or ethnic community as a social group whose members share a sense of common origin, claim a common and distinctive history and destiny, possess one or more distinctive characteristics and feel a sense of collective uniqueness and solidarity'.

Ethnicity and Family: Ethnicity cannot be separated from our families for the diverse process of socializing children in ethnically diverse families has far reaching consequence. This in part explain the concept "ethclass" which explains the role that social class membership plays in defining the basic condition of life influenced by ethnicity at the same time that it accounts for differences between groups at the same social class level.

Studies of Stratification-Unequal access to resources which are both material and non-material have to therefore take a account of ethnicity. As Sharman says "an ethnic groups may be considered as a stratum in a given system of social stratification. It is possible because ethnicity is accompanied with class and power".

Ethnic nationalism is a form of nationalism wherein the "nation" is defined in terms of ethnicity. Whatever specific ethnicity is involved, ethnic nationalism always includes some element of descent from previous generations. Furthermore, the central theme of ethnic nationalists is that nations are defined by a shared heritage, which usually includes a common language, a common faith, and a common ethnic ancestry." It also includes ideas of a culture shared between members of the group, and with their ancestors, and usually a shared language; however it is different from purely cultural definitions of "the nation" (which allow people to become members of a nation by cultural assimilation) and a purely linguistic definitions (which see "the nation" as all speakers of a specific language). The central political tenet of ethnic nationalism is that each ethnic group on earth is entitled to self-determination. The outcome of this right to self-determination may vary, from calls for self-regulated administrative bodies within an already established society, to an autonomous entity separate from that society, to a sovereign state removed from that society. In international relations, it also leads to policies and movements for irredentism to claim a common nation based upon ethnicity. In scholarly literature, ethnic nationalism is usually contrasted with civic nationalism. Ethnic nationalism bases membership of the nation on descent or heredity often articulated in terms of common blood or kinship rather than on political membership. Hence, nation-states with strong traditions of ethnic nationalism tend to define nationality or citizenship by jus sanguinis (the law of blood, descent from a person of that nationality) while countries with strong traditions of civic nationalism tend to define nationality or citizenship by jus soli (the law of soil, birth within the nation-state). Ethnic nationalism is therefore seen as exclusive, while civic nationalism tends to be inclusive. Rather than allegiance to common civic ideals, then, ethnic nationalism tends to emphasise shared narratives and common culture. For example, Germany is often cited as an example of ethnic nationalism; German citizenship is open to "ethnic Germans" (e.g. descendents of Germans living in the former Soviet Union). The theorist Anthony D. Smith uses the term 'ethnic nationalism' for non-Western concepts of nationalism as opposed to Western views of a nation defined by its geographical territory. Diaspora studies scholars extend this non-geographically bound concept of "nation" among diasporic communities, at times using the term ethno nation or ethno nationalism to describe a conceptual collective of dispersed ethnics. There are also subtle forms of ethnic nationalism present in immigration policies. States such as Armenia, Bulgaria, Croatia, Finland, Germany, Hungary, Ireland, Israel, Romania, Serbia, and Turkey provide automatic or rapid citizenship to members of Diasporas of their own dominant ethnic group, if desired. For example, Israel's Law of Return, grants every Jew the right to settle in Israel and automatically acquire citizenship. A nation-state for the ethnic group derives political legitimacy from its status as homeland of that ethnic group, from its protective function against colonisation, persecution or racism, and from its claim to facilitate the shared cultural and social life, which may not have been possible under the ethnic group's previous status as an ethnic minority. Ethnic nationalism has sustained criticism because of its use by extremists to advocate racist agendas and genocide, such as the case of Nazi Germany and its extermination of millions of Jews and other ethnic and cultural groups during the Holocaust. More recent acts of violence that used ethnic nationalism as a justification include ethnic cleansing such as the Rwandan Genocide in 1994 and the Genocide in Bosnia and Herzegovina in 1995. A long-standing and on-going example of this phenomenon is found in the ethno nationalist project to create a Jewish state in Palestine.

Ethnic group is a group of humans whose members identify with each other, through a common heritage that is real or presumed. Ethnic identity is further marked by the recognition from others of a group's distinctiveness and the recognition of common cultural, linguistic, religious, behavioural traits as indicators of contrast to other groups. Ethnicity is an important means through which people can identify themselves. According to "Challenges of Measuring an Ethnic World: Science, politics, and reality", a conference organised by Statistics Canada and the United States Census Bureau (April 1–3, 1992), "Ethnicity is a fundamental factor in human life. It is a phenomenon inherent in human experience." However, many social scientists, like anthropologists Fredrik Barth and Eric Wolf, do not consider ethnic identity to be universal. They regard ethnicity as a product of specific kinds of inter-group interactions, rather than an essential quality inherent to human groups. Processes that result in the emergence of such identification are called ethno genesis. Members of an ethnic group, on the whole, claim cultural continuities over time. Historians and cultural anthropologists have documented, however, that often many of the values, practices, and norms that imply continuity with the past are of relatively recent invention. According to Thomas Hylland Eriksen, until recently the study of ethnicity was dominated by two distinct debates. One is between "primordialism" and "instrumentalism". In the primordial's view, the participant perceives ethnic ties collectively, as an externally given, even coercive, social bond. The instrumentalist approach, on the other hand, treats ethnicity primarily as an ad-hoc element of a political strategy, used as a resource for interest groups for achieving secondary goals such as, for instance, an increase in wealth, power or status. This debate is still an important point of reference in Political science, although most scholars' approaches fall between the two poles. The second debate is between "constructivism" and "essentialism". Constructivists view national and ethnic identities as the product of historical forces, often recent, even when the identities are presented as old. Essentialists view such identities as ontological categories defining social actors, and not themselves the result of social action. According to Eriksen, these debates have been superseded, especially in anthropology, by scholars' attempts to respond to increasingly politicised forms of self-representation by members of different ethnic groups and nations. This is in the context of debates over multiculturalism in countries, such as the United States and Canada, which have large immigrant populations from many different cultures, and post-colonialism in the Caribbean and South Asia.

Q10. Write a note on the relationship between gender and stratification. [June 08, Q. 15]

Ans. In conventional class analysis, women generally, and wives in particular, took the social class position of the males in their family or household (Hakim, 2007)," this was due to the fact that the male was the worker and brought in all the income for the family. If a females' husband were a lawyer, after marrying, she would inherit all of his worth and class status once they become a union. Initially before marriage, the father was the provider of the household so, a young woman would hold the social class of her father until later, after marriage, their husband's social class. "This was essentially because occupation, or any other status in the public sphere, was taken as the most obvious indicator of a family's or household's social class/status in modern capitalist societies. Women were mostly housewives and did the household chores and cared for the family, so without any other form of income it would be hard to be in a high social class without a working husband." The feminist movement challenged the conventional class analysis. Due to the rising female employment rates in modern western societies, a new situation arose in which couples would be dual-career as well as dual-earner, besides the traditional one earner per couple. Women in relationships could financially contribute and no longer where financially dependent on their spouse. Thus, it was no longer appropriate to classify wives by their husband's social status or occupation. This was a big start for many women. Women now had a choice as to how they wanted to contribute to their family. Women could choose to fulfill the homemaker role or be a career woman and contribute financially to the relationship/family. It also created of equality within the couple, because they could get out and work as well instead of solely caring for the children and family. Her previous occupation, household chores, became shared between the husband and wife. This gave the woman an opportunity to make something of herself and not have to rely on her husband's earnings.

2 Explaining Social Stratification

Q1. Discuss the Max Weber's concept of class.

Ans. Maximilian Carl Emil Weber (21 April 1864–14 June 1920) was a German lawyer, politician, scholar, political economist and sociologist, who profoundly influenced sociological theory. Weber's major works deal with rationalisation in sociology of religion, government, organisational theory, and behavior. Marx saw class divisions as the most important source of social conflict. Weber's analysis of class is similar to Marx's, but he discusses class in the context of social stratification more generally. Class is one dimension of the social structure. Social status, or "social honor," is another. Both are significant contributors of social difference. Weber's treatment of class and status indicates the manner in which the material basis of society is related to the ideological. Social conflict can result from one or the other, or both. Social action is motivated by both, though in some cases more one than the other. By bringing in status, Weber provides a more flexible view of the details of social differences, and their implications for the lived experience of social actors.

Class: Weber identified three aspects of class: **(i)** a specific causal component of actor's life chances **(ii)** which rests exclusively on economic interests and wealth, and **(iii)** is represented under conditions of labor and commodity markets. The possession of material resources, accumulated by advantage in the market place, results in distinctive qualities in terms of the standard of living. The possession of property defines the main class difference, according to Weber. The owners of property have a definite advantage, and in some cases a monopoly on, action in the market of commodities and, especially, labor. They have privileged access to the sources of wealth creation, by virtue of ownership and control of the markets. Weber identified a subdivision among property owners based on the means of their wealth creation. Entrepreneurs use wealth in commercial ventures. Rentiers profit by interest on their property, through investments or rent of land. Both forms of ownership yield advantages resulting from the ability to convert property to money. The property-less class is defined by the kinds of services individual workers provide in the labor market. Workers are classified as skilled, semi-skilled and unskilled. These distinctions are based on the value of different kinds of labor. Different wages result in different qualities in terms of the standard of living. Weber did not believe that class interests necessarily led to uniformity in social action. Neither communal nor societal action is the inexorable result of class interest. Weber challenges, here, the Marxian notion of the primarily material basis of social action. He is not denying it outright, but rather, introducing an element of unpredictability. Weber did not believe that proletarian revolutionary action would arise as a certain result of structural contradiction. Communal or societal action may develop from a common class situation in certain conditions. Weber believed that the general cultural conditions played a large role in this determination. Intellectuals occupy a key position in this regard. Weber argued that the extent of the contrasts between the property owners and the property-less workers must become transparent to the workers in order for collective action around the issue of class to occur. Intellectuals function either to call attention to or explain these contrasts, or, to obscure them. For communal or societal action to take place, the workers must not only recognize the differences in wealth and opportunity, but these differences must be seen as the result of the distribution of property and economic power. If the differences are believed to be a natural characteristic of society, as a given fact, then only occasional and irrational action is possible. Very often, collective action centers on the labor market. Workers seek higher wages, and see this as the goal of their struggle. Most class antagonism, Weber noted, is directed at managers, rather than at owner's stockholders and bankers because they appear to be have the power to set the price of labor power.

Q2. State Marx's views on social stratification with reference to class. [June 08, Q. 8]

Ans. The class system is universal phenomenon denoting a category or group of persons having a definite status in society which permanently determines their relation to other groups. The social classes are de facto groups (not legally or religiously defined and sanctioned) they are relatively open not closed. Their basis is indisputably economic but they are more than economic groups. They are characteristic groups of the industrial societies which have developed since 17th century. The relative importance and definition of membership in a particular class differs greatly over time and between societies, particularly in societies that have a legal differentiation of groups of people by birth or occupation. In the well-known example of socioeconomic class, many scholars view societies as stratifying into a hierarchical system based on occupation, economic status, wealth, or income.

According to Ogburn and Nimkoff a social class is the aggregate of persons having essentially the same social status in a given society. Marx defined class in terms of the extent to which an individual or social group has control over the means of production. In Marxist terms a class is a group of people defined by their relationship to the means of production. Classes are seen to have their origin in the division of the social product into a necessary product and a surplus product. Marxists explain history in terms of a war of classes between those who control production and those who actually produce the goods or services in society (and also developments in technology and the like). In the Marxist view of capitalism this is a conflict between capitalists (bourgeoisie) and wage workers (proletariat). Class antagonism is rooted in the situation that control over social production necessarily entails control over the class which produces goods in capitalism this is the exploitation of workers by the bourgeoisie. Marx saw class categories as defined by continuing historical processes. Classes, in Marxism, are not static entities, but are regenerated daily through the productive process. Marxism views classes as human social relationships which change over time, with historical commonality created through shared productive processes. In 17th century, farm labourer who worked for day wages shares a similar relationship to production as an average office worker of the 21st century. In this example it is the shared structure of wage labour that makes both of these individuals "working class". Maclver and Page defines social class as any portion of the community marked off from the rest by social status. Max Weber suggest that social classes are aggregates of individuals who have the same opportunities of acquiring goods, the same exhibited standard of living. He formulated a three component theory of stratification with social, status and party classes (or politics) as conceptually distinct elements.

· Social class is based on economic relationship to the market (owner, renter, employee, etc.).

· Status class has to do with non-economic qualities such as education, honour and prestige.

· Party class refers to factors having to do with affiliations in the political domain.

According to Weber a more complex division of labour made the class more heterogeneous. In contrast to simple income—property hierarchies, and to structural class schemes like Weber's or Marx's, there are theories of class based on other distinctions, such as culture or educational attainment. At times, social class can be related to elitism and those in the higher class are usually known as the "social elite". For example, Bourdieu seems to have a notion of high and low classes comparable to that of Marxism, insofar as their conditions are defined by different habitus, which is in turn defined by different objectively classifiable conditions of existence. In fact, one of the principal distinctions

Bourdieu makes is a distinction between bourgeoisie taste and the working class taste. Social class is a segment of society with all the members of all ages and both the sexes who share the same general status. Maclver says whenever social intercourse is limited by the consideration of social status by distinctions between higher and lower there exists a social class.

Q3. Describe the functionalist theory of stratification.
[Dec 07, Q. 3][June 07, Q. 2]

Ans. The functionalist theory of social inequality holds that stratification exists because it is beneficial for society. Society must concern itself with human motivation because the duties associated with the various statuses are not all equally pleasant to the human organism, important to social survival, and in need of the same abilities and talents.

Parsons' approach: The sociologist Pitirim Sorokin is often credited with first developing and then using the concept of stratification in empirical work, the clearest lineage emerges in the work of Talcott Parsons and that of his students. In his essay 'An analytical approach to the theory of social stratification', Parsons wrote: 'Social stratification is regarded here as the differential ranking of the human individuals who compose a given social system and their treatment as superior and inferior relative to one another in certain socially important respects.' Parsons then wrote that the 'status of any given individual in the system of stratification in a society may be regarded as a resultant of the common valuations underlying the attribution of status to him in dimensions such as achievements, possessions, authority, and power. In 1945 Parsons's students, Kingsley Davis and Wilbert Moore, wrote 'Some principles of stratification' in which they specified a clear conception of the sources and inevitably of stratification. Adopting the functionalist framework championed by Parsons, Davis and Moore maintained that society is a functioning social system, directly analogous to a living organism, which survives because it determines necessary social positions, recruits appropriate individuals to fill each position, and induces individuals to perform their assigned duties. To foster efficiency, the social system attaches differential rewards to alternative positions, where the sizes of the rewards are based on:

(a) the functional importance of the position to the society as a whole and ***(b)*** the counterfactual scarcity of individuals willing to take the position in the absence of appropriate rewards. Davis and Moore claimed that 'Social inequality is thus an unconsciously evolved device by which societies insure that the most important positions are conscientiously filled by the most qualified persons.' Thirteen years after his initial essay on the topic, and eight years after the seminal Davis and Moore piece, Parsons began 'A revised analytical approach to the theory of social stratification' with the bold assertion: 'It has come to be rather widely recognized in the sociological field that social stratification is a generalized aspect of the structure of all social systems, and that the system of stratification is intimately linked to the level and type of integration of the system as a system.' Parsons then discussed how societies cope with the functional necessity of stratification by developing norms and value standards that, by and large, attribute differences in attainment to differences in achievement.

Parsons and his colleagues assumed that moderately high levels of intergenerational mobility are essential for the efficiency and integration of society. Functionally important positions must be staffed by the most qualified individuals and hence based on past achievements rather than social origins. And, to ensure integration and social order, reward for achievement rather than reward for social origins must be reasonably expected and then observed. In later work, Parsons (1959) specified the social processes that develop and then transmit these norms of achievement in his essay 'The school class as a social system'. He argued that schools serve two primary functions in society – socialisation and allocation – which they fulfil in a simultaneous four-part process: ***(a)*** emancipation of children from exclusive attachment to their parents, ***(b)*** inculcation of values and norms that cannot be taught by parents, ***(c)*** differentiation of the school class on actual achievement and on differential valuation of achievement, and finally ***(d)*** an allocation of individuals to positions in the adult role system. Parsons wrote: 'Differentiation of the class along the achievement axis is inevitably a source of strain, because it confers higher rewards and privileges on one contingent than on another within the same system. As a result of this scholarship, the term 'stratification' gained popularity in sociology, becoming the name for the entire sub-field of inquiry concerned with the causes and consequences of inequality. Thereafter, the term diffused throughout the social sciences and was drawn upon by historians and anthropologists to frame comparative studies of inequality. Within economics, the term has been used less frequently and with no consistent definition. For early studies of racial–ethnic inequality, one can find the term used in the dissimilar work of Closson (1896) and Myrdal (1944).

More recently, the term has been used to refer to the determinants of labour market earnings that arise from family background rather than one's own skills.

Q4. Explain the Davis and Moore's theory on stratification.

Or

[June 09, Q. 11][June 07, Q. 2]

List the functional prerequisites of Davis and Moore.

Ans. Stratification is the division of a society into hierarchical layers on the premise of religious beliefs, affiliation, or faith practices. According to Kingsley

Davis and Wilbert E. Moore "the reason why religion is necessary is apparently to be found in the fact that human society achieves its unity primarily through the possession by its members of certain ultimate values and ends in common. Furthermore, Davis and Moore contend that it is "the role of religious belief and ritual to supply and reinforce this appearance of reality" that these "certain ultimate values" have. This is one possible explanation for why religion is one of the underlying factors which links various forms of inequality into a chain of stratification.

Parsons stressed on the stratification in society. He showed that it was inevitable in every society. Davis and Moore elaborated on this and try to examine how stratification becomes effective in any society. In this way the attempt to extend Parsons argument. The main problem they pose is why do certain positions carry different degrees of prestige? And, how do individuals get into these positions?

The authors support Parson's view that the basis of the existence of societies in order and stability. All societies have their own functional prerequisites which help them survive and operate effectively. Let us elaborate on this point. Societies are not more collection of individuals. These individuals have to perform specific tasks so, that the requirements of society are fulfilled. There are thus a number of activities that exist in society. A society needs workers, industrialists, managers, policemen, teachers, students artisans and so on. Different individuals who have specialized skills do these different types of work. Therefore the first functional prerequisite of any society is of allocating these different roles effectively. This will ensure that the right people are placed in proper position.

There are four aspects of the above-mentioned functional prerequisite. Firstly, all roles in society must be filled. All societies have different types of occupations. These occupations are necessary for their existence. Hence it is necessary to ensure that these occupations are not enough. If the wrong people (i.e. people who do not have the requisite skills) are selected for the tasks there will be instability in society. This in especially true if these positions are important. For example if a power generation company employs a well known novelist, who has no idea of power generation, the work of the company will suffer and there will be instability not only in the company but in supply of electricity. Therefore the second factor is that the most competent people must fill in the positions. Thirdly, in order the best people are selected for the job it is necessary to train them for it. Training therefore is an effective means of ensuring that the best people are selected. In the case of that novelist who is made the head of a power generation company, had he undergone training for fulfilling the needs of that position he could be regarded as the best person. Lastly, the roles must be performed conscientiously.

Functions of Stratification: Davis and Moore stated that all societies need some mechanism for ensuring that the best people are selected for the positions and they perform well. According to them the most effective means for ensuring this is social stratification. This system is effective because it offers unequal rewards and privileges to the different position in society. If all people are given the same rewards then there will be no motivation for people to work harder. There may also be a tendency for people to avoid taking up positions of responsibility or challenging jobs. They know that no matter how well they perform and no matter what position they occupy they will get the same rewards. Therefore stratification is necessary for the efficient functioning of the system. The main contributions of a system of unequal rewards are two-fold. Firstly it motivates people to fill certain positions. When positions carry higher rewards people put in greater efforts become qualified for positions. For example if the position of a lecture carries higher rewards than other professions bright students will strive to fulfil the qualifications for becoming lecturers. In this way society will get better teachers. Secondly, the rewards must be unequal even after fulfilling the position so that the persons who are appointed are motivated to improve their performance further. If lecturers are rewarded for their teaching and research activities through promotions and increased salaries, they will perform their duties better as they would like the higher rewards. In this manner the system of stratification, based on unequal rewards, is beneficial for societies. Davis and Moore explain that this system of stratification holds true for both modern societies based on competition and for traditional societies that are based on ascription. In modern societies people occupy positions according to their skills and qualifications. Those who are better qualified get better rewards and they occupy positions of prestige. In traditional societies positions are ascribed through birth. In traditional caste oriented Indian society people occupied their position not due to their competence but through the status they had by birth. The son of a labourer would become a labourer even if he had the intelligence to do other type of superior work. Similarly, the son of a landlord would become a landlord even if he were totally incompetent for the job. In such a system the provision of unequal rewards would have no effect in improving the efficiency of the system. However Davis and Moore argue that in such societies the stress is on performance of duties attached to the positions. Thus, even though the son of a labourer will remain a labour, if he performs his duties well he will be rewarded though other means.

Q5. What does Coser mean by the function of conflict? [Dec 08, Q. 14]
Ans. L.Coser was born in Berlin. He was the first sociologist to try to bring together structural functionalism and conflict theory; his work was focused on finding the functions of social conflict. Coser argued - with Georg Simmel

- that conflict might serve to solidify a loosely structured group. In a society that seems to be disintegrating, conflict with another society, inter-group conflict, may restore the integrative core. For example, the cohesiveness of Israeli Jews might be attributed to the long-standing conflict with the Arabs. Conflict with one group may also serve to produce cohesion by leading to a series of alliances with other groups. Conflicts within a society, intra-group conflict, can bring some ordinarily isolated individuals into an active role. The protest over the Vietnam War motivated many young people to take vigorous roles in American political life for the first time. Conflicts also serve a communication function. Prior to conflict, groups may be unsure of their adversary's position, but as a result of conflict, positions and boundaries between groups often become clarified, leaving individuals better able to decide on a proper course of action in relation to their adversary.

Function of Conflict: The function of conflict in establishing and maintaining group identities is quite clear in Marx's theory of class. For him classes constitute themselves only through conflict with another class. Individuals may store common objective positions with others and yet may not be aware of the communality of interests. It is a class-in-itself. They become a class i.e. class for itself, only when they carry out a common battle against another class.

Let us now turn to the caste system and the role of conflict within it. Let us recall the second function mentioned above, namely 'reciprocal repulsions'. Coser believes that conflict between castes not only establishes distinctiveness and separateness of the various castes but also ensures the stability of the total Indian social structure.

This is possible as a result of a balance of claims made by rival competing castes. Members of the same caste are drawn together in a solidarity resulting from their common hostility and rejection of members of other castes. Hierarchy of positions in the system is maintained because of the rejection by the subgroups or castes in the society of each other.

Conflicts and Rejections: The discussion so far has focused on the conflicts and rejections of strata of one another and the functional consequences following from them. To recapitulate, two such functions have been mentioned. First conflict with other groups leads to integration and solidarity within the group. Secondly, the system as a whole is maintained by a balance of a versions the groups have for one another.

An important qualifications is required at this stage for the foregoing discussion. Sometimes, out-groups instead of becoming targets of hostility and rejection, actually become positive reference groups to the group in question (cf. Merton). The out-group may be emulated for purposes of becoming its member in future. Merton calls this anticipatory socialisation. Coser, however, believes that such may not be the case for the caste system where caste positions are fixed for life and there is little possibility of moving from one caste to another. M.N. Srinivas believes, however, that a ritually lower caste may try to adopt the rituals and life styles of higher castes in order to improve the position of the caste in the hierarchy of castes. This he calls the process of 'sanskritisaion'. The open class system, has bounded strata; some movement, both upward and downward is possible. Such mobility, in fact, is an ideal, although in practice there may not be substantial movement. In such a situation, hostility between classes is mixed with positive attraction to the higher classes. The sentiments of hostility towards higher classes do not necessarily mean rejection of the values of these groups but represent a 'sour grapes' attitude: 'that which is condemned is secretly coveted'.

Q6. What are the views of Coser and Dahrendorf's on social classes? [Dec 08, Q. 2]

Ans. First of all let us examine the ideas contained in his 'Theory of Social Classes and Class Conflict'.

The objective of the exercise is an examination and explanation of structure changes in terms of group conflict. Since the primary interest is on conflict and its consequences, following the coercion model, it is taken as present throughout social structure i.e. ubiquitous. All the elements of the social structure e.g. roles, institutions norms have to do something or with instability and change.

Every theory, however rudimentary it may be, uses a set of concepts which have to be clearly defined so that the statements showing the inter relationships can be clearly understood. Dahrendorf is one of the rare authors who has deliberately chosen to practice what the methodologists often preach but seldom practice.

Since, it is a theory dealing with conflict concepts like power, authority have to find a place.

Following Marx's ideas on the existential basis of consciousness, class consciousness and fake class consciousness (cf "class-in-itself" and "class-for-itself") Dahrendorf distinguished between latent and manifest interest.

Latent interests are those interests about which the incumbents of the two espousing position of domination and subjection are unaware. In contrast the manifest interests are articulate and conscious to the individual and lead to opposition to the other. Corresponding to the two kind of interests, collectivities can be classified. The collectivity of individuals having common latent interests is called a quasi group, on the other hand, that which shares manifest interests is called interest groups.

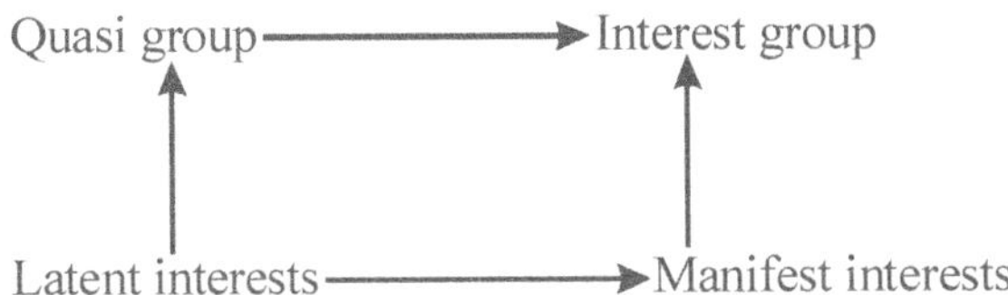

(note that if latent interests become manifest due to structural dynamics of opposition, quasi groups become interest groups)

Dahrendorf on Social Class: Social classes then are such organized or unorganized collectives which share latent or manifest interests which arise from the authority structure of imperatively coordinated associations (I.C.A.)

A few important points to note are:

i) Social class does not encompass all or even most members of a society as a whole. It has relevance only for the given ICA.

ii) Given the authority structure of an ICA of domination and subjection, only two classes are emergent.

iii) Social classes are always conflict groups.

Group conflict is the antagonistic relationship between organized collectivities as is based on patterns of social structure. (Not random, not based on psychological factors). In a given I.C.A. class conflict which arise from the authority structure is endemic and ubiquitous. The presence and acting out of class conflict has consequences for structural change. This change can be in the social institutions and/or norms and values. Change can take place in varying degrees of suddenness or radicalness or both. (Note the departure from Marx formulation that structural change is always revolutionary i.e. sudden, radical and violent).

A model of conflict group formation, 'in very imperatively coordinated association, two quasi groups united by common latent interests can be distinguished. Their orientations of interest are determined by possession of or exclusion from authority. From these quasi groups, interest groups are recruited, the articulate programs of which defined or attack the legitimacy of exciting authority structures. In any given association, two such groupings are in conflict.

Consequences for Social Structure: Once conflict groups of the class type are formed in an I.C.A. i.e. in two opposing groups, how does the conflict interaction proceed? What will be the consequences for the social structure in which group conflict is rooted? There are the questions that any theory of conflict has to answer. Dahrendorf has attempted to do so.

To begin with, one asks the question regarding the intensity of conflict (which involves 'costs' in case of defeat which factors affect it positively and negatively. Dahrendorf believes that the intensity of class conflict decreases to the extent that conditions for class organisation are present and vice versa. For example, if the workers have opportunities of forming unions and negotiate with management, the worker management conflicts will be less intense. Similarly, in states where people can freely form parties and civic association will have less intense conflict, similarly, intensity of group conflict will diminish when the classes in different associations are not superimposed. For example the factory workers are also not from an ethnic minority or low caste. If there is superimposition of the two, the conflict will be more intense.

The intensity of class conflict is also affected by the fact of whether or not different group conflicts in the same society are dissociated. As an example let us suppose, that there are three major kind of conflicts in a society: class conflict, ethnic conflict and regional, say north-south conflict. If the incumbents of position of domination are also from dominant ethnic group and from the north, and those of subjection from a particular subordinate ethnic group and from the south, the intensity of class conflict will be very high.

The factors that affect the intensity of class conflict, Dahrendorf, then moves on to examine the variables affecting the violence of conflict. He rejects Marx's position that all class conflicts are violent. It also does not mean that it is absent. What is believed is that the degree of violence varies from peaceful to bloody revolutionary conflict.

The conditions of class organisation prevalent in an ICA is negatively related to the violence of class conflict (cf unionisation and peaceful collective bargaining in a factory). Dahrendorf also believes that if relative deprivation replaces absolute deprivation in the subject classes, the violence of class conflict is reduced. Yet another factor affecting the degree of violence is the regulation of conflict, By regulation of conflict is meant the mechanisms and procedures that deal with the expression of conflict and not either with its resolution or suppression. To begin with, both parties must recognize that the conflict is real and necessary. Calling the other party's claim as 'unrealistic' is not regulation. It must be recognized that the 'other' has a case. Conflict regulation is more likely to occur when the opposing groups are organized as interest groups. In case of unorganized groups regulation is difficult. For example if there is only one workers' union in a factory, both the management and workers can work out effective strategies for dealing with the issues involved in conflict. Finally, if both the parties agree on certain formal 'rules of the game', conflict is better regulated. As in most democratic countries of the world, India has evolved procedures for industrial conflict regulation e.g. negotiations, mediations, arbitration and adjudication; strike being the last resort.

As class conflict takes place in an association, given its varying intensity and violence, it has consequences for the structure. Two kind of structure changes have been identified by Dahrendorf: suddenness and radicalness. The term structure change is to be applied when there are changes in the personnel position of domination and subjection in I.C.A.s. An extreme case will be when all the positions of authority are takes over by members of the erstwhile subject class, such as for example, in a revolution. More often than not, however, there is partial replacement.

By radicalness of structure change is meant the significance of consequences and ramifications of such change. It should be noted that many sudden changes may not necessarily be radical.

Q7. Discuss the synthesis between the functionalist and conflict approaches to the study of stratification. [June 08, Q. 5][Dec 07, Q. 4]

Ans. Functionalist Theories: Talcott Parsons believe that order, stability and cooperation in society are based on value consensus that is a general agreement by members of society concerning what is good and worthwhile. Stratification system derives from common values it follows from the existence of values that individuals will be evaluated and therefore placed in some form of rank order. Stratification is the ranking of units in a social system in accordance with the common value system. Those who perform successfully in terms of society's values will be ranked highly and they will be likely to receive a variety of rewards and will be accorded high prestige since they exemplify and personify common values. According to Kingsley Davis and Moore stratification exists in every known human society. All social system shares certain functional prerequisites which must be met if the system is to survive and operate efficiently. One such prerequisite is role allocation and performance. This means that all roles must be filled. They will be filled by those best able to perform them. The necessary training for them is undertaken and that the roles are performed conscientiously. Davis and Moore argue that all societies need some mechanism for insuring effective role allocation and performance. This mechanism is social stratification which they see as a system which attaches unequal rewards and privileges to the positions in society. They concluded that social stratification is a device by which societies insure that the most important positions are conscientiously filled by the most qualified persons.

Conflict Theories: According to Karl Marx in all stratified societies there are two major social groups: a ruling class and a subject class. The ruling class derives its power from its ownership and control of the forces of production. The ruling class exploits and oppresses the subject class. As a result, there is a basic conflict of interest between the two classes. The various institutions of society such as the legal and political system are instruments of ruling class domination and serve to further its interests. Marx believed that western society developed through four main epochs-primitive communism, ancient society, feudal society and capitalist society. Primitive communism is represented by the societies of pre-history and provides the only example of the classless society. From then all societies are divided into two major classes - master and slaves in ancient society, lords and serfs in feudal society and capitalist and wage labourers in capitalist society.

Weber sees class in economic terms. He argues that classes develop in market economies in which individuals compete for economic gain. He defines a class as a group of individuals who share a similar position in market economy and by virtue of that fact receive similar economic rewards. Thus, a person's class situation is basically his market situation. Those who share a similar class situation also share similar life chances. Their economic position will directly affect their chances of obtaining those things defined as desirable in their society. Weber argues that the major class division is between those who own the forces of production and those who do not. He distinguished the following class grouping in capitalist society:

Luhmann's System theory: Niklas Luhmann (December 8, 1927 - November 6, 1998) was a German sociologist, and a prominent thinker in sociological systems theory. Luhmann was born in Lüneburg, Germany, where his father's family had been running a brewery for several generations. After graduating from the Johanneum school in 1943, he was conscripted as a Luftwaffenhelfer in World War II and served for two years until, at the age of 17, he was taken prisoner of war by American troops in 1945. After the war Luhmann studied law at the University of Freiburg from 1946 to 1949, when he obtained a law degree, and then began a career in Lüneburg's public administration. During a sabbatical in 1961, he went to Harvard, where he met and studied under Talcott Parsons, then the world's most influential social systems theorist. Luhmann's Systems theory was based on, what he called, the "evolution of communication": from oral communication, over writing systems towards electronic media and parallel with the evolution of society through functional differentiation. In his theory there are three strands:

1. Systems theory as societal theory

2. Communication theory and

3. Evolution theory

which weave through his entire work. The core element of Luhmann's theory is communication. Social systems are systems of communication, and society is the most encompassing social system. Being the social system that comprises all (and only) communication, today's society is a world society. A system is defined by a boundary between itself and its environment, dividing it from an infinitely complex, or (colloquially) chaotic, exterior. The interior of the system is thus a zone of reduced complexity: Communication within a system operates by selecting only a limited amount of all information available outside. This process is also called "reduction of complexity." The criterion according to which information is selected and processed is meaning (in German, *Sinn*). Both social systems and psychical or personal systems operate by processing meaning. Furthermore, each system has a distinctive identity that is constantly reproduced in its communication and depends on what is considered meaningful and what is not. If a system fails to maintain that identity, it ceases to exist as a system and dissolves back into the environment it emerged from. Luhmann called this process of reproduction from elements previously filtered from an over-complex environment autopoiesis (pronounced "auto-poy-E-sis"; literally: self-creation), using a term coined in cognitive biology by Chilean thinkers Humberto Maturana and Francisco Varela. Social systems are *autopoietically closed* in that they use and rely on resources from their environment; yet those resources do not become part of the systems' operation. Both thought and digestion are important preconditions for communication, but neither appears in communication as such.

Luhmann likens the operation of autopoiesis (the filtering and processing of information from the environment) to a program, making a series of logical distinctions. Here, Luhmann refers to the British mathematician G. Spencer-Brown's logic of distinctions that Maturana and Varela had earlier identified as a model for the functioning of any cognitive process. The supreme criterion guiding the "self-creation" of any given system is a defining binary code. This binary code, is not to be confused with the computers operation: Luhmann (following Spencer-Brown and Gregory Bateson) assumes that auto-referential systems are continuously confronted with the dilemma of disintegration/ continuation. This dilemma is framed with an ever-changing set of available choices; everyone of those potential choices, can be the system's selection or not (a binary state, selected/rejected). The influence of Spencer-Brown's book, *Laws of Form*, on Luhmann can hardly be overestimated. Although Luhmann first developed his understanding of social systems theory under Parsons' influence, he soon moved away from the Parsonian concept. The most important difference is that Parsons used systems as a merely analytic tool to understand certain processes going on in society; Luhmann, in contrast, treats his vision of systems ontologically, saying that "systems exist", that is Luhmann in fact suggests to change the ontological paradigm with the paradigm of systems theory: the difference system/environment (which also signifies a relationship). Another difference is that Parsons asks how certain subsystems contribute to the functioning of overall society. Luhmann starts with the differentiation of the systems themselves out of a non-descript environment. He does observe how certain systems fulfill functions that contribute to "society" as a whole, but this is happening more or less by chance, without an overarching vision of society. Finally, the systems' autopoietic closure is another fundamental difference from Parsons' concept. Each system works strictly according to its very own code and has no understanding at all for the way other systems perceive their environment. For example, the economy is all about money, so there is no independent role in the economic system for extraneous aspects such as morals. One seemingly peculiar, but within the overall framework strictly logical, axiom of Luhmann's theory is the human being's position outside any social system, initially developed by Parsons. Consisting of "pure communicative actions" (a reference to Jürgen Habermas) any social system requires human consciousnesses (personal or psychical systems) as an obviously necessary, but nevertheless environmental resource. In Luhmann's terms, human beings are neither part of society nor of any specific systems, just as they are not part of a conversation. Luhmann himself once said concisely that he was "not interested in people". That is not to say that people were not a matter for Luhmann, but rather, the communicative actions of people are constituted (but not defined) by society, and society is constituted (but not defined) by the communicative actions of people: society is people's environment, and people are society's environment. Thus, sociology can explain how persons can change society; the influence of the environment (the people) onto the system (the society), the so-called *"structural coupling"*. Luhmann was devoted to the ideal of non-normative science introduced to sociology in the early 20th century by Max Weber and later re-defined and defended against its critics by Karl Popper. However, in an academic environment that never strictly separated descriptive and normative theories of society, Luhmann's sociology has widely attracted criticism from various intellectuals, perhaps most notably from Jürgen Habermas.

Lenski's power and privilege: It is in the works of Gerhard Lenski that one finds a most systematic attempt at developing a synthesis of the different theories of social stratification. In the introductory chapter of his well known book *Power and Privilege: A Theory of Social Stratification,* Lenski clarifies that his attempt at developing a synthesized theory of social stratification focuses on three important questions. First, he focuses on the causes of stratification rather than its consequences as has been done by most others. Second, as is suggested in the title of his focus, his main focus is on power and privilege rather than prestige. Finally, he equates social stratification with distributive process in human societies-the process by which scarce goods and values are distributed.

Historically speaking, the question of distribution and social inequality assume significance only when the societies begin to produce surplus, i.e., more than what is required for the survival of the given population. The core question for Lenski is 'who gets what and why?' his answer is rather simple and clear. "The distribution of rewards in a society is a function of the distribution of power". This answer is counter posed to the answer suggested by the structural functionalists who explain the differential distribution of rewards in terms of functional needs of the social system. Though his answer to the question of 'who gets what and why?' appears to be rather simple, his overall theory of social stratification is quite an elaborate one. Lenski has offered a multidimensional view of the working of the distribution system that determines the structure of power and privilege in society.

Lenski's notion of class, however, is very different from that Karl Marx or Max Weber. While Marx and Weber define class primarily in economic terms and treat it as being a part of the economic system of the society, Lenski uses the term in a very broad sense and emphasizes more on its political dimension. For Lenski, stratification is a multidimensional phenomenon and therefore he rejects a single dimensional definition of class. Human societies are stratified in various ways, and each of these alternative modes of stratification provides a basis for different conception of class. Thus, classes are not merely aggregation of individuals who share common economic status in society or a common position in the structure of production. There can be different types of classes, i.e., political classes, ethnic classes and prestige classes.

He defines class as "an aggregation of persons in society who stand in a similar position with respect to some form of power, privilege or prestige" (Lenski, 1966:74-75). However, he clarifies that if one has to explain the phenomenon of social stratification or answer the question 'who gets what and why? Power and class must be our chief concern. Prestige and privilege are largely determined by the distribution of power. By power, Lenski means all those individuals who have access to the institutional sources of power or who have the legitimate right or capability of using force. Thus, in his definition of class, the most crucial element is that of power.

However, the manner in which he defines power and class, a single individual can be member of more than one class. For example, in contemporary Indian society, an individual can be a member of the middle class with respect to property holdings, a member of the working class by virtue of his job in a factory and a member of subordinate ethnic class in terms of his being a dalit by caste. Each of the major roles of occupies, as well as his status in the property hierarchy influences his chances of obtaining the things he seeks in life and thus each places him in a specific class. This tendency towards multidimensionality of class statuses, according to Lenski becomes more pronounced as one moves from technologically primitive societies to technologically advanced societies.

He further argues that every unequal or stratified system has a potential of conflict. The members of every class share common interests with one another, and these shared interests constitute a potential basis of hostility toward other classes. The members of a given class have a vested interest in protecting and increasing the values of their common resources and in reducing the value of the resources of the opposite classes. However, he does not claim that classes always act together or that they are aware of their common interests. Nor are they always hostile to the opposite classes. A given class structure spells out the possibilities that could be realised, but there is nothing inevitable about them. The final element in his theory of social stratification is the concept of **class systems.** A class system, according to Lenski is defined as 'a hierarchy of classes ranked in terms of some single criterion'. However, there is no single class system. He argues that once we recognize the fact that power has diverse basis, and that these are not always reducible to some single common denominator, we are forced to think in terms of series of class hierarchies and class systems.

Berghe Synthesis:

In one of his research articles, 'Dialectic and Functionalism: Toward a Theoretical Synthesis' Published in the American Sociological Review in 1963. Pierre van den Berghe tried to identify the common elements in the two major traditions of sociological theorizing by using the Hegelian concept of synthesis. He argues that Functionalism and Marxian conflict theory each stresses one of two essential aspects of social reality. "Not only does each theory emphasize one of two aspects of social reality which are complementary and inextricably intertwined, but some of the analytical concepts are applicable to both approaches" (Berghe, 1963: 703). However, it is not enough to say that the two theories are complementary. One should be able to show their reconcilability. According to Berghe, by retaining and modifying elements of the two approaches, one can develop such a unified theory of society. He shows that the two theories converge on four important points.

First, both the approaches are holistic in character as they both look at society as a system with interrelated and interdependent parts. However, the two theories have opposite views on the interrelationship of different parts. While functionalism emphasizes on the reciprocal interdependence of parts, the dialectical theory talks about the conflicted relations among the different parts of the system. However, both the theories have been criticized for overemphasizing one at the cost of the other. The concept of system thus needs to include both, interdependence as well as conflict.

Second, their concern with regard to conflict and consensus also tends to overlap. Whereas functionalism regard consensus as major focus of stability and integration, the dialectical theory views conflict as a source of disintegration and revolution. However, according to Berghe, the two can be reconciled into a single theory. For example, Coser has pointed the integrative and stabilizing aspect of conflict. Instead of leading to disintegration, conflict can help the system to retain a dynamic equilibrium. Furthermore, in a number of societies, conflict is institutionalized and ritualized in a manner that seems conducive to integration. In industrial societies, for example, the existence of trade unions of the working class help in regulating industrial relations and they work as safety values against the possibility of a disintegrative kind of class conflict. Similarly, excessive unity among different groups can also lead to inter-group conflict in a plural society where diverse cultural groups live together.

Thirdly, both functionalism and the conflict/dialectical theory share the evolutionary notion of social change. Though their notion of stages and processes involved in the course of historical change differ, they both nevertheless believe in the idea of progress. Class struggle, functionalists attribute this change to a continuous process of social differentiation. However, as Berghe argues, the two theories of change have at least one important point in common: both theories hold that a given state of the social system presupposes all previous stages, and hence, contains them, if only in residual or modified form.

Fourthly, Berghe claims that both functionalism and dialectic-conflict theories are based on "an equilibrium model". In the case of functionalism, this is obvious. But the dialectic sequence of thesis-antithesis-synthesis also involves a notion of equilibrium. The dialectic conceives of society as going through alternating phase of equilibrium and disequilibrium. While the notion of equilibrium in the dialectical theory is different from the classical notion of dynamic equilibrium, the views are neither contradictory nor incompatible with a postulate of long-range tendency towards integration.

3 Ethnic Stratification

Q1. Define ethnicity. **[Dec 07, Q. 9(b)][Dec 06, Q. 3]**

Ans. The terms "ethnicity" and "ethnic group" are derived from the Greek word *ethnos*, normally translated as "people" or "tribe". The term "ethnic" and related forms were used in English in the meaning of "pagan/ heathen" from the 14th century through the middle of the 19th century. This practice was derived from New Testament Greek, which used the plural *ethne* to render the Hebrew *goyim* (or non-Jew). The modern usage of "ethnic group", however, reflects the different kinds of encounters industrialized states have had with subordinate groups, such as immigrants and colonized subjects; "ethnic group" came to stand in opposition to "nation", to refer to people with distinct cultural identities who, through migration or conquest, had become subject to a foreign state. The modern usage of the word is relatively new—1851 — with the first usage of the term *ethnic group* in 1935.

Q2. Discuss about the early conceptions of ethnicity.

Ans. An ethnic group is a group of humans whose members identify with each other, through a common heritage that is real or presumed. Ethnic identity is further marked by the recognition from others of a group's distinctiveness and the recognition of common cultural, linguistic, religious, behavioral traits as indicators of contrast to other groups. Ethnicity is an important means through which people can identify themselves. According to "Challenges of Measuring an Ethnic World: Science, politics, and reality", a conference organised by Statistics Canada and the United States Census Bureau (April 1–3, 1992), "Ethnicity is a fundamental factor in human life: it is a phenomenon inherent in human experience." However, many social scientists, like anthropologists Fredrik Barth and Eric Wolf, do not consider ethnic identity to be universal. They regard ethnicity as a product of specific kinds of intergroup interactions, rather than an essential quality inherent to human groups. Processes that result in the emergence of such identification are called ethno genesis. Members of an ethnic group, on the whole, claim cultural continuities over time. Historians and cultural anthropologists have documented, however, that often many of the values, practices, and norms that imply continuity with the past are of relatively recent invention.

According to Thomas Hylland Eriksen, until recently the study of ethnicity was dominated by two distinct debates. One is between "primordialism" and "instrumentalism". In the primordial's view, the participant perceives ethnic ties collectively, as an externally given, even coercive, social bond. The instrumentalist approach, on the other hand, treats ethnicity primarily as an ad-hoc element of a political strategy, used as a resource for interest groups for achieving secondary goals such as, for instance, an increase in wealth, power or status. This debate is still an important point of reference in Political science, although most scholars' approaches fall between the two poles. The second debate is between "constructivism" and "essentialism". Constructivists view national and ethnic identities as the product of historical forces, often recent, even when the identities are presented as old. Essentialists view such identities as ontological categories defining social actors, and not themselves the result of social action. According to Eriksen, these debates have been superseded, especially in anthropology, by scholars' attempts to respond to increasingly politicised forms of self-representation by members of different ethnic groups and nations.

Q3. Explain the concept of ethnic stratification.

[June 08, Q. 9][Dec 06, Q. 3]

Or

Discuss Ethnicity as the basis of social stratification.

Ans. Stratification is a system whereby people are unequally ranked and rewarded on the basis of wealth, power and prestige. It is part of every society and may take various forms like class, gender, race and, of course, ethnicity. The earlier studies of stratification used to focus on the phenomena of caste and race while gender and ethnicity were treated as side issues. However, of late not only have ethnicity and gender been getting some attention in stratification analysis, but ethnic stratification is even replacing class as the foremost form of social division since now property relations tend to be determined by ethnic ranking instead of it being the other way round. The model of internal colonialism is used to analyse ethnic resurgence and conflicts by highlighting the dominant group's political control over, economic exploitation of and cultural domination over the minority groups, and their ideological justification of this unequal relationship. Ethnic stratification shares a lot of things with the other forms of stratification, such as, ranking, inequality, discrimination, exploitation etc.

Ethnic Nationalism: Membership of an ethnic group tends to determine a person's status in society. This can occur in two ways. Social rewards like money, prestige and power are often allocated along ethnic lines. Secondly, in most societies one or more ethnic groups dominate others in economic, political and cultural matters. Ethnic politics can, therefore, take the appearance of ethnic stratification resulting in the emergence of ethnic nationalism. Ethnic identity may sometimes be related to political necessities and demands. This happens when minority groups try to play the ethnic card in order to acquire a better deal for themselves in a plural society. However, some ethnic groups go a step further and demand a say in the political system or control over a piece of territory or even demand a national status, i.e., country of their own. If they succeed in achieving any of these objectives they become a nationality or a nation.

Nation and Ethnic Group: The concepts of nation, nation-state, nationality, national minority etc. arose with the rise of capitalism in Western Europe and spread to the rest of the world. Nation is derived from the Latin word *nasci* meaning to be born and Latin noun *nationem,* i.e., breed or race. It is a historically evolved, stable uniformity of languages, territory, economic life and psychological makeup which can be seen in the form of a common culture. More importantly, it is a type of ethnic community which is politicized and has universally accepted group rights in a political system.

Oommen (1997) holds that nation and ethnic group share many features but differ on a crucial point, namely, territory. An ethnic group becomes a nation only when it identifies itself with a territory. Contrarily, a nation becomes an ethnic community when the members are separated from their homeland. No single feature of ethnic groups can be identified as being more important than the others. Each gains importance in different situations. But a nation cannot be a nation without territory. Thus, he calls ethnic groups 'passive nations', groups with potential to become nations while nations are 'active ethnicity' as they emerge out of ethnic elements. Bacal (1997) too, offers the terms 'micro-nations' and 'macro-ethnies' for ethnic groups and nations, respectively supporting Oommen's emphasis on territory being the key factor in differentiating the two.

Nationalism and Ethnicity: Nationalism refers to the expressed desire of a people to establish and maintain a self-governing political entity. It has proven to be one of the most powerful forces in the contemporary world, both a creator and destroyer of modern state. Nationality and ethnicity are related, yet different. Ethnicity may become nationalism and nationalism is always based on real or assumed ethnic ties. Yet, at the heart of nationalism lie in the three themes of autonomy, unity and identity. Autonomy implies an effort by a people to determine their own destiny and free themselves from external constraint. Unity means ending internal divisions and uniting, and identity involves an effort by a group to find and express their authentic cultural heritage and identity (Cornell and Hartman, 1988). Thus, nationalism is a form of ethnicity in which a particular ethnic identity is crystallized and institutionalized by acquiring a political agenda. Nations are created when ethnic groups in a multi-ethnic state are transformed into a self-conscious political entities. Hence, it is the goals of sovereignty and self-determination that set nationalism apart from ethnicity.

Development of a Nationality: According to Brass (1991) there are two steps in the formation of a nationality. First there is transformation of an ethnic category into a community which involves changes like creation of a self-conscious linguistic unity, formation of a caste association etc. this happens in the early stages of modernisation in multi-ethnic societies where social divisions of various kinds are still prevalent. The second stage involves the articulation and acquisition of social, economic and political rights for the members of the group or for the group as a whole. When the group succeeds by its own efforts in achieving and maintaining group rights through political action and political mobilisation, it goes beyond ethnicity and establishes itself as a nationality.

However, why does ethnicity become nationality? This question is answered by the *relative deprivation approach* which focuses our attention of the feeling of frustration caused by the differences between what people feel they legitimately deserve and what they actually get. Similarly, when subjugated groups fail to achieve success according to the norms established by the dominant group the nature of their response tends to be ethnic antagonism which may take the form of: **a)** struggle of the indigenous people's right to their land and culture, **b)** efforts by minority groups to procure equal economic, political and cultural rights; **c)** competition by ethnic groups for obtaining scarce resources; and **d)** movements for a separate nation.

Ethno-Nationalism: The Indian Case: Sharma (1991) has described how ethnic antagonism has posed four serious challenges to the Indian state. These are:

Casteism: A curious mix of ethnic identity and modern interests in which the ethnic group uses the caste ideology to further its economic and political interests, e.g., a political party asking for votes of a particular caste group.

Communalism: The "unholy" alliance between religion and politics in which religion may be used for political or economic gains, e.g., the Hindutva concept used by the BJP.

Nativism: The 'sons of the soil' concept in which regional identities become the source of ethnic strife, e.g., the movement in Assam to expel the 'foreigners' from Bengal.

Ethno-nationalism: The transformation of an ethnic group to a nationality which may start demanding autonomous governance in a particular territory or even secession, separation and recognition as a sovereign nation, e.g., the movement in Kashmir and Punjab.

Q4. Discuss the concept of social movement with reference to tribes in India. [June 08, Q. 2]

Ans. The word "tribe" is generally used for a "socially cohesive unit, associated with a territory, the members of which regard them as politically autonomous". Often a tribe possesses a distinct dialect and distinct cultural traits. The term 'primitive tribes' was often used by western anthropologist to denote "a primary aggregate of peoples living in a primitive or barbarous condition under a headman or chief". Various anthropologists define tribe as a people at earlier stage of evolution of society. The tribes are considered to be a complete society amongst them. They are a complete society within themselves. The forest (territory) occupies a central position in tribal culture and economy. The tribal way of life is very much dictated by the forest right from birth to death. It is ironical that the poorest people of India are living in the areas of richest natural resources. Tribes have been living in forests and have been protecting them. They have an inherent right over that, which does not require a piece of paper to establish its legitimacy. Their cultural identity has to be restored at any cost, by the state. These tribes are engrossed in their culture, which when taken away cannot be returned in any other form. No rehabilitation is sufficient and no monetary benefit is capable of restoring the same. Thus, the state has no right to do something which it cannot undo. Tribes are a part of society and any step for development of society, must include even the tribals and not just the state holders. This is what is called an egalitarian society and is in accordance with our constitutional scheme.

In spite of the protection given to the tribal population by the Constitution of India (1950), tribals still remain the most backward ethnic group in India. Tribal development policies and programmes in India assumed that all the tribals will develop and will integrate themselves with the so-called mainstream. This has happened only in a symbolic way. One must consider tribal life and culture to be as worthy as any other culture. Displacement cannot be a precondition for the tribal people to get access to basic public facilities like health care, education or transport. It is their right as citizens, to get these facilities wherever they are. This is the duty of a welfare state. In the similar way no tribal can be asked to leave the forests, so that the selfish needs of some are satisfied. They are the son of soils, the preserver of natural recourses and a living example of their culture and identity, which cannot be encroached under any circumstance. Moreover, with asking them to leave from their territory, we are not respecting their relationship with their eco-system (including their IPRs), which will become of major importance in the coming years. An experience in India is worth sharing. It relates to a medicine basic active ingredient is an extract from a plant, trichopus zeylanicus, found in the tropical forests of southwestern India and collected by the Kani tribal people. Scientists at the Tropical Botanic Garden and Research Institute (TBGRI) in Kerala learned of the plant, which is claimed to bolster the immune system and provide additional energy, while on an expedition with the Kani in 1987. These scientists isolated and tested the ingredient and incorporated it into a compound, which they christened "Jeevani", the giver of life. The tonic is now being manufactured by a major Ayurvedic drug company in Kerala. In 1995, an agreement was struck to share the license fee and 2% of sales of the product as royalty that was receivable by TBGRI, on a fifty-fifty basis with the tribe. Thus, these tribes are a store house of much traditional knowledge, which should not be allowed to get buried under the developmental scheme. This is likely to be a "I don't disagree with the fact that we have to develop. But no national development can be carried out at the cost of its own nationals" issue. The courts have to take up these issues and provide relief. The courts also have not showed a positive sign on this subject. The recent Narmada issue is a leading example of the same. The tribal does not believe that the State – the Courts – can give him justice. While this lack of faith has historical roots, the positions taken by the Courts in recent years, especially with respect to mass displacement, have only further strengthened this belief. There are various figures regarding the extent of displacement in the country. Walter Fernandez pegs it at 300 lakhs of people, while another study put the figure at 164 lakhs, of whom only 25% could be resettled. Despite these mind-boggling figures regarding the extent of decimation of tribal communities, the Courts have consistently held that these Projects serve a public purpose, and are necessary for the "welfare of the nation". When these questions are consistently answered by the Courts to the detriment of the tribal, is it logical to expect the tribal to have 'faith in the judicial system'. Hence, immediate steps are required at the hands of judiciary and the state. That is, tribes cannot be a subject of development; rather they have to be a part of development.

Q5. Discuss tribal social stratification systems in the context of North-East India. [Dec 08, Q. 3]

Ans. The system of social stratification covers two main dimensions, the traditional system of stratification based on age, sex, kinship, etc. and the stratification emerging in the society as a result of the influence of a number of modernizing process, education, industrialisation, occupational differentiation, status hierarchies associated with parliamentary democracy, government employment etc. which tend to stratify the society in terms of new class and status hierarchies modifying, reinforcing or undermining the traditional hierarchical divisions.

Traditional the tribe of the North-East have not been homogeneous egalitarian units. A number of factors have contributed to the development of the stratification system among the different tribal communities, most important being lineage, relationship to land, ritual status, position of economic, social and political dominance. The manner in which these factors are distributed leads to the formation and perpetuation of hierarchies within the various tribal groups and of the dominance of one tribal group over the other. Among the Garos, for example, the land meant for shifting cultivation and homestead plots was the property of seven lineages (Mahari) known as a king.

Mizo Administration: The Mizos had a well established system of administration through their chiefs. All activities in the life of a village involved are around the chief and his house. Each village was ruled by its chief. It was the normal practice that the son of a chief was given on marriage a certain number of households by his father to set up their own village and become independent. Generally, the youngest or the eldest son depending on the clan would remain with the father to succeed him and all his property on death.

Among the Silos hereditary succession is through the youngest while for the Paite it is the eldest. In his work of administration the chief was assisted by council of eldest known as Upa and Zawlbuk, the youngmen's dormitory. Upa were given preference in the choice of field for Jhums and favour at the time of feast or any other functions organized or patronized by the chief. The other important functionaries in the village were the Tlangau (the village crier), the Third ending (the village Blacksmith) and the Puithiam (the village priest) each of these functionaries received a basketful of Paddy for performing professional work for the members of the village. Similarly the Zawlbuk was an important institution and played a very crucial role.

The Mizo chiefs also had certain rights and privileges like **(i)** Fathang (paddy tax); **(ii)** Schhiah (meat tax) **(iii)** Salam (fee in the form of fine) **(iv)** building and repairing of chiefs house whenever asked to do so. The chiefs also granted the privileges to a class of farmers called Ramhual and Salen who the first choice of jhum fields.

However after independence it was through the internal struggle, awareness, growth of urbanisation and emergence of middle class with its aspirations that the institution chieftainship was abolished giving rise to stratification on the basis of class and other new emerging interests.

Power and Prestige Among Nagas: Among the Nagas too this inequality if reflected through the unequal sharing of power, prestige and wealth, largely acquired through the feast of merit where, 'perishable food substances were redistributed which has social function to secure symbolic prestige, and honoured alliances during the war as well peace for example the Semas were differentiated in term of **(i)** Kekami (chiefs), **(ii)** Chockomi (chiefs associated) **(iii)** Mughamis (Orphens or commoner), **(iv)** Akahemi (chiefs dependents) and **(v)** Anukeshimi (chiefs fields cultivators). Haimendorf has shown how the institution of chiefs survived among the knoyaks on the principle of purity of blood.

Further Haimendorf's (1992: 29, 286-313, 315-323) elaborate study of Arunachal Pradesh drew attention to the prevalence of similar trends there too. The most important tribes of the region are the Apatanis who live in seven villages ranging in size from 160 to 1000 houses. The Apatanis are agriculturists and live in a rigidly stratification society. There are primarily two Apatanis are agriculturists and live in a rigidly stratification society. There are primarily two classes differing in status: an upper class whose members owned a large part of the land and wield political power in class and village and lower class which used to consist of few men owning their own land as well as domestic slaves. The primary difference being between the Mate. Mite-Guth (Patricians) and the Mura, Cuchi (slaves/connoners).

The Jaintias and Khasis: The Jantias too had a more elaborate stratification system. They were differentiated between.

i) Raja (king),

ii) Dolois (Governor),

iii) Wahen Ch Nong (Village headman),

iv) Myntries, Patas, Laskars, Sangat, Maji (who are commoners and include all categories of officials.).

Tilput Nongbri has discussed an interesting aspect of the stratification system of the Tribals in the context of gender. She mentions that tribal customary laws like the non-tribal societies deny them equal right to property. This discrimination is specially meted out in the case of inheritance laws, where women are entitled only to maintenance rights and expenses. In matrilineal society too, in the context of land, a sharp distinction is made between 'ownership' and 'control'. Thus, while ownership is passed on through women, the control rests with men e.g. the Khasi, Jaintia, Garo, Rabha etc. Similarly where women posses usufructory rights in the patriarchal societies, they are subject to a number of conditions like their remaining unmarried, having no brothers, being widowed and forced to marry a prescribed in. Similarly, women face a bias in the allocation and management of common property resources. Women also face discrimination in matters of marriage and divorce. The practice of bride price by which women become almost like commodities is particularly delimiting. The women also face the problem of being treated as threats to their descent group and ethnic identity particularly in the context of the demographic repercussion of a women's marriage with the outsiders have made many men want to change the matrilineal system of inheritance to matrilineal thus weakening its base.

Traditional Ranking Systems: All these examples show elaborate and varying traditional ranking systems conditioned by the particular ecological and historical circumstances of different tribes. The beginning of the colonial rule and its ending at the time of independence of the country led to a number of important changes which shook the carefully protected relatively isolated world of the North-East tribals. These included linking up the tribals with colonial system of administration which meant opening up further towards. Shillong, Calcutta, Delhi and even London, the coming in of the Christian Missionaries, introduction of the market economy, the formalisation and consolidation of status hierarchy within the tribes by the British for their administrative and political convenience, extension of protective discrimination and development schemes for backward areas and finally participation in the democratic process in independence India and resulting changes at various levels.

Q6. Write briefly about the salient features of Tribal Social movement in North-East India. [Dec 08, Q. 13]

Ans. We need to bear in mind the unique geo-political and historical background of the tribal people of the North-East in order to understand the specificity and very different character of the tribal movements of this region from those of other areas. These background factors include:

i) Because of their location of international borders, many of these tribal communities played the role of bridge and buffer communities and so had developed bonds with certain groups across the borders.

ii) British colonial administration followed a policy of insuring economic social and political isolation on these tribes from the rest of the country. The tribal areas were categorized as excluded or partially excluded areas and contacts of the outsiders with these areas were strictly regulated, particularly in the excluded areas where no outsiders could enter without obtaining a permit. Thus, their areas not only remain unaffected by the political influence of the freedom struggle in the country, but also developed apprehensions about maintaining their own separate identity and political autonomy in relation to independent India.

iii) Unlike the tribals of middle India, tribals in the North-East have throughout constituted an overwhelming majority (expect in Tripura) and being free from exploitative economic and social contacts with their Assamese neighbours including alienation of their land and forests, failed to develop agrarian and millenarian movements which frequently characterized the tribals of other regions of the country.

iv) Spread of the Christianity and mission education gave the tribals a distinctive sense of identity and made them apprehensive about their future in Independent India.

v) Influence of the second world war as threatres of war came close to their habitat in the North-East.

vi) Impending independence of India and resulting heightening of political consciousness and struggle.
vii) After independence there was open unrestricted contact between the tribals and outsiders. A number of traders, refugees and other migrants began to settle in the area, acquiring land and resources. All these generated fears of being swamped by outsiders and losing land, forests and other resources to the outsiders.
viii) The impact of modernisation of Tribal life and social institutions, especially the conflict between members of the growing middle class and traditional chiefs as well as dislocations of the traditional pattern of land control and land relations.
Depending on the particular circumstances and objective of the individual movements, many of these factors indifferent combinations affected the formation and development of the different tribals movement. Because of the characteristic conditions of their genesis, thrust of these movements has been largely political, centering on issues of identity and security', with 'goals ranging from autonomy to independence and means from constitutional agitation to insurgency'. Although a majority of the movement have also centred on issues of language, script and cultural revival, the same political struggle appears to have been reflected in these movements also. We will now look at some of the movements in detail to understand their specificity.
The Naga Movement: A large number of factors acted as catalysts for the Naga Movement. These were:
i) fear of the losing special privileges bestowed upon them by the British,
ii) the danger of erosion cultural autonomy and district 'ethnic identity,'
iii) fear of losing the customary ownership of the hills,
iv) The spread of Christianity,
v) Development of format education in the Naga Hills, and
vi) Reaction to the formation of complex political structures.
Though the Naga ethnic identity and the movement were sharply articulated after independence, the roots were sworn with the formation of the Naga Club in 1918 at Kohima. The first taken up the club was a memorandum submitted to the Simon commission in 1929 seeking the continuity of the direct British Administration of the hills and number of other issues. The memorandum was signed by representatives of most of the Naga tribes.
A very important role in the resurrection of Naga identity was played by Zapu Phizo, who had assisted the Japanese and the INA with the hope of getting help to form a sovereign Naga State (Verghese 1994: 85). Their was a great deal of debate over what the Naga's wanted after British lift India. The issue centred primarily on autonomy Vs Independence.
The Nagas boycotted the first General Election in 1952 and the District Council Scheme. This agitation took a violent turn when Phizo announced the formation

of a Republican Government of Free Nagaland at 'Kautaga' on September 18th, 1954. In this endeavor the moderate elements like Sakhrie were completely outnumbered. Soon, he was assassinated and underground gorilla warfare began in earnest. The army was called out to aid the civilian government on August 27th. 1955. Gradually the gorilla struggle lost momentum but the people continued to suffer acute hardship under harsh army control. This situation became a rallying point for the moderates who abandoned independence and discussed the protect their heritage and way of life. A Naga Peoples' convention was called in Kohima in August 1957. It was a conglomeration of 1760 delegates representing all the tribes in the Naga Hills and Tuensang district of NEFA. After a long deliberation, the council decided to seek a single Naga Hills – Tuensang administrative unit within the Indian Union. The NHTA was created as an autonomous district directly administered by the governor of Assam on behalf of the President. This convention was followed by two more conventions. The deliberation of the October 1959 convention led to a historic landmark agreement with the government of India in July 1960. Under the agreement the NHTA was to be redesigned as Nagaland and became an independent state in December 1963. Even as the elections took place to the assembly, the underground movement continued. Several inconclusive rounds of the talks were held between the underground leadership and the Government of India. A peace mission was set up in 1964 which had J.P. Narayan, B.P. Calika, Rev. Michael Scott and Shandkaro Dev as its members. All these activities and efforts finally culminated in the Shillong accord of November 11, 1975.

Under this agreement the underground accepted the constitution of India deposited their arms, security forces halted their operations and gave enough time to the underground organisations to formulate other issues for discussion for the final settlement to take place. Though this accord brought peace to the area, a section of the underground under the Nationalist Socialist Council of Nagaland set up in 1980 is still struggling for a sovereign state.

Tribal Policy in Tripura: Tripura represents an example of a state which despite being ruled by a tribal ruler followed policies which reduced its original tribal inhabitants to a minority. The state consisted of nineteen major tribes of which the Tripura is to which the ruler belonged were the most dominant. Due to a variety of historical reasons most tribals had come under the influence of Hinduism, particularly Vaishnavism. For economic reasons the Maharaja, who had zamidaris in the adjoining districts of Comilla, Noakhali and Chittagong, invited the Bengali peasants from there to develop settled agriculture in Tripur. They were known as Ziratia tenants and, they apart from promotion agriculture, generated much needed revenues for the state. For humanitarian considerations also the ruler allowed the Bengali refugees to settle in his kingdom and reclaim forest lands for cultivation. Similarly a number of entrepreneurs were encouraged to establish tea gardens. Bengali being the language of the administration a number of Bengali professional and white collared workers, teachers and other also got settled in the state.

This process changed the demographic profile of the state, the tribals who constituted 64% of the population in 1974 were only 36% of the population in 1911, and by 1931 the number of immigrants from various other regions mostly Assam and Bengal had risen to 114, 383. However the maharaja of Tripura in his proclamation of 1931 and 1943 reserved certain area almost 5050 sq. km. For settled agriculture of five designated tribes the Tripuris, Reangs, Jamatis, Naotis and Halams.

i) This demographic charge meant an increasing dominance and control of immigrants in various departments particularly the market and the credit system as well as professional and service sector. This also resulted in large number of tribals being pushed back to the interior, tremendous pressure on land, increase in mortgages and indebtedness, banning of slash and burn cultivation, increased alienation of land and transfer from tribals to non-tribals. Thus, 'the changing demographic balance, economic pressures created by the sudden influx of population, and the spread of education, combined to generate new impulses, a mix of expectations and discontents' (Verghese 1994:171).

The first response to this unrest was the formation of the tribal militant organisation the Seng Krak in 1947. This was followed by two other tribal bodies, the Adivasi Samiti and the Tripura Rajya Admivasi Sangh, both of which came together in 1954 in the Adivasi Sansad. The Easter India Tribal Union also established its branch in Tripura and contested election in 1957 and 1962. Similarly the communists had established a strong presence in Tripura forming the Rajya Mukti Parishad in 1948 and taking up the cause of the tribals vis-à-vis the non-tribals, communist leaders. The split and decline in the communist party and the reemergence of the congress as a result of changing equations created a lot of disillusionment and resentment among the younger generation who formed the Tripura, Upajati Juba Samita (TUJS) under Samachran Tripua on June 10, 1967. TUJS is a political organisation of the Tribals, With a four point agenda **(a)** creation of an autonomous district council for tribals under the sixth schedule of the constitution **(b)** restoration of tribal lands illegally transferred to the non-tribals **(c)** recognition of the Kek-Barak language **(d)** adoption of Roma Scupt.

ii) The TUJS campaigned massively for the fulfillment of its demands. Resorting to agitation, propaganda, petitions, dharnas and protest, through phases of upswings and downswings, the TUJS managed to retain its hold and work for the cause of tribal upliftment as Tripura became a fully fledged state in 1972. The 1977 elections saw the recovery of the communists who were returned back to power marginalizing both the congress and the TUJS.

The CPM government made a number of moves to restore and strengthen the tribal position. Among them being the recognition to the Kek-Barak language, measures to implement the agrarian laws on illegally alienated lands, set in motion the process of forming an autonomous hill council. Through these moves were welcomed by the tribals and the moderate section of the TUJS, a section of radicals smarting under the declining influence of the TUJS, came into prominence under the leadership of a Christian Missionary Vijay Kumar Rankhel, who saw the bond of Christianity as an important vehicle to forge unity and assertion among the tribal. He also sought the help of the MNF and other organisations to train the TUJS volunteers. He become the self-styled leader of the Tripura Tribal National Front and the Tripura Sena. The secession and independence of Tripura became important goals for him. This revival of the movement coincided with the movement against foreigners in Manipur, Meghalaya and Assam. The TUJS Conference of March 1980 gave a call for the deportation of all foreigners came to Tripura after 15 October 1949. The violent agitation was begun by a call for boycott of foreigners, particularly traders and protests outside important government offices. A lot of violence took place against the Bengali and other settlers who countered it through the Arma Bengali. The carnage reached a crescendo in almost a month. The fuse being ignited by the Lembucherra incident.

iii) The Dinesh Singh Committee on Tripura set up by the centre saw the real solution of the problem in the economic development of the region. It took note of the transformation brought in the state as a result of inroads made into tribal society by traders lend grabbers, refugees and missionaries. The committee made an elaborate list of suggested short and long term measures to ameliorate the problem. These included elimination of disparities, restoration of land to the tribals and ensuring their rehabilitation. The TUJS disassociated itself from the militant Tripura National Volunteers led by Rankhal and called a peaceful agitation for implementation of the Dinesh Singh Committee report, a judicial inquiry into the June incident and the formation of Tribal Area Autonomous Council, while the Anti-foreigners agitation, was put on hold. After a period of intense struggle the TNV militants finally negotiated a settlement with the government on Aug. 12, 1988. Under the agreement promised speedy action in the restoration of alienated lands, the formation of a Autonomous district council, stringent measures to prevent infiltration from across the border, etc.

iv) However, not all factions of the TNV were satisfied with this agreement. They established breakaway groups to continue the agitation like the All Tripura Tribal Force (which signed agreement with the state in 1993), the National Liberation Front of Tripura. The Tripura Rajya Raksha Bahini Tripura State Volunteers, Tripura National Democratic Tribal Force. However, the intensive, conviction and commitment of the agitation has waned. But the groups continue to survive patronized and supported simultaneously by different political parties and underground movements across the borders who provide resources and ammunition. (317-339; Doley 1998: 30-32; Verghese 1994: 165-195).

Tribal Struggle in Manipur: Manipur has a long history of struggle. The prominent among them being the Zeliangrong Naga uprising (1930-32), the Kuki rebellion (1917-19), the women agitation, Meiti state committee and a number of other agitations. Manipur was a princely state which merged with India in 1949, remained a UT till finally granted statehood in 1972. To account for the agitations to resurface in the state, Kabui relates it to crisis of identity, weakness of the Indian political system, economic exploitation, corruption, unemployment and influence of foreign power and ideology (cf. Doley 1998: 21). The various agitations launched in the state were.

i) The Meitei State Committee was formed in 1967 in protest at Manipur's merger with the Indian Union. This organisation gradually became a revolutionary body seeking an independent Manipur governed on the lines of a Socialist ideology developed by Irabot Singh. The movement weakened and the committee surrendered in 1971. This movement failed as result of **(a)** low level of education of leaders **(b)** lack of clarity about the objectives of the movement **(c)** lack of strong infrastructural organisation and support. (Doley 1998:24).

ii) The Kukis in Manipur revolted against the British in 1917-19 in response to the alien intervention in the traditional pattern of and way of life of the tribal people. Though this response was suppressed by the British. It found expression against the treatment of the melties by the government became an important turning point in the agitation. A fillup has been provided by the growing prominence of the Sanmahi cult, which explodes the myth of the Aryan origin of the Meities who converted to Hinduism in the eighteenth century. An important role has been played by the Manipur National Front which aims to revive the Mongoloid heritage which would unit the Sanamahis as well as other Mongoloid people of the NE. The front, as it tries to go back to its own tribal religion, seeks to get rid of the borrowing and domination and exploitation imposed on them by Brahmin and Vaishnav practices. The resurgence of the Sanamahi cult revived the Meteir script, language and literature, thus given from to a distinct Metei identity. At the same time this assertion was also a reaction against Hindus and outsiders. It emphasized the glory of Manipur and its cultural distinction from India. An offshoot of the emergence of Metei, Nationalism has been the gradual erosion of the word Manipur and Manipuri and its replacement by Kangleipak and Metei respectively (Kabui: 1983, p.236-237) which can only be achieved by the formation of a Meitei homeland.

All these factors have contributed to the spread of insurgency in Manipur, of the two main organisations active in the state, the people's revolutionary party of Kangleipak (PREPAK) and PLA (people's liberation army), PREPAK is seen as a Marxist-Leninist party closely linked to Meitei revivalism while the PLA has radical ideology and a strong rural base and prefers to propagate communist ideology and integrated insurgent groups across the N.E. Thus, the Meities represent an interesting group at the cross roads who have revived their traditional religion and yet are unable to get the status of tribals which they aspire for and failure to achieve which prevent them from getting privileges under the sixth schedule (Doley 1998: 22-27, Verghese 1994: 113-134; Kabui 1983: 234-237; 1992:5357)

Resurfaced with the Kuki National Assembly in 1946, which gradually articulated a political demand for a autonomous district or state for Kuki Inbals in order to fully reaplise the culture and glory of their own culture and may of life. (Doley 1998: 25).

iii) The Manipur women protested against the British regarding Rice Trading and the British export policy. The immediate cause of the movement was the shortage of foodgrains in Manipur due to the vagaries of the weather; the high price of rice in the local market due to exports and the pressure of the vested business interests. It was one Manipuri woman, Aribam Chaotian Devi, who organized a few women to stop selling rice to the mill owners. A chain reaction followed and other women got involved in the agitation. Though this was suppressed by the British in 1941 but left its impact on the administrative set up and cultural pattern of the state. (Doley 1998: 26-27).

iv) The Zeliangrong movement was started by three tribal groups the Zemei, Liangmei and the Rongmei who together were called the Zeliangrong. This movement began essentially as a social reform movement and was led by a young Rongmel Nagar Jadonang and his cousin Rani Gaidinliu. They formed the Heraka cult which sought to abolish some cuational customs, and to reform and revive the traditional religion, as a response to Hinduism and impact of Christianity. The movement was also anti- British and anti-Kuki, and it sought to establish Naga rule by forging a single Zeliangrong identity Jadonang's subsequent arrest and executive gave a jolt to the movement. However, his cousin Gainilue carried it forward linking it to the struggle against British rule and civil disobedience movement of the Congress (Kubui 1982:56), She was, however, imprisoned for almost 14 years and in the mean time the movement lost much of its steam. It gradually got converted to a purely peaceful movement and various tribal organisations like the Kabnui Samity (1934), Kabui Naga Association (1946), Zeliangrong Council (1947) Manipur Zeliangrousn Union (1947) all came into the picture with the objective of overthrowing the British rule. After more than two decades the aim of the movement became political, seeking the creation of a separate Zeliengrong Administrative Unit consisting of the Zeliangrong inhabited areas of Manipur, Nagaland and Assam's Cachar hills.

Q7. Write a short note about the Bodo movement.

Ans. Bodoland is an area located in the north bank of Brahmaputra river in the state of Assam in north east region of India, by the foothills of Bhutan and Arunachal Pradesh; inhabited predominantly by Bodo language speaking ethnic group. Currently the hypothetical map of Bodoland includes the Bodoland Territorial Areas District (BTAD) administered by the non-autonomous Bodoland Territorial Council (BTC). The map of Bodoland overlaps with the districts of Kokrajhar, Baksa, Chirang and Udalguri in the state of Assam. At present, Kokrajhar serves as the capital of Bodoland. The early history of Bodos is largely unknown. By definition, Bodos do not display tribalistic culture or rituals in that they do not live in caves or jungles or go hunting wild animals. For century's majority Bodos remained as farmers, cultivators, and peace loving society. Like many cultures in the world today, Bodos are also ethnocentric or nationalist society. Cultural assimilation with Assamese was not productive. In brief, before the British Raj, Bodo-kachari Kingdom may have included a vast area extending far and beyond Assam, a small province in the North-East India. History suggests that Dimapur was the capital of Bodo-Kachari kingdom. The British-India colonial rulers effectively adapted divide and rule policy for over 300 years. It is likely that Bodo- The official Bodoland Movement for an independent state of Bodoland started on March 2nd, 1987 under the leadership of Upendranath Brahma of ABSU. The ABSU created a political organisation, the Bodo Peoples' Action Committee (BPAC), to spearhead the movement. The ABSU/BPAC movement began with the slogan "Divide Assam 50-50". The ABSU/BPAC leadership of the movement ended with the bipartite Bodo Accord of February 20, 1993 and the creation of the BAC. The accord soon collapsed amidst a vertical split in ABSU and other Bodo political parties brought about mainly by the split between S K Bwiswmuthiary and Premsingh Brahma, and violence erupted in Bodo areas leading to a displacement of over 70,000 people Kachari were lagging behind their fellow Indians in terms of education and employability. Since the time of British Raj, Assam is known to produce oil and natural gas, and Assam tea. Before independence (1947), North-East India was a remote place.

Compared to other parts of India, such as West Bengal and Maharashtra, education came to North East India only after Indian independence in 1947. Even after India obtained independence, most administrative positions were filled by immigrants from West Bengal, East Bengal (now Bangladesh), and other parts of India. When India obtained independence, B The official Bodoland Movement for an independent state of Bodoland started on March 2nd, 1987 under the leadership of Upendranath Brahma of ABSU. The ABSU created a political organisation, the Bodo Peoples' Action Committee (BPAC), to spearhead the movement. The ABSU/BPAC movement began with the slogan "Divide

Assam 50-50". The ABSU/BPAC leadership of the movement ended with the bipartite Bodo Accord of February 20th, 1993 and the creation of the BAC. The accord soon collapsed amidst a vertical split in ABSU and other Bodo political parties brought about mainly by the split between S K Bwiswmuthiary and Premsingh Brahma, and violence erupted in Bodo areas leading to a displacement of over 70,000 people were not represented by within the government. Following Indian independence, the Bodos were given opportunity to take advantage of scheduled tribe (ST) status. This process lead to the creation of tribal belts and blocks, protected lands meant for farming and grazing, specifically for the Bodo people. The official Bodoland Movement for an independent state of Bodoland started on March 2, 1987 under the leadership of Upendranath Brahma of ABSU. The ABSU created a political organisation, the Bodo Peoples' Action Committee (BPAC), to spearhead the movement. The ABSU/BPAC movement began with the slogan "Divide Assam 50-50". The ABSU/BPAC leadership of the movement ended with the bipartite Bodo Accord of February 20th, 1993 and the creation of the BAC. The accord soon collapsed amidst a vertical split in ABSU and other Bodo political parties brought about mainly by the split between S K Bwiswmuthiary and Prem Singh Brahma, and violence erupted in Bodo areas leading to a displacement of over 70,000 people.

Q8. Describe religious ethnicity in the context of Punjab.[June 08, Q. 4]
Ans. The **Punjabi people** are an Indo-Aryan ethnic group from South Asia. In recent times, however, the definition has been broadened to include also emigrants of Punjabi descent who maintain Punjabi cultural traditions, even when they no longer speak the language. Punjabis make up almost 45% of the population of Pakistan. The Punjabis found in Pakistan are composed of various social groups (caste) and economic groups.

The present day Punjab is a rather small state located in the northwest of India. Despite it being relatively small in size, the state of Punjab occupies an important place in the India politics. The state is located on India's border with Pakistan. The effects of the partition of the sub-continent in 1947 were felt the most in Punjab. A large number of people migrated from both sides of the "new" border. Most importantly for us, Punjab is one of the states of India where a majority of the population belongs to a minority religion. Nearly sixty percent of Punjab's population is that of the Sikhs. Not only that, the state has also witnessed various ethnic mobilisations during the late nineteenth century. But the most important separatist movement occurred during the decade of 1980s. As a consequence of these mobilisations, the Sikhs of Punjab acquired a separate ethnic and religious identity.

Q9. Describe the historical background to religious ethnicity in Punjab.

Ans. The term 'Punjab' emerged during the Mughal period when the province of Lahore was enlarged to cover the whole of the Bist Jalandhar Doab and the upper portions of the remaining four doabs or interfluves. 'Punjab' is thus actually co-terminous with the Mughal province of Lahore, that is, the Mughal Lahore became known as the province of Punjab. The boundaries of Punjab changed several times thereafter, under Maharaja Ranjit Singh, the British and in independent India. The religious movements during these centuries, as well as the freedom movement in the rest of India had important affects on the economic and social life of the province. British rule in Punjab introduced new institutions and technologies. The colonial state subscribed to the values of humanism, rationalism and progress. Yet the state was geared towards using its technological and industrial superiority to perpetuate its own domination and maximise its economic advantages. Thus, an increase in agrarian production meant that the surplus was taken away by foreign agencies. The network of perennial canals built by the new state, combined with new agricultural techniques, implements and seeds, made Punjab agriculturally the best-developed region of India. The bulk of its agricultural surplus entered foreign trade. The commercialisation of agriculture transformed the large peasant proprietor in the upper doabs and the canal colonies into a producer for the world market. But the small peasant often had to depend on the moneylender to meet the fixed revenue demand. Thus, notwithstanding agricultural expansion and increase in production, an overwhelming proportion of the actual cultivators in colonial Punjab began to exist at the level of subsistence. As machine-made goods became available, the traditional artisan was faced with a shrinking market. As his incomes fell he began to look for opportunities outside the village community. However, not many opportunities were available since industry was slow to grow in Punjab. An increasing number of artisans thus became skilled and unskilled labourers on construction sites, railway tracks and railway workshops. Some migrated to the British colonies in Africa, Latin America and South-east Asia in search of work. However, others took to the new education and became professionals like teachers, lawyers and engineers. Some turned to petty trading and jobs related to industry; others joined the police, army and civil administration. Indeed, the new education became the single most important means of effecting a change in occupation. The colonial state took two policy decisions regarding education: one, that it was the responsibility of the state to impart education to the people, and two, that it should focus mainly on Western knowledge and English language. The system of education, thus, was aimed primarily to provide manpower for the administrative, technical and military requirements of the colonial state. The content of education developed by the government was totally secular, consisting of natural and social services, languages and literature. However, Christian missionaries were not only allowed but also encouraged to undertake educational projects. Often, the evangelical content of their educational programme motivated English-educated Punjabis to devise their own programmes of education. By 1900, several educational institutions came up in the Punjab under the aegis of the Arya Samajis, Singh Sabhas and Islamic Anjumans. The 20th century saw the extension of private enterprise in education along with an enlargement of the educational responsibilities of local bodies, particularly through municipalities. The principle of free elementary education for boys was conceded in 1919 and for girls in 1940. In this instance, humanism and progress were allowed to triumph over the needs of the colonial state. A similar tendency is evident in the sphere of medicine and health. By the time the British annexed Punjab, the idea of regular Western-style hospitals for Europeans and soldiers was well established. Within the first two decades of British rule in Punjab, civil hospitals and dispensaries of different grades were established mainly at the district and tehsil headquarters, and a medical school was set up in 1860 at Lahore. Dispensaries and hospitals were also run by the missionaries and charitable institutions, which received some assistance in the form of grants-in-aid. However, most of these dispensaries catered to the urban population. Municipalities were expected to take care of sanitation. There was great disparity between the privileged enclaves occupied by the Europeans and congested urban centres and far flung rural areas in which Punjabis lived. Notwithstanding the number of hospitals and dispensaries in colonial Punjab, elementary health care reached only a small proportion of the population. Rural people suffered more than urban and women suffered more than men.

Punjab in Independent India: In 1947, 13 out of 29 British districts of Punjab in undivided India came to East Punjab, which was renamed Punjab (India) on 26 January 1950. In 1948, the former princely states were organized separately as Himachal Pradesh and PEPSU (Patiala and East Punjab States Union), the latter merging with Punjab in 1956. Following the Akali agitation for a Punjabi-speaking state, and the Reorganisation Act of 1966, the territory of Punjab was bifurcated into the linguistic states of Punjab and Haryana, with the remaining hill areas going to Himachal Pradesh. Post-bifurcation, Punjab came to have an area of 50,362 sq. kilometres which was one-seventh of its size before independence. The new state was divided into eleven districts, including Rup Nagar, created as part of the reorganisation. Structurally, the development blocks which were introduced in 1952 presented the only new feature up to this period. Following the re-organisation, Punjab took centre stage in the Green Revolution launched by the Government of India and the states. Much of what has happened in Punjab subsequently owes its origins, nature and impact in some direct or indirect way to the Green Revolution.

India has gone from a food-deficit to a food surplus country largely because of the agricultural transformation of Punjab. The economic transformation of rural Punjab is basically a story of agricultural transformation. During the 1960s a fundamental change occurred in the institutional and economic infrastructure due to massive public investment. There was irrigation and power development, agricultural research and extension services, and the strengthening of the co-operative credit structure. Already, consolidation of holdings and the predominance of owner farmers had created crucial pre-requisites for the Green Revolution.

Punjab led the country's Green Revolution of the 1960s and earned for itself the distinction of becoming India's 'bread basket'. The Green Revolution introduced a new technology of production in agriculture. The technology consisted of a package of inputs, such as, high-yielding varieties of seeds, chemical fertilisers, pesticides, insecticides, weedicides, machines like tractors, threshers, pumpsets/motors, combine harvesters/reapers and others. The proper usage of these inputs required an assured irrigation system, a peasantry with the will and capacity to adopt the new technology and a government willing to lend its support and investment. All these conditions were present in Punjab.

In fact, before the Green Revolution, Punjab had experienced certain developments that set the stage for its rapid spread. Before Independence, Punjab's agriculture had been dominated by peasant proprietors (Singh, 1989). The rapid settlement of land claims after the partition of the state, and the completion of the consolidation of land holdings by the end of the 1950s created a favourable man-land ratio. The fragmentation of land holdings seen in other states of India was thus taken care of. This encouraged peasant proprietors to invest in land improvement and adopt new technologies, as their holdings had become economically viable. Land reform measures also encouraged several land owners to reclaim their land from tenants for self-cultivation (Gill, 2001). Punjab was also a major beneficiary of British investment in irrigation works and development of canal colonies where peasants from the east and central Punjab were resettled.

In the post-Independence period, canal irrigation was further developed by the state. By 1960-61 the net sown area irrigated in Punjab had gone up to 54 percent. During the British period, agriculture in Punjab, particularly in the canal colonies was largely commercialised. The peasants who migrated to Indian Punjab from western Punjab in 1947-48 during partition were experienced in and geared towards commercial agricultural production.

Thus, even before the availability of the Green Revolution technology, Punjab was showing signs of rapid agricultural development. Between 1953-55 to 1963-65, the index of agricultural production of all crops experienced a growth rate of 4 percent compared to 2.2 percent at the all India level (Singh, 2001).

These conditions in Punjab were accompanied by an official policy of strengthening and promoting agricultural research and extension. The College of Agriculture at Ludhiana was converted into the Punjab Agricultural University (PAU) in 1962. PAU was put in charge of agricultural research and education in the state and played an active role. It is renowned for its work on high yielding varieties of seeds and technical innovations like fertiliser drills and threshers. Simultaneously, the government invested massively in rural development, ranging from irrigation works, drainage of rain water, reclamation of land to solve the problem of land salinity. To promote investment at the farm level, arrangements were made for credit on long and short term crop loans through land mortgage, banks and a network of cooperative credit societies. High-yielding dwarf varieties of wheat from the International Centre for Maize and Wheat Improvement (CIMMYT) Mexico, were introduced leading to bumper crops. The availability of assured irrigation for fertile lands provided a conducive environment that enabled a dynamic peasantry to accept innovations in seed technology. Several farmers already possessed the immediate capacity (supported by the government) to make the necessary investments in the new technology. These initial innovators were immediately imitated by other farmers, irrespective of the size of their holdings, when they observed the sudden jumps in per hectare yield.

The impact was dramatic. Between 1965-66 and 1970-71 the per hectare yield of wheat doubled, from 1104 kg per hectare in 1965-66 to 2238 kg in 1970-71. Following the success of the new technology in wheat in the mid-1970s, a breakthrough was achieved in dwarf high-yielding varieties of paddy. After wheat, paddy provided a major push to agricultural prosperity in the state. By the mid-1980s, except for the southern parts of Punjab, the state began to follow a 'wheatpaddy rotation' pattern in cultivation, and, as a consequence Punjab became the food bowl of the country. It became the largest contributor to the central pool of procurement of food grains both for food security, as well as for running the public distribution system of food grains. With the minimum support price for wheat and paddy combined with the procurement system of the union government, crop production was greatly supported.

The Green Revolution has been the backbone of Punjab's development. It increased cropping intensity from 126 percent in 1960-62 to 185 percent in 1996-97, and the net sown area as a percentage of the geographical area rose from 75 to 85 during this period. The number of tractors rose from 10,646 in 1962-65 to 234,006 in 1990-93 and pumps sets from 45,900 to 721,220. Fertiliser (NPK) consumption increased from 30,060 tonnes in 1962-65 to 1212,570 tonnes in 1990-93. Consumption of chemical inputs also increased.

Militancy has left an indelible mark on Punjab and has had drastic social, political and economic consequences. After Partition, it was militancy that once again revived communal identities as masses were mobilised to protect the Sikh identity and establish its difference from Hindus.

Rise of Militancy: Militancy in Punjab had its origin in several social, historical, religious, political, cultural, riparian and linguistic factors, combined with simmering frustrations and feelings of identity crisis. It would be inaccurate to attribute the rise of terrorism only to economic factors.

The dominant theme that unites all these explanations is the emerging centrality of Sikh religion and Sikh identity. Sikh identity, as a separate identity, was an idea used by communal forces to propagate ideas that all Sikhs should have common social, economic and political interests and, should therefore unite against the State which was seen as representing the interest of the Hindu majority. Religion was manipulated to suit the political ambitions of a few. Thus, "exploitation of religion for political gains has become a permanent feature of our political system, posing a serious threat not only to the national unity, but also to the purity of religion and sanctity of religious places."

Jurgensmeyer's explanation that militancy drew on a religious sanction for violence in times of perceived threat is also significant. He says the perceptions of those who participated in militancy in the name of religion were crucial. In his opinion, Sikh militants felt they were justified, to a certain extent, when they claimed that they acted as a result of religious conversions which, they felt were going on at this time, even while upholding notions of Indian secularism. He stressed that the militant movement in Punjab was an instance of a religious struggle emanating from a perceived threat and that religion was used to legitimise violence.

There are scholars who view economic and regional disparities as being the real cause for the rise of militancy. These explanations argue that although the Green Revolution was a success, it failed to provide sustainable and homogeneous development throughout the state. The effects of the Revolution also produced far reaching social changes. Environmentalist Vandana Shiva, an advocate of this argument says that the Green Revolution led to a destruction of the community and a consequent homogenising of social relations, purely on communal criteria. Thus, an overriding concern with economic growth, with total disregard to environmental and social factors led to a collapse of the community, giving rise to a violent situation. Gupta (1992) is also of the view that the Green Revolution failed to distribute benefits equally and thus made communal mobilisation possible.

Other scholars believe that communal mobilisation among the Sikhs occurred as a result of the anxieties generated by the process of modernisation. Sikhs feared being assimilated into Hinduism (Bomwall, 1985). They feared that in the name of national integration, their identity would be submerged within that of the majority community.

In conclusion, it can be said that militancy grew from a growing distrust with the state and its initiatives. It also grew from a deep dissatisfaction with the perceived discriminatory policies practiced by the government and a lack of a responsive political will to address the needs of the people. The only successful policy had been the Green Revolution and even this was riddled with problems. It had created a vast mass of restless, unemployed youth who now became the cadres for the militant movement.

Militancy and Human Rights: However, the militant movement lost direction. It was not only the security forces that the militants targeted. Even common people, Hindus and Sikhs, living in Punjab and the neighbouring states, became victims of their terrorist activities. Since the militants largely came from rural areas of Punjab and they often used these villages as their hiding places, the security forces too began to harass the average citizen. People of Punjab nearly forgot what it meant to live in peace. Their basic human rights were being violated both the terrorists and the security forces. Extortion kidnapping and indiscriminate killings became regular features of everyday life in the state. The militants also tried to impose a moral code of conduct on the common Sikhs. The Sikh women were directed against wearing "western-style" dresses. They also issued directives on things like how the Sikh weddings should be arranged. The common Sikhs did not approve of these "reforms" initiated by the militants. The democratic political process had come to a halt in the state and no elections were held for a long time. The militant's movement for an independent state of Khalistan could gain only limited support from the common Sikhs in Punjab. Though many Sikhs were angry at the Central Government particularly for the army action of Golden Temple and the massacre of Sikhs in Delhi in November 1984, they were also unhappy with politics of militancy. In the absence a popular political base, the Khalistan movement began to disintegrate by the late 1980s. The militant groups got divided and started attacking each other. The state police used this opportunity to repress the militants with force. In some cases the police even recruited ex-militants to fight the terrorist groups in Punjab. By early 1990s, most of the groups had either disintegrated or had been physically eliminated, directly or indirectly, by the security forces. The militant Sikh movement was thus over without having achieved anything at all political terms the democratic process was revived in the state and the Akalis came back to power in the state in 1996.

Implications of Militancy: Though politically movement failed and could not achieved anything concrete for the Sikhs, its implications for the community as well as for the country were many. It created an unprecedented sense of political crisis all over. Those in academics and in policy-making began to review the process of nation building in India afresh. For the Sikh community, the crisis of 1980s was a testing time. Apart from tragedies like the "Operation

Bluestar" and the anti-Sikh riots in Delhi and in other parts of India, the "crisis" redefined their identity. Their sense of being a minority ethnic group became much more acute. Not only the Sikhs began to see themselves as being a distinct minority; others also began to see them in similar light. The "Operation Bluestar" and the anti-Sikh riots in different parts of India provided them for the first time, with a proof of their being discriminated against as a community which also reinforced their sense of a collective identity. They began to see their status as being much closer to the notion of an ethnic minority. To put it in different words, the militant movement and the crisis of 1980s furthered the process of minoritisation of the Sikhs in India.

The Sikhs constitute a little more than two percent of the total population of the country, nearly 75 percent of the live in the state of Punjab and the rest 25 percent in different part of the country and the globe. Since they continue to be in majority in the state of Punjab, for a large majority of the Sikhs their sense of being a minority is not experienced in everyday life. However at the level of consciousness, they continue to see themselves as an ethnic minority.

Q10. Write briefly on linguistic ethnicity and the state. [Dec 08, Q. 12]

Ans. Linguistic Ethnicity and the State: British administration never saw linguistic ethnicity of political organisation of a state. Most of the state in the Pre British period and also during British administration was by and large historical accidents. Inadvertently, reorganisation of Bengal was instrumental in promoting the policy of State restructure by India National Congress on the basis of vernacular. It was in the Montagu Chemsford report 1918, that first evidence of vernacular movement in India were recorded. Despite this paradigm shift, the Government of India Act 1919 made no significant move to promote regional languages. In 1920, Mahatma Gandhi favoured formation of linguistic provinces, even though he was apprehensive that favouring formation of linguistic provinces may interfere with his plans to promote Hindustani, as a national language. However, Gandhi's tactical nod and Nehru's grudging approval led to the reorganisation of Indian national Congress on linguistic provincial basis. Twenty-one provincial congress committee were created. By 1927, Congress passed a resolution asking for creating of linguistic provinces for Andhra, Utkal (Orissa), Sindh and Karnataka.

However, congress continued to pursue its policy of linguistic province and demanded two more provinces of Andhra and Karnataka. Kerala followed suit in 1938 demanding an autonomous linguistic province for Malayalam speaking people. Second World War provided a brief interlude to growing demand for linguistic provinces. In 1945-46, once again, in its election manifesto, congress retreated its view that administrative units should be constituted as far as possible on a linguistic and cultural basis. Some British historians in their postcolonial interpretations have talked about hidden and ulterior motives in these demands. According to Robert D. King: "the drive for linguistic states or provinces lay aspirations grounded not so much in language as in caste and communal rivalries, in grappling for privilege.

Q11. Discuss about the Dravida Munnetra Kazhagam (DMK) movement.

Ans. Dravida Munnetra Kazhagam (literally "Dravidian Progress Federation") (founded 1949, Tamil Nadu, India) is a regional political party in the state of Tamil Nadu in India. It also has presence in nearby union territory of Puducherry. It is a Dravidian party founded by C. N. Annadurai as a breakaway faction from the Dravidar Kazhagam (known as Justice Party till 1944) headed by Periyar. Since 1969, DMK is headed by M Karunanidhi, the current Chief Minister of Tamil Nadu.

The north-south divide on the language issue dates back to the days of early western scholars like Roberto di Mobili (1577-1656) Constanius Beschi (1680-1743, Rev. Robert Caldwell (1819-1891). Caldwell was originally responsible for developing the theory that Sanskrit was brought to South India by Aryan Brahman colonists. They also developed a peculiar type of Hinduism that encouraged idol worship. Tamil was cultivated by the native inhabitants who were addressed as Sudras by the Brahmans. Inherent in this were traces of brahmanical dominance, because the original inhabits were infact Chieftains, Soldiers, Cultivators etc. Brahman immigrants failed to conquer these 'Tamilians'. According to the locality, should be substituted. (cf. Eugenc Jrschick 1969:276). Thus, it becomes obvious that the linguistic ethnicity in the South is rooted in caste politics.

Mountstaurt Elphinstone Grant Duff, Governor of Madras in 1886, in his address to the graduates of the University of Madras said: "It was these Sanskrit speakers, not Europeans, who lumped up the Southern race as Rakshusas demons. It was they who deliberately grounded all social distinctions on varna, colour". Inferring from these details Barnett concludes, 'The ideological category "non Brahmian" therefore, was proceeded by the development of a sense of a Dravidian cultural history separate, distinct, and perhaps superior to that of the South Indian Brahmins'. It was this cultural history that led to the formation of the south Indian Liberal Federation (Justice Party) in 1916, started as a reactionary movement challenging supremacy of Brahmins in elite occupations, its political discourse remained in English and not in Tamil. From this one may interpret that post-independence linguistic movements were anti-Hindi and pro-English but not necessarily pro-Tamilian.

Earliest reference to importance of Tamil language is found in an article published in Dravidan dated September 29th, 1920 that expressed satisfaction in the proposal of setting a Tamil university. The decision was taken at the Trichnapoly non-Brahmin conference. The article argued; " Tamil in not properly encouraged in the present universities, and that many foreign Aryans, who wielded an influence in the university, brought the language to its present low condition. The article further stressed that the Tamilians will attain progress and acquire political influence only when the Tamil language is approved.

These anti-Brahmanical sentiments were further strengthened by the formation of Self-Respect League in 1924 by E.V. Ramasami. The movement was an attempt to develop viable cultural alternatives. It did radicalize social and political consciousness among non Brahmins. The importance of self-respect movement declined with the rise of pragmatic congress politics. The non brahmanical wing of the congress party became active in the 1930's and 1940's with the rowing realisation that congress will be the ruling party in independent India. The leading non-Brahmin Communities of Kammas and Kapoos was pro-congress. In 1936, Congress won the elections in Madras presidency, under the Government of India act 1935. C. Rajagopalcharia became the premier of Congress government. It is at this point in history that the Dravidian independence movement was born. The agitation was the result of introduction of Hindustani in certain schools as a compulsory subject. Kudi Arsu Revolt and Justice were opposing Hindi and Hindustan as northern Aryan languages since early 1920's. The language issue thus became a convenient rallying point for the non-congress political parties. The intensive agitation followed. Political parties in opposition picked outside 'Premier's' residence. Demonstrations were held outside certain high schools. This was followed by number of meeting and processions. The most provocative slogan used in these demonstrations was, "Down with the Brahmin Raj'. A report prepared by the home department in 1939, recorded that 536 persons were arrested during this agitation. The agitation which was pronounced in 1938, dimmed comparatively in 1939. Two significant events of this period were the rise of C.N. Annaduri as a skilled agitationist and the conference of the title of Periiyar to E.V. Ramasami at the Tamil Nadu Women's Conference held in November 1939. Tamil speaking districts of Madras Presidency namely North Areot. Salem, Trichinoploy, Tanjor, Madurai and Ramnad. The demand Dravida Nadu separation day was proclaimed on July 1, 1939. E.V. Ramasami articulated the connection between the need for separation and the language issue. The slogan 'Dravida Nadu for Dravidians' was earned as a response to Brahmincal political dominance and penetration of Aryan ideas into Tamilian culture. The anti-Hindustani agitation was interrupted due to second world war. The Congress organized 'Quit India' movement and did not support British war efforts. On the other hand E.V. Ramasami openly came in support of the British and also met cripps commission and persisted with his demand for a separate Dravida Nadu.

Radicalisation of the Dravidian ideology occurred mainly in the 1930s, but had its roots in activities of E.V. Ramasami, reaching as for back as the 1924 founding of Kudi Arasu. During the 1930s, despite increasing congress popularity as manifested in the 1936 electoral victory and the cleavage between radicals and moderates in the Dravidian movement, "Dravidian" political identity remained salient.

Birth of DMK Movement: The Dravidar Kazhagam (DK) was founded at Party's Salem conference in 1944. Though Ramasami was elected as the president of the Justice party in 1938, after the anti-Hindustani agitation, while he was in Jail, his ability to generate support was insignificant. When the party re-named itself as DK, Annadurai's influence on the political agenda of the party became distinct, Annadurai realised that old Justice party lacked mass base, as it was perceived to be a party of the rich. He made consistent efforts to promote populist schemes for the uplift of now-growing anti-British feelings among the common people. However, Party President Ramasami and C. Annaduri publicity disagreed on Party's political stand on the day of India's independence, the August 15, 1947 formal split occurred in DK. The DMK emerged as the new party and nearly 75,000 of DK members switched party loyalitics. Though the agenda of both the parties remained similar, DMK gained immense political mileage with the publication of Aryan illusion by C. Annaduri, which was banned in 1952 for being inflammatory.

Role of Universal Primary Education: In July 1952, C. Rajagopalchari, Congress government's chief-Minister promoted a programme of universal primary education. According to this programme; children were suppose to spend half-day in school and the other half of the day at their traditional occupations. This was labeled as 'caste based education' by DMK and a massive agitation was launched. Also at the same time, DMK started demanding change in the name of the town Dalmiapuram to Kallakudi in Trichy district. This was demanded because Dalmia was a north-Indian cement magnate. These were the first post-independence period developments in which the dominance of the north in the Southern states was challenged. The protest were significantly violent. Hundreds of people were injured and at least nine demonstrators died.

They included many Tamil scholars in their rank and file. Tamil literature and linguistics witnessed a renaissance with the publication of Mursoli, Mam Nadu, Dravida Nadu and Manram as party papers and magazines. Drama and other fold medium was used extensively to promote Tamil awareness. Poverty and alienation of Tamils was highlighted through plays like Parasakti which was written by Karunanidhi in 1952 and in which Shivajee Ganeshan started. The mass appeal and the mass communication media carried DMK ideology to every household in Madrsas. It was under these influences that the Tamil language issue assumed violent proportions in 1965.

The Language Issue: The language issue became very complex. It no longer restricted itself to DMK's concern for Tamil language and the opposition of Tamil to Hindi, Tamil to Sanskrit, Hindi to English or Tamil to English. But in it were incorporated elements to student politics. (Barnett, 1976:129). Regional identities assumed proportions of subnationalism. DMK pointed out that 'Hindi speaking' areas constituted only one region of the country. Dominance of a regional language and its compulsory knowledge for recruitment to government jobs created immense insecurity among the student community of the southern states. On January 26, 1969, when protest march was organized, a DMK supporter self-immolated, calling his actions a protest against the imposition of Hindi at the altar of Tamil. Between January 26th and February 12th four more DMK supporters committed suicide. These self-immolations became highly patriotic events among the students in the state. Even though DMK leader C. Annadurai condemned these politically motivated self-immolation bids, the anti-Hindi 'Martyrs' provided student leadership legitimacy for wider and open political participation. This encouraged the Tamil Nadu students Anti-Hindi Agitation council to take an independent stand with or without DMK support. For the first time Dravid cultural movement found support outside DMK. Both Kamraj of the congress and Annadurai of DMK evoked the central congress leadership to reassure the students in the state, that the assurance given by Pt. Nehru in 1963, about the associate status of English will not be revoked. During this period about 900 arrests were made in Madras city and nearly 200 people arrested in Madurai. In Madras, a ban was imposed on Public meeting till February 15th.

Schools and colleges were re-opened on February 8th. But students refrained from attending classes on a call given by Tamil Nadu student Anti-Hindi agitation. They demanded a constitutional amendment for retaining English as the language for official communication. Lawyers joined their cause on February 9th and refrained from attending courts. Violence followed. A bus was burnt in Trichy. Two post-offices attacked and the appeals made by Annadurai went unheard. From February 10 through 12, what followed was mayhem. Public buildings, Police Stations, Trains, Busses, Post-offices, factories were looted and burnt. According to official estimates 70 people died. This included three children who were killed by Police firing. Ten thousand people were arrested. Property worth ten million rupees was destroyed. The lumpen elements from the slums and streets joined the mob-violence. Two constables in Madurai were beaten to death by the police. DMK's role in these events was not hidden. Though openly they condemned the violence, the violence of 1965 ensured DMK popularity. It also opened vistas for DMK's debacle. DMK now realised that they could no longer sustain a radical agenda which was based on separatist leanings. Hence, they moderated their stance on issues of political autonomy.

Also, at the same time necessity of keeping language issue alive, by protecting Tamil interests was not lost sight of and for this law abiding citizens like lawyers were roped in for a movement of sustained protest.

It was in the wake of these events, that Lal Bahadur Shastri, then Prime-Minister of India, in a nationwide broadcast on February 11th 1963; reaffirmed Nehru's assurance to the student community and made the following statements. "For an indefinite period I would have English as an associates language because I do not wish the people of non-Hindi areas to feel that certain doors of advancement are closed to them. I would have it as an alternative language as long as people require it, and the decision for that I would leave not to the Hindi knowing but non Hindi knowing people......".

Policy on Language Issue: Policy decisions stated by Shastri in this regard were:

i) every state can transact its business in the language of its choices or English.

ii) interstate communication could be in English or accompanied by an authentic translation.

iii) non-Hindi states could correspond with the center in English.

iv) transaction of business at the central level would be in English.

v) although recruitment exams for central service posts were in English, in 1960, it was decided that Hindi was to be permitted as an alternate. This was followed by a reassurance given by Shastri to non-Hindi speaking students that their interests would be protected at all expense.

Q12. Describe the Punjabi Suba movement and other linguistic movement.

Ans. Punjabi Suba was a proposed state in northwest India. It was proposed by Shiromani Akali Dal in 1966. The Punjabi Suba movement resulted in the trifurcation of the Indian Punjab region into three states: Punjab (India), Himachal Pradesh and Haryana.

Linguistic issues

In the 1950s and 1960s, linguistic issues in India caused civil disorder when the central government declared Hindi as the national language of India. The nationwide movement of linguistic groups seeking statehood resulted in a massive reorganisation of states according to linguistic boundaries in 1956. At that time, Indian Punjab had its capital in Shimla, and though the vast majority of the Sikhs lived in Punjab, they still did not form a majority. The Akali Dal, a Sikh dominated political party active mainly in Punjab, sought to create a Punjabi Suba, or a Punjabi-speaking state. This case was presented to the States Reorganisation Commission established in 1953. It is generally believed that many Punjabi-speaking Hindus declared Hindi as their mother tongue in the censuses of 1951 and 1961, and therefore the census figures did not support the case for a Punjabi speaking state. The demand for adoption of Punjabi for Punjabi-speaking areas first created and later intensified the rift between Hindus and Sikhs of Punjab.

The States Reorganisation Commission, not recognizing Punjabi as a language that was distinct grammatically from Hindi, rejected the demand for a Punjabi suba or state. Another reason that the Commission gave in its report was that the movement lacked general support of the people inhabiting the region. Many Sikhs felt discriminated against by the commission.

Punjabi Suba movement

The Akal Takht played a vital role in organizing Sikhs to campaign for the Punjabi suba. During the course of the campaign, twelve thousand Sikhs were arrested for their peaceful demonstrations in 1955 and twenty-six thousand in 1960-61. Finally, in September 1966, the Punjabi suba demand was accepted by the central government and Punjab was trifurcated under the Punjab State Reorganisation Bill. Areas in the south of Punjab that spoke a language that is a derivative of Braj formed a new state of Haryana and the Pahari- and Kangri-speaking districts north of Punjab were merged with Himachal Pradesh, while the remaining areas formed the new Punjabi speaking state, which retained the name of Punjab. As a result, the Sikhs became a majority in the newly created state with a population of a little over sixty percent.

River waters dispute

Before the creation of the Punjabi suba, Punjab was the master of its river waters (The North Indian rivers Sutlej, Beas, Ravi did not flow through any other state for any length). The trifurcation of the state led to three competing demands for these river waters, and the central government decided to step in. The central government against the provisions of the Indian constitution introduced sections 78 to 80 in the Punjab Reorganisation Act, 1966, under which the central government "assumed the powers of control, maintenance, distribution and development of the waters and the hydel power of the Punjab rivers." Many Sikhs perceived this division as unfair and as an anti Sikh measure, since the vast majority of the people of Punjab is dependent on agriculture.

Akali Dal's demands

The Akali Dal led a series of peaceful mass demonstrations to present its grievances to the central government. The demands of the Akali Dal were based on the Anandpur Sahib Resolution, which was adopted by the party in October 1973 to raise specific political, economic and social issues. The major motivation behind the resolution was the safeguarding of the Sikh identity by securing a state structure that was decentralised, with non-interference from the central government. The Resolution outlines seven objectives.

1. The transfer of the federally administered city of Chandigarh to Punjab.

2. The transfer of Punjabi speaking and contiguous areas to Punjab.

3. Decentralisation of states under the existing constitution, limiting the central government's role.
4. The call for land reforms and industrialisation of Punjab, along with safeguarding the rights of the weaker sections of the population.
5. The enactment of an all-India gurdwara (Sikh house of worship) act.
6. Protection for minorities residing outside Punjab, but within India.
7. Revision of government's recruitment quota restricting the number of Sikhs in armed forces.

The Wall Street Journal, noted:

"The Akali Dal is in the hands of moderate and sensible leadership...but giving anyone a fair share of power is unthinkable politics of Mrs. Gandhi [the then Prime Minister of India]...Many Hindus in Punjab privately concede that there isn't much wrong with these demands. But every time the ball goes to the Congress court, it is kicked out one way or another because Mrs. Gandhi considers it a good electoral calculation."

The assassination of Lala Jagat Narain

In a politically charged environment, Lala Jagat Narain, the owner of the Hind Samachar group of newspapers and member of indian National Congress, was assassinated by Sikh militants in September 1981. In September 1981, Bhindranwale was arrested for his alleged role in the assassination but was later released by the Punjab State Government, as no evidence was found against him.

The Khalistani movement can be considered to have effectively started from this point. Though there were a number of leaders vying for leadership role, most were based in United Kingdom and Canada, and had limited influence. In Punjab, Bhindranwale was the unchallenged leader of the movement and made his residence in the Golden Temple in Amritsar. By convention, the Indian Army and the Punjab Police would not enter this religious building.

Dharam Yudh Morcha

In August 1982, the Akali Dal under the leadership of Harcharan Singh Longowal launched the Dharam Yudh Morcha, or the "battle for righteousness." Bhindranwale and the Akali Dal united; their goal was the fulfillment of demands based upon the Anandpur Sahib Resolution. In two and a half months, security forces arrested thirty thousand Sikhs.

In November 1982, Akali Dal announced the organisation of protests in Delhi during the Asian Games. The police were instructed to stop all buses, trains and vehicles that were headed for Delhi and interrogate Sikh passengers. The Sikhs as a community felt discriminated against by the Indian state. Later, the Akali Dal organised a convention at the Darbar Sahib attended by 5,000 Sikh ex-servicemen, 170 of whom were above the rank of colonel. These Sikhs claimed that there was discrimination against them in government service.

Religious confusion

During this turmoil, the Akali Dal began another agitation in February 1984 protesting against clause (2)(b) of Article 25 of the Indian constitution, which ambiguously states "the reference to Hindus shall be construed as including a reference to persons professing the Sikh, Jaina or Buddhist religion", though it also implicitly recognizes Sikhism as a separate religion with the words "the wearing and carrying of kirpans shall be deemed to be included in the profession of the Sikh religion.".

The Akali Dal members demanded that the constitution should remove any ambiguous statements that use the word Hindu to refer to the Sikhs. For instance, a Sikh couple who marry in accordance to the rites of the Sikh religion must register their marriage either under the Special Marriages Act (1954) or the Hindu Marriage Act – the Akalis demanded replacement of such rules with Sikhism-specific laws. However, their demands were not taken seriously, and several Akali leaders were arrested for burning the Indian constitution in protest. Thus, the Indian Government's implicit defining of its Sikh citizens as being part of the Hindu community created discontent among Sikhs, who feared a loss of identity.

Gender Differentiation and Ethnicity

Q1. Explain the biological and sociological theories of sex roles.

Ans. Biological Theory of Sex Roles: George Peter Murdock sees biological differences between men and women as the basis for sexual division of labour in society. Men have more physical strength and therefore they take such roles which require physical strength. Women can bear children and therefore they are associated with activities that are related to the raising of family.

Lionel Tiger and Robin Fox say that biological factors programme human behaviour though there may be cultural variations. They call it "human biogrammer" and there is some difference in the biogrammer of men and women.

Talcott Parsons characterizes women's role in the family as "expressive" which provides emotional support and warmth necessary for socialisation of the child. The man's role on the other hand is "instrumental" as the bread winner of the society. Both the expressive and instrumental roles are essential and they complement each other.

Sociological Theory of Sex Roles: According to a British sociologist Ann Oakley, sex is a biological term and gender is a cultural term. Gender refers to the sex of an individual after socialisation.

Oakley argues that division of labour is not universal. She disagrees with Murdock. She regards it as a myth that women are biologically incapable to carry out heavy and demanding work. She also noted that employment of mothers is not detrimental to the children's development. According to her Parson's explanation of woman's "expressive role" and men's instrumental role, is for the convenience of men.

Emile Durkhiem, one of the founding fathers of sociology, said that in the primitive societies men and women were fairly similar in strength and intelligence and only as civilisation progressed new codes evolved which restricted women from working outside home. Thus, they became weaker and less intelligent.

The process of socialisation begins the moment a person is born. Sex roles are learned activities as children are socialized into these roles. Thus, sex role allocation is a social phenomenon and is in fact learned behaviour. Women for centuries have been socialized into passive roles.

Q2. Describe the impact of development on women.

Ans. Impact of Development on women: Indian demographers have proposed several hypotheses to explain the declining sex-ratio, and five of these suggest important contributing factors.

i) females are under enumerated in the Indian census.

ii) The general mortality rates of females are higher than those of males.

iii) Indian families prefer sons and female infants are consequently neglected leading to higher female mortality.

iv) Frequent and excessive child bearing has an adverse effect on the health of women.

v) Certain diseases have higher incidence in women.

This raises the whole question of attitudes towards females and the role of women in Indian society.

It is hard to avoid the conclusion that a preference for boys lies at the heart of the inferior status of women and girls in India and many other countries. Equally disturbing are the increasing indications that when public services ranging from medical and health facilities to agricultural extension projects are provided in the course of development efforts, they may either reinforce the traditional male biases or diminish the status that women enjoyed in the traditional society.

Female Infanticide and Child Neglect in Rural India: It is beyond doubt that systematic indirect female infanticide exists today in India in addition to the sex selective abortion (i.e. female foeticide) and female infanticide (killing of a child less than one year of age). It was found that in certain villages in Rajasthan there were no female children. In Salem district in Tamil Nadu female infanticide is openly practiced.

The indirect female infanticide accomplished by nutritional and health care deprivation of children results in higher mortality rates of daughters than sons. In several parts of rural India there is a strong preference for sons. Sons are considered as economic assets, they are needed for farming and for income through remittances if they leave the village etc. Sons play important roles in local power struggles over rights to land and water. Sons stay with the family after their marriage and thus maintain the parents in their old age, daughters marry out and cannot contribute to the maintenance of their natal households. Sons bring in dowries with their brides, daughters drain family wealth with their required dowries and constant flow of gifts to their family of marriage after the wedding. Sons, among Hindus are also needed to perform rituals which protect the family. After the death of the father, daughters cannot perform such rituals. The extreme son preference is more prevalent among upper castes and classes then the lower castes and classes.

Gender Household and Kinship: Let us now take the example of Taiwanese women. These women marry into the household of their husbands. According to Wolf a Taiwanese wife must pay homage to her husband's ancestors, obey her husband and mother in law, and bear children for her husband's patrilineage. After Taiwanese wife gives birth to a son, her status in the household begins to change and it improves during her life course as she forges what Wolf calls a uterine family-a family based on the powerful relationship between mothers and sons. When a Taiwanese wife becomes a mother in law she achieves the greatest power and status within her husband's household.

Views of Engels Leacock: According to Engels Leacock the early communal society was self sufficient. Men and women work together and neither of them were dependent on each other. Thus, there was a reciprocal division of labour. Also there was no distinction between the public world of men work and private world or women's household work. Both the sexes produced the good necessary for livelihood. Thus, in this type of society, goods were produced only for consumption to satisfy everyday needs. Later on as the process of industrialisation began goods were produced on a large scale, concepts of trading and exchange became common. Slowly in order to maximize their profits the capitalists started exploitation of the women and workers. This led to the isolation of family as separate unit and the women were then confined to their families and thus the place of work and residence was separated.

Equality and Inequality: The Sexual Division of Labour and Gender Stratification: In most societies certain tasks are predominantly assigned to men while others are assigned to women. In European and American cultures it used to be considered "natural" for men to be the family bread winners, women were expected to take care of the home and raise the children. An underlying assumption of this division of labour was that men were dominant because their contribution to the material well being of the family was more significant than that of women. Women were dependent on men an therefore automatically sub-ordinate to them.

The "naturalness" of this division of labour has been called into question as women increasingly enter the labour force. However has this significantly altered the status of women within their families and in the wider society? Or has it simply meant that women are now working a double day, performing domestic tasks that are negatively valued and not considered work once they get home from their "real" day's work? If employment enhances the social position of women, why is it that women still earn only 65% of what men earn for the same work? Why is there still a high degree of occupational segregation by gender?

What precisely is the relationship between the economic roles of women and gender stratification?

Cross cultural research on the sexual division of labour attempts not only to describe the range of women's productive activities in societies with different modes of subsistence, but also to assess the implications of these activities on the status of women.

The Cultural Construction of Gender: We all live in a world of symbols that assign meaning and value to the categories of male and female. Despite several decades of consciousness raising in the United States, advertising on television and in the print media perpetuates sexual stereotypes. Although "house beautiful" ads are less prominent as women are increasingly shown in workplace contexts, body beautiful messages continue to be transmitted. In children's cartoons women are still helpless victims who the fearless male hero must rescue. Toys are targeted either for little boys or little girls and are packed appropriately in colours and materials culturally defined as either masculine or feminine. Argues that women because of their reproductive roles, are universally viewed as being closer to nature while men are linked with culture. She defines culture in terms of human consciousness including the products of the same like, technology which is used to control and harness nature. That which is cultural and subject to human manipulation is assigned more worth than that which is natural, hence women and women's roles are degraded or devalued, whether explicitly or implicitly.

Q3. Write a short note about the colonialism and development.

Ans. A global world based on complex political and economic relationship. Although most of the colonized world achieved independence by the 1960's, the economic domination of the capitalist world system that was initiated during the colonial period had not been significantly altered. In the late twentieth century an imbalanced relationship between the countries of the industrial or "developed" world and the developing or Third World remains. How have the men and women of the developing world experienced the continuing impact of the penetration of capitalism and the integration of their societies into the global economy.

In many parts of the world, originally egalitarian gender relationships have been replaced by more hierarchical ones, and women have consequently been marginalized, removed from the positions of economic and political decision making that they held in the pre colonial period.

If women got any attention it was as mother and housekeepers in family planning projects and in training programs for home economics. Male centered development programs often resulted in new division of labour between the sexes, by which the depending of women on men greatly increased.

Greater female dependency on men has also resulted from the process of urbanisation, from the shift from household to factory and industry, from the introduction of cash crops. In some societies women have lost their traditional rights to land and men, though continuing to rely on women's traditional assistance, claim the entire income from the cash production export crops for themselves.

Q4. How is gender identities formed? Explain. [June 09, Q. 2]

OR

Discuss the formation of gender identity in society. [Dec 08, Q. 11]

Ans. Gender identity (otherwise known as **core gender identity**) is the gender(s), or lack thereof, a person self-identifies as. It is not necessarily based on biological fact, either real or perceived, nor is it always based on sexual orientation. The gender identities one may choose from include: male, female, both, somewhere in between ("third gender"), or neither. *Gender identity* was originally a medical term used to explain sex reassignment surgery to the public. The term is also found in psychology, often as *core gender identity.* Sociology, gender studies and feminism are still inclined to refer to gender identity, gender role and erotic preference under the catch-all term *gender*. The term is also used in gender taxonomy. The formation of a gender identity is a complex process that starts with conception, but which involves critical growth processes during gestation and even learning experiences after birth. There are points of differentiation all along the way, but language and tradition in many societies insist that every individual be categorized as either a man or a woman, although there are societies, such as the Native American identity of a two-spirit, which include multiple gender categories. When the gender identity of a person makes him/her a woman, but his/her genitals are male, (s)he will likely experience what is called gender dysphoria, i.e., a really deep unhappiness caused by his/her experience of him/herself as a woman and her lack of female genitals and breast(s). Some research has been done that indicates that gender identity is fixed in early childhood and is thereafter static. This research has generally proceeded by asking transsexuals when they first realised that the gender role that society attempted to place upon them did not match the gender identity that they found in themselves and the gender role that they chose to live out these studies estimate the age at which gender identity is formed at around 2-3. Such research may be problematic if it made no comparable attempt to discover when non-transsexual people became aware of their own gender identities and choice of gender roles. Some critics question this research, claiming that the studies suffer from a sampling bias. The acquisition of hormone replacement therapy and sexual reassignment surgery is generally controlled by doctors. One of the questions some doctors ask to distinguish between "real" transsexuals and others is to ask them when they first felt identification with the opposite sex. The researchers may then be unintentionally eliminating some subjects from consideration when they try to determine a typical time of gender identity formation. There is also a possibility of reporting bias, since transsexuals may feel that they must give the "correct" answers to such questions in order to increase the chances of obtaining hormones. Patrick Califia, author of *Sex Changes* and *Public Sex*, has indicated that this group has a clear awareness of what answers to give to survey questions in order to be considered eligible for hormone replacement therapy and/or sexual reassignment surgery: None of the gender scientists seem to realise that they, themselves, are responsible for creating a situation where transsexual people must describe a fixed set of symptoms and recite a history that has been edited in clearly prescribed ways in order to get a doctor's approval for what should be their inalienable right. Richard C. Friedman, in *Male Homosexuality* published in 1990, writing from a psychoanalytic perspective, argues that sexual desire begins later than the writings of Sigmund Freud indicate, not in infancy but between the ages of 5 and 10 and is not focused on a parent figure but on peers. As a consequence, he reasons, male homosexuals are not abnormal, never having been sexually attracted to their mothers anyway.

Q5. Discuss about the concept of body.

Ans. Concept of Body: The body is, clearly a medium of culture. In the sense, we take care of our body and maintain it, eat, dress, and adorn ourselves, communicate with others, and so on. However, the body is not only a text of culture. It is also more directly, a 'locus of social control' so that we are not what we want to be but are made through culture. This is what Foucault calls the 'decile body' which is regulated by the norms of cultural life.

In the Indian context, an important work on the body in contemporary times is David Arnold's *Colonizing the Body.* He emphasizes the importance of the body as a site of colonizing power and of contestation between the colonized and the colonizers.

Sociological Understanding of Body: Anthropologists and sociologists have commented on the marked of woman's body by caste, religious belief, social norms and practices and on how woman's embodiment and her sexuality serve as important boundary markers. The female sexuality is controlled by caste and class factors is an indisputable fact. A woman's body and sexuality are in any case under the controlling purview of men. It is an assertion not only of patriarchal power but also of social control. Woman is allowed little or no space for an independent, self-perceived articulation, definitionor expression of her sexuality. Her body becomes an instrument and a symbol for the community's expression of caste, class and communal honour. Chastity, virtue and above all, purity are extolled as great feminine virtues embodying the honour of the family, community and nation. In a sense, woman's body is often no longer her body but has been taken over by the community, of both men and women, establish and legitimize its image in society.

To the extent that woman's body is the foundation on which gender equality is built, established and legitimized, understanding the female body in different contexts, setting and situations is important.

Communicative Body: Only when we view the female body as communicative or lived body that we can begin to understand the implications of both the social construction of lived experience as well as women's own perceptions and articulations of their embodiment. The gender is inscribed on woman in everyday life both socially as well as through her life experiences, perceptions, desires, fantasies. It is in this sense that gender identity is truly both constructed and lived. The internalisation of representation of the female body by women appears to be fundamental to the formation of feminine identity.

Q6. Explain the role of social institutions in gender identity formation. [Dec 07, Q. 2]

Ans. Within the India sub-continent there have been infinite variations on the status of women diverging according to cultural milieu. Family, structure, class, caste, property rights and morals".

Gender and Caste

In order to properly assess the position of women in ancient society, a brief reference to stratificatory system as expressed through varna and caste system in necessary. Features like caste endogamy as mechanism of recruiting and retaining control over the labour and sexuality of women exist. Concepts of purity and pollution segregating groups and also regulating mobility of women are very crucial. Caste not only determines social division of labour but also sexual division of labour. Certain tasks have to be performed by women while certain other tasks are meant for men. In agriculture, for instance, women can engaged themselves in water regulation, transplanting, weeding but not in ploughing. Also with upward mobility of the group, women are immediately withdrawn from the outside work. Overt rules prohibiting women from specific activities and denying certain rights did exist. But more subtle expression of patriarchy was through symbolism giving messages of inferiority of women through legends highlighting the self-sacrificing, self-effacing pure image of women and through the ritual practices which day in and out emphasized the dominant role of a woman as a faithful wife and devout mother.

The linking of women and shudras together is one more evidence of the low position of women. Prescription and prohibitions for shudras and women were same on many occasions. The prohibition of the sacred thread ceremony for both women and shudras, similar punishment for killing a shudra or a woman, denial of religious privilege etc. are some of illustrations which indicate how caste and gender get entrenched.

Gender and Religion

In most of the religions, we find the great philosophical and theological teaching about the essential sameness of human nature, of the intrinsic worth of all human beings as everyone, woman just as much as man, is endowed with a soul, a divine spark, or is part of the same atman. This lofty ideal is often of very little practical consequence, however, in actual practice, much of the ethical teaching and the religious counsels reflect the social position of women in a particular environment. As a result, we also possess many sacred texts which relegate women's place to a lower or secondary rank to man. Such texts are frequently quoted as the spiritual basis for the legitimisation of women's low status through the ages; they are the sacred authority which teaches that woman's status has to be low and unequal to that of man.

One important point in understanding the value structure in Indian society is the dual concept of the female in Hindu philosophy; on the one hand, woman is fertile, benevolent, bestower of prosperity; on the other hand she is considered aggressive, malevolent and destructive. This dual character manifest in the goddesses also, as there are dangerous, aggressive, malevolent goddesses like Kali and Durga; there the equally important goddesses like Laxmi, Saraswati, Mariamman who are benevolent. In short, the value structure by presenting the dual character of women seems to have been successful in creating a myth that India women possess power, may be not in visible terms. However, it is a very valuable concept in understanding the seemingly high and really inferior position of women in India. Hence, we have the paradoxical situation that in some religious teacings, an idealized exaltation of women in her role as mother and wife occurs; in some instances, an ideal of woman in her eternal essence is projected when in actual social life subjugation is woman's common lot.

Today, with an altogether different situation in society, the religions, are faced with an entirely new challenge. Since, the social economic and political emancipation of women has become widely accepted, new pressures from the social environment are affecting all the religious traditions and the inadequacy of their traditional teaching regarding the general status or image of woman is being fundamentally questioned.

Gender and Marriage Regulations

The concept of annloma and pratiloma marriage by definition denigrates women. A marriage where a boy of upper caste marries a girl of lower caste is approved and called anuloma. While marriage of women ritually pure groups with men of lower ritual status were considered pratiloma. Most serious punishments like excommunication and even death could be evoked for transgressing the norms. Physical mobility is also restricted through caste norms. The significant symbol of the low status of women in society is that the women of lower castes are accessible to men to higher status, while there is a very severe punishment for men of lower castes who dare to approach any women of higher groups.

Marriage at an early date, marriage within the caste and even in the subcaste, prohibition of pratiloma, marriage where a woman of higher caste marries a man of lower caste, marriage as a sacrament whereby a women is bound in wedlock till she dies, were all practices which suggest the control of sexuality.

Q7. Describe the gender inequality in terms of production and reproduction issues.

Ans. Motherhood: Motherhood is the central fact of female existence because it is the most authentically biological experience that differentiates a woman from man. A women's role in the reproduction of human beings far outweighs that of a man. It is invariably a woman who mothers. Motherhood and mothering are usually perceived as naturally related. This bringing forth of new life and its sustenance, so essential to human survival, paradoxically, become instruments of subordination. Maternal responsibility is used as an alibi to exclude a woman from power, authority, decision and a participatory role in public life. Further, motherhood and mothering are not controlled by her. Glancing specifically at the situation of India women, Krishnaraj argues that what was, originally, a source of women's power, viz., her procreative role has rendered her powerless, that is especially subject to male domination. Perceived as a field in possession of the owner of seed (read semen), a woman's motherhood renders her especially susceptible to male control and domination. Deprived of minimum safety nets such as nourishment, safe birthing, adequate anti-natal care, child care facilities, motherhood renders working Indian women, especially in poor rural areas, extremely vulnerable. State sponsored incentives to motherhood both as ideology and material help are also questioned as patriarchal, denying women the ability to render motherhood as materially empowering.

Heredity: From ancient times the process of human reproduction in India has been conceived of in terms of male seed germinating in the female field. This can be seen in texts used during rituals of marriage and other crises of life many of which are of vedic origin, and the great epic of Mahabharata. The law books, particularly Manu Smriti, use it as the basis of determining the status of the offspring of mixed unions and for assessing the propriety of the types of mixed unions.

The conception of the process of human reproduction seems to have formed part of both the literate tradition and people's consciousness through the ages. Leela Dube, argues that though medical science as expressed in Ayurveda recognized a woman's contribution to heredity, it was propagated in popular culture that the child carried the man's blood, as semen was believed to a product of his blood. In many matrilineal tribes, the superior reproductive role of women is recognized.

The underlying implications of the metaphor of conception as the seed sown in the soil are used for biological symbolisation of descent, to understand the nature of relations between the sexes and their relative rights and positions. Two things emerge from this. First, an essentially unequal relationship is reflected in an emphasized through the use of these symbols; and second, the symbolism is utilizing the culture to underplay the significance of women's contribution to biological reproduction. While tying her down to the supreme duty of motherhood, this symbolism is instrumental in denying her the natural right over her own children. Also in creating and sustaining an ideology in which strategic resources of both types – material as well as human remain in the hands of men.

Fertility Performance: Allowing for variations of behaviour across regions and between higher and lower caste, it is generally true that in India, a woman's sense of personal growth is related to her fertility performance and the social standing, she achieves as a mother of sons. High fertility in sex segregated society affects the status of woman in several ways. First, the birth of the first child at a very early age and repeated pregnancies combined with malnutrition leads to high maternal mortality and fetal wastage. Second, women are so completely tied down by child care, house work and agricultural labour that few options are open to them for their personal growth apart from their main role of wife-mother. Third, since such high value is attached to the destined for marriage and motherhood at an early age. This pattern of early marriage and the attitude to female education is largely responsible for the high female illiteracy rate.

Gender Inequality: Issues of Production: Man's rights over the woman do not relate only to her sexuality and reproduction capacity, but encompass her productive capacities and labour power also. Just as he is entitled to have control over her sexuality and over the product of her sexuality, he is entitled to have control over her labour and also the proceeds of her labour. The extent of her actual participation in the process of production does not decide the worth of her contribution for she is a dependent as far as the productive resources are concerned and works as a family labourer. She is perceived as a dependent in respect of shelter also, for it is the husband's right, both by law and custom, to establish a matrimonial home. The notion that man is the provider of shelter and staple food is firmly rooted in the minds of the people. It is not surprising therefore that a woman's role in cultivation and other over her earning for the she lives in her man's house and eats his produce even though all the while she also earns. This logic is applicable even where the woman is earning through wage labour. The non-recognition or gross under recognition of woman's contribution to economy is not unconnected with the patriarchal ideology being propagated through various methods.

Because occupational segregation based on a sex-typed division of labour, high proportion of educated women are found in such female occupations as nursing, teaching and clerical work: less number of women seek career in engineering, technology and science, in politics and administration. There are several reasons why this pattern of occupational segregation and the exclusion for women from positions of executive authority and leadership are maintained. First, socialisation in the family and education in the school reinforce "gender roles", that is, cultural/ definitions of the traits and behaviour that are considered appropriate for men and women. In school, girls are encouraged to aspire to a limited range of occupations which are believed to be "feminine" and compatible with the demands of their primary gender roles of housewife and mother. Also the increase in the number of women in the profession and the service sector has not lead to sexual equality in the distribution of occupational position having power, status and privilege.

Q8. What do you understand by Women's empowerment?

[June 08, Q. 3][Dec 07, Q. 9(a)]

Ans. The empowerment of women occurs in reality, when women achieve increased control and participation in decision making that leads to their better access to resources, and therefore, improved socio-economic status. Empowerment is a multi-faceted, multi-dimensional and multi layered concept.

Women's Empowerment: Women's empowerment is a process in which women gain greater share of control over resources - material, human and intellectual like knowledge, information, ideas and financial resources like money - and access to money and control over decision-making in the home, community, society and nation, and to gain 'power'. According to the Country Report of Government of India, *"Empowerment means moving from a position of enforced powerlessness to one of power.* THE Experts on gender issues hold that women's advancement involves the process of empowerment and define it as a process, by which women achieve increased control over public decision making. The male domination of society and government are often seen for the purpose of serving male interests and in the continued subordination of women. The experts also inform that there are five levels of the women's empowerment framework, namely- welfare, access, conscientiousness, mobilisation and control. Welfare means an improvement in socio-economic status, such as improved nutritional status, shelter or income, which is the zero level of empowerment, where women are the passive recipients of benefits that are 'given' from on high. Access to resources and services stands for the first level of empowerment, since women improve their own status, relative to men, by their own work and organisation arising from increased access to resources and services. Conscientisation is defined as the process, by which women collectively urge to act to remove one or more of the discriminatory practices that impede their access to resources. Here, women form groups to understand the underlying causes of their problems and to identify strategies for action for gender equity. Mobilisation is the action level of empowerment by forging links with the larger women's movement, to learn from the successes of women's similar strategic action elsewhere and to connect with the wider struggle. Control is the level of empowerment when women have taken action so that there is gender equality in decisions making over access to resources, so that women achieve direct control over their access to resources. But one needs to understand that these five levels of women's empowerment are not really a linear progression but helical and circular along with being interconnected. The empowerment occurs when women achieve increased control and participation in decision making that leads to their better access to resources, and therefore, improved socio-economic status.

Q9. Explain the various approaches for empowering women.

Ans. The central challenge the practitioners interested in empowering women seeks to address is: how best to overcome or transform the causes of sub-ordination or oppression of women.

Shrilatha Batliwala's Study of Employment of Women in South Asia: In her study on the empowerment of women in South Asia, Srilatha Batliwala distinguishes between three different non-government organisations (NGO) approaches. The integrated development approach, the economic approach and the consciousness raising cum research and resource agency approach adopted by some NGOs which do not directly operate at the grass roots level. According to Batliwala there are two types of empowerment:

a) Economic Empowerment

b) Total Empowerment

The Government and various agencies feel that by providing various resources i.e. through integrated rural development programmes or entrepreneurial development programmes women can be empowered. But economic empowerment does not always lead to total empowerment or enhanced status. Some of the women belonging to affluent families may have the resources but have no decision making rights in their families and thus are not empowered. Thus, lack of resources is not causes of dis-empowerment but it is the result dis-empowerment. The causes are historical factors like low status of women, male dominated society etc. therefore only economic empowerment may not result in total empowerment i.e., woman may become economically independent but still she may not have decision making power in her family and her husband or father may control the household.

As Batliwala also observes – the distinctions between these approaches can only be made conceptually. In practice, these distinctions often get blurred. Most development programmes combine some mix of these approaches. Under Batliwala's typology the experiences documented here would be classified as integrated rural development or economic approaches. However, all of them build upon an initial underlying base of consciousness – raising and organizing. And all of them explicitly or implicitly attribute women's disempowerment to multiple factors and not any single factor.

Sydney Schuler and Syed Hashemi's Study on Empowerment of Women in Rural Bangladesh: In their study on empowerment of women in rural Bangladesh, Sydney Schuler and Syed Hashemi focus on empowerment as experienced by women members of Bangladesh Rural Advancement Committee (BRAC) and Grameen Bank, both of which have been characterized as adopting individuals economic approaches. According to them there are six specific components to female empowerment in Bangladesh namely:

1) a sense of self and vision of a future,
2) mobility and visibility,
3) economic security,
4) status and decision making power within the household,
5) ability to interact effectively in the public sphere, and
6) participation in non-family groups.

Among the example of collective empowerment and action they report cases of women's groups taking action against the husbands of group members who beat or divorce their wives, or women groups fielding their own candidate and voting with their own minds in local elections.

Even these individuals economic approaches can have collective political effects.

Leslie Calman's Study of Women's Movement in India: Leslie Calman in her study of women's movement in India sees two major ideological and organisational tendencies within the movements.

i) Large urban bases – which focuses on issues of rights and equality, and
ii) Both rural and urban based which emphasizes empowerment and liberation.

According to Calman women's rights advocates, see women's concerns as issues of civil and political rights i.e. the aim for equality under the law. The women's empowerment advocates on the hand, see women's concerns as issues of economic and social rights i.e. the right to a livelihood and to determine one's future and aim at the personal and community empowerment of poor women.

The first step in organizing for empowerment is to get groups of women to analyse their common problems and then collectively to seek solutions. Under Calman's classification SEWA (Self Employed Women's Association) is a leading example of a empowerment organisation, even 'Proshika' would be classified as an empowerment organisation by Calman.

5 Explaining Caste in Indian Society

Q1. Discuss the concepts of Varna and jati with suitable illustrations.
[June 07, Q. 6]

Ans. Jati (the word literally means *births*) is the term used to denote communities and sub-communities in India. It is a term used across religions. In Hindu society, each jâti typically has an association with a traditional job function, although religious beliefs (e.g. Sri Vaishnavism or Veera Shaivism) or linguistic groupings define some jatis. A person's surname typically reflects a community (jati) association: thus *Gandhi* - greengrocer, *Dhobi* - washer man, *Srivastava* = military scribe, etc. In any given location in India 500 or more jatis may co-exist, although the exact composition will differ from district to district. Many jâtis found today in India could fit into one varna (occupation categorisation) or another as described in Hinduism, similar to communities of old that had fit into a Varna. This indicates that Hindu society since pre-historic times had a very complex economy. One non-sacred text, the Laws of Manu, c. 200, codified the social relations between communities although this book was never followed by any society since it was much less important than the sacred Hindu texts of the Vedas. It is believed that the jati system ossified from an original occupation-based classification into a hereditary classification. Originally, the jati was effectively a system similar to guilds, and was associated with occupation. For example, as a general rule goldsmith, carpenters and barbers form separate communities. Most communities with a significant number of members are divided into sub-communities. The development of sub-communities could arise because of these reasons:

· Geographical separation: For example purabia (eastern) or pachchaia (western) sections of some communities.

· Variation in standards of conduct: For example, disagreements over the permissibility of widow marriages caused some communities to subdivide.

In several cases, merging of sub-communities have been recorded. A *jâti* could originally change their occupation and thus association with a varna. Marriages would occur usually within one's community, or sometimes between communities. At one time there was considerable interest in relative ranking of communities (jâtis). There are several ways ranking can be done.

1. By public reputation of the community in a region,

2. By wealth and influence,

3. Food relationship: Members of a lower community will accept water-based (kachcha) food prepared by members of a higher community.

A consequence of the 3rd rule was that Brahmins were often employed as cooks. The rule was often not applicable if the food items are dry (e.g. roasted grains) or cooked with oil/ghee (pakka). There are now several thousand communities and sub-communities in India. A jâti is defined by the mutual interaction among the members of the community. The two most common bonds are:

1. "Roti" (bread): dining together.

2. "Beti" (daughter): intermarrying together,

Varna and Jati: Ancient Hindu scriptures have the citations of four 'varnas' or colour, which is the basic social class in the caste system in India. Bhagavad gita says that varnas are decided on the grounds of Guna which is the amalgamation of the five elements of ether, air, fire, water and earth, and Karma which is the concept of action. The works of Brahmins, Kshatriyas, Vaishyas, and Shudras are different, in harmony with the three powers of their born nature. Four varnas that are mentioned by other shastras are the Brahmins destined as teachers, scholars and priests , the Kshatriyas- kings and warriors , the Vaishyas were the trading class and the Shudras were agriculturists, service providers, and some artisan groups. These are further classified into 'jatis'. Another group excluded from the main society was called Parjanya or Antyaja this is the group of former "untouchables" (now called Dalits) who were considered either the lower section of Shudras or beyond the caste system altogether. Varna and jati are both different concepts. Varna actually unifies the Hindu sub communities or jatis into the four groups. Jati or community is an endogamous group where the members marry within themselves. Then there is a further division of the sub communities into exogamous groups in terms of 'gotras'. There are exactly thousands of sub-castes or 'jatis' in India, often with particular ecological ranges and a governmental or corporate structure. Jatis are the way in which caste is embodied for most practical purposes. A question about the proper Varna to which a particular jati belongs can be raised though very infrequently. It is possible to rank the jatis in relation to each other.

Q2. Discuss the critiques of Dumont's theory of caste. [June 07, Q. 8]

Ans. Dumont's Theory: To sum up Dumont's theory, we can identify the following core points that he makes:

· The Hindu caste system could not be explained in terms of politico-economic factors. Caste was not just another form of class or an extreme form of stratification.

· It should be explained in terms of its underlying structure of ideas and values, i.e., the ideology.

· The nature of the value system (ideology) and the framework of social organisation in the traditional societies were totally different from that of the modern societies of the West.

· The ideology of the Hindu caste system was that of hierarchy. The structure of hierarchy was explained in terms of the dialectical relationship (unity and apposition) between the "pure" and "impure". Pure was superior to the impure.

· One of the core features of caste system was the distinction that it made between status and power. It was the ideology of hierarchy (that allocated status to different groups in society) that was more important than the material position of a person in the caste system. Priest, at least in principle, was superior to the king.

Criticisms of Dumont's Theory: Dumont's book *Homo Hierarchicus* has been widely acclaimed as the single most important contribution to the study of the Hindu caste system. His explanation of caste in terms of "purity" and "pollution" has become a part of the common sense sociology. However, his theory has also been one of the most controversial pieces of work. He has been criticized on various grounds. Among those who have critically examined his thesis and questioned his explanation of caste include scholars like Gerald Berreman, Dipankar Gupta, Andre Beteille and Joan Mencher. They have all themselves been students of the Indian society and have found problems with Dumont's arguments at different levels, empirically, logically, and ideologically. Following are some of the common points that have been raised by different scholars against Dumont's work.

i) It does not correspond with the lived reality of caste: It has been pointed out by his critiques that much of Dumont's theory has been derived from the study of some selective classical Hindu texts. He has ignored the large amount of empirical literature that was available to him, produced by professional social anthropologists in from village studies and monographs. These monographs provided graphic details of the ways in which caste system functioned at the micro-level. Their description of the system did not confirm his theory. Interestingly, as pointed by Gupta, even when Dumont was aware of the existence of these facts, he constructed them in a manner that their impact was marginalized. Though Dumont explicitly states that his attempt was to understand the underlying structure of the system and not the way caste was practiced in every day life, he nevertheless aspires to make generalisations that have empirical value. He wants us to believe that his theory truly explains the essence of caste.

Moreover, as Berreman rightly points out, caste did not exist except empirically, in the lives of people as they interacted with each other. 'The human meaning of caste for those who lived it was power and vulnerability, privilege and oppression, honour and denigration plenty and want, reward and deprivation, security and anxiety. As an anthropological document, a description of caste which failed to convey this was a travesty in the world today'.

Further, Dumont has tried to develop a theory of caste that was supposed to apply to the entire Indian subcontinent. However, at empirical level, there existed significant variations in the system of caste hierarchy from region to region. While there were some regions of India where Brahmins had indeed been considered the superior most, there were other regions where they did not command much respect, such as, in the north-western region of Indian.

ii) Status and power are not independent of each other: Dumont's theory of caste stands on the premise that in the Indian society, the ritual hierarchy functioned independently of the considerations of power and wealth. This premise has been the most contentious issue among his critics. They find it simply not being applicable to the actual structure of social inequalities in the Indian context. Berreman has, for example, argued that the power-status opposition is a false dichotomy in the context of caste. The two, Berreman insists, went together everywhere and the Indian case was no exception. Power and status were two sides of the same coin. He cites the example of the integration of Gonds, a tribal group into the caste system. They were generally incorporated into the caste system as untouchables. In areas where they had retained power in the form of land, they were treated differently. In such case they were given much higher status in the local caste hierarchy and were called Raj Gonds. Similarly, Gupta has pointed out that 'the rule of caste was obeyed when it was accompanied by the rule of power'.

iii) Dumont's theory represents a Brahmanical perspective on caste: Dumont has been widely criticized for presenting a partial and a biased view of the system. Since his theory was largely derived from the classical Hindu texts, produced invariably by the upper caste Brahmins, his theory allegedly reflected the bias that the upper caste themselves had vis-à-vis the system. It may be worthwhile to quote once again from Berreman. He writes:

Dumont relies heavily on some classical Sanskritic texts ignoring others, a technique that is inevitable with such sources, but which enables one to 'prove' almost anything one wishes. The result is that he conveys a view of caste which is artificial, stiff, stereotypical and idealized. It is a view that confirms rather closely to the high-caste ideal of what the system of Hindu India ought to be like according to those who value it positively.

Another scholar, Joan Mencher, who conducted her field-work among the lower castes in Tamil Nadu found that from the point of view of people at the lowest end of the scale, caste had functioned and continued to function as a very effective system of economic exploitation.

iv) Dumont works with a false dichotomy between the "traditional" and "modern" societies: Dumont has also been criticized for treating Indian society as being fundamentally different from the West. He works with a much-criticized notice of a dichotomy between the modern societies of the West and the traditional societies of the Third World. His theory is based on the assumption that while the modern societies of the West were characterized by the ideas of individualism and egalitarianism, and traditional societies, in contrast, were characterized by conceptions of the collective nature of man, by the primacy of social rather than individual goals, and thus by hierarchy. As an implication of this, traditional societies like India get represented as knowing nothing about the values of equality and liberty. While traditional societies like India projected as being closed and unchanging, the West was presented as being progressive and open.

v) Dumont's theory given no agency to the individuals who practice it: Dumont's notion of traditional society is such that it gave no recognition to the individual choice. According to Berreman: 'The people who comprise the system were depicted as unfeeling, regimented automatons ruled by inexorable social forces, confirming unquestioningly and unerringly to universal values'. Such a notion of the "traditional" Indian society could be easily contradicted by the empirical studies carried out by professional social anthropologists. These studies showed that the Indian people were 'as willful, factionalized and individually variable as people anywhere else'.

vi) Dumont does not acknowledge the social movements against the caste ideology: Critics have also pointed out that the oppressive side of the caste system and the various oppositional movements against it are not Epiphenomenal to caste, as has been suggested by Dumont. There was a long list of social mobilisations against Brahminical dominance in modern as well as in the pre-modern India. From Buddhism to Bhakti to Sikhism neo Buddhism, there had been strong, and to some extent successful opposition to the caste ideology. There was no place for such realities in Dumont's depiction of the Indian society and in his theory of the caste system.

Q3. Show the role of purity and pollution in caste hierarchy.

[Dec 08, Q. 5][June 08, Q. 12]

Ans. Purity and Pollution: Many status differences in Indian society are expressed in terms of ritual purity and pollution. Notions of purity and pollution are extremely complex and vary greatly among different castes, religious groups, and regions. However, broadly speaking, high status is associated with purity and low status with pollution. Some kinds of purity are inherent, or inborn; for example, gold is purer than copper by its very nature, and, similarly, a member of a high-ranking Brahman (see Glossary), or priestly, caste is born with more inherent purity than a member of a low-ranking Sweeper (Mehtar, in Hindi) caste. Unless the Brahman defiles himself in some extraordinary way, throughout his life he will always be purer than a Sweeper. Other kinds of purity are more transitory—a Brahman who has just taken a bath is more ritually pure than a Brahman who has not bathed for a day. This situation could easily reverse itself temporarily, depending on bath schedules, participation in polluting activities, or contact with temporarily polluting substances. Purity is associated with ritual cleanliness—daily bathing in flowing water, dressing in properly laundered clothes of approved materials, eating only the foods appropriate for one's caste, refraining from physical contact with people of lower rank, and avoiding involvement with ritually impure substances. The latter include body wastes and excretions, most especially those of another adult person. Contact with the products of death or violence are typically polluting and threatening to ritual purity. During her menstrual period, a woman is considered polluted and refrains from cooking, worshiping, or touching anyone older than an infant. In much of the south, a woman spends this time "sitting outside," resting in an isolated room or shed. During her period, a Muslim woman does not touch the Quran. At the end of the period, purity is restored with a complete bath. Pollution also attaches to birth, both for the mother and the infant's close kin, and to death, for close relatives of the deceased. Members of the highest priestly castes, the Brahmans, are generally vegetarians (although some Bengali and Maharashtrian Brahmans eat fish) and avoid eating meat, the product of violence and death. High-ranking Warrior castes (Kshatriyas), however, typically consume non vegetarian diets, considered appropriate for their traditions of valor and physical strength.

A Brahman born of proper Brahman parents retains his inherent purity if he bathes and dresses himself properly, adheres to a vegetarian diet, eats meals prepared only by persons of appropriate rank, and keeps his person away from the bodily exuviate of others.

If a Brahman happens to come into bodily contact with a polluting substance, he can remove this pollution by bathing and changing his clothes. However, if he were to eat meat or commit other transgressions of the rigid dietary codes of his particular caste, he would be considered more deeply polluted and would have to undergo various purifying rites and payment of fines imposed by his caste council in order to restore his inherent purity.

In sharp contrast to the purity of a Brahman, a Sweeper born of Sweeper parents is considered to be born inherently polluted. The touch of his body is polluting to those higher on the caste hierarchy than he, and they will shrink from his touch, whether or not he has bathed recently. Sweepers are associated with the traditional occupation of cleaning human feces from latrines and sweeping public lanes of all kinds of dirt. Traditionally, Sweepers remove these polluting materials in baskets carried atop the head and dumped out in a garbage pile at the edge of the village or neighborhood. The involvement of Sweepers with such filth accords with their low-status position at the bottom of the Hindu caste hierarchy, even as their services allow high-status people, such as Brahmans, to maintain their ritual purity.

However, castes associated with ruling and warfare—and the killing and deaths of human beings—are typically accorded high rank on the caste hierarchy. In these instances, political power and wealth outrank association with violence as the key determinant of caste rank.

Maintenance of purity is associated with the intake of food and drink, not only in terms of the nature of the food itself, but also in terms of who has prepared it or touched it. This requirement is especially true for Hindus, but other religious groups hold to these principles to varying degrees. Generally, a person risks pollution—and lowering his own status—if he accepts beverages or cooked foods from the hands of people of lower caste status than his own. His status will remain intact if he accepts food or beverages from people of higher caste rank. Usually, for an observant Hindu of any but the very lowest castes to accept cooked food from a Muslim or Christian is regarded as highly polluting.

In a clear example of pollution associated with dining, a Brahman who consumed a drink of water and a meal of wheat bread with boiled vegetables from the hands of a Sweeper would immediately become polluted and could expect social rejection by his caste fellows. From that moment, fellow Brahmans following traditional pollution rules would refuse food touched by him and would abstain from the usual social interaction with him. He would not be welcome inside Brahman homes—most especially in the ritually pure kitchens—nor would he or his close relatives be considered eligible marriage partners for other Brahmans.

Generally, the acceptance of water and ordinary foods cooked in water from members of lower-ranking castes incurs the greatest pollution. In North India, such foods are known as *kaccha khana* , as contrasted with fine foods cooked in butter or oils, which are known as *pakka khana* . Fine foods can be accepted from members of a few castes slightly lower than one's own. Local hierarchies differ on the specific details of these rules.

Completely raw foods, such as uncooked grains, fresh unpeeled bananas, mangoes, and uncooked vegetables can be accepted by anyone from anyone else, regardless of relative status. Toasted or parched foods, such as roasted peanuts, can also be accepted from anyone without ritual or social repercussions. (Thus, a Brahman may accept gifts of grain from lower-caste patrons for eventual preparation by members of his own caste, or he may purchase and consume roasted peanuts or tangerines from street vendors of unknown caste without worry.)

Water served from an earthen pot may be accepted only from the hands of someone of higher or equal caste ranking, but water served from a brass pot may be accepted even from someone slightly lower on the caste scale. Exceptions to this rule are members of the Waterbearer (Bhoi, in Hindi) caste, who are employed to carry water from wells to the homes of the prosperous and from whose hands members of all castes may drink water without becoming polluted, even though Water bearers are not ranked high on the caste scale.

These and a great many other traditional rules pertaining to purity and pollution constantly impinge upon interaction between people of different castes and ranks in India. Although to the non-Indian these rules may seem irrational and bizarre, to most of the people of India they are a ubiquitous and accepted part of life. Thinking about and following purity and pollution rules make it necessary for people to be constantly aware of differences in status. With every drink of water, with every meal, and with every contact with another person, people must ratify the social hierarchy of which they are a part and within which their every act is carried out. The fact that expressions of social status are intricately bound up with events that happen to everyone every day—eating, drinking, bathing, touching, talking—and that transgressions of these rules, whether deliberate or accidental, are seen as having immediately polluting effects on the person of the transgressor, means that every ordinary act of human life serves as a constant reminder of the importance of hierarchy in Indian society.

There are many Indians, particularly among the educated urban elite, who do not follow traditional purity and pollution practices. Dining in each others' homes and in restaurants is common among well-educated people of diverse backgrounds, particularly when they belong to the same economic class. For these people, guarding the family's earthen water pot from inadvertent touch by a low-ranking servant is not the concern it is for a more traditional villager. However, even among those people whose words and actions denigrate traditional purity rules, there is often a reluctance to completely abolish consciousness of purity and pollution from their thinking. It is surely rare for a Sweeper, however well-educated, to invite a Brahman to dinner in his home and have his invitation unself-consciously accepted. It is less rare, however, for educated urban colleagues of vastly different caste and religious heritage to enjoy a cup of tea together. Some high-caste liberals pride themselves on being free of "casteism" and seek to accept food from the hands of very low-caste people, or even deliberately set out to marry someone from a significantly lower caste or a different religion.

Q4. Explain the meaning of caste.

Ans. India is also home to a large and diverse population that has added to its vibrant character since ages. There are about 3,000 communities in India. So wide and complex is the mix of the Indian population that two-thirds of her communities are found in the geographical boundaries of each of her states. They are a mingling of the Caucasoid, the Negrito, the Proto-Austroloids, the Mongoloid and the Mediterranean races. The tribals constitute eight percent of the total population of India.

Based on their physical type and language, we can easily divide Indian people into four broad classes. First, a majority of high class Hindus, who live in North India and whose language is derived from Sanskrit. Secondly, those who live in that part of India that is south of the Vindhyas and whose languages - Tamil, Telugu, Kannada and Malayalam are entirely different from Sanskrit. These are known by the generic name of "Dravidians". Thirdly, primitive tribes living in hills and jungles of India constitute eight percent of the total population in India. The Kols, Bhils and Mundas belong to this class. Fourthly, there are a people with strong Mongolian features inhabiting within India the slopes of the Himalayas and mountains of Assam. The Gorkhas, Bhutiyas and Khasis are striking examples of this.

To add all this, India is perhaps the only place in the world where twenty religious streams flow together. If that sounds clichéd, here is a surprising piece of information. About 500 communities of India say they follow two religions at the same time! India has a population of over 1 billion people, the majority of whom are Hindus. The caste system in India is a social system where people are ranked into groups based on heredity within rigid systems of social stratification. The caste is a group whose members are restricted in their choice of occupation and degree of social participation. Marriage outside the caste is prohibited. Social status is determined by the caste of one's birth. The Indian term for caste is jati, which generally designates a group varying in size from a handful to many thousands. There are thousands of such jatis, and each has its distinctive rules and customs. Varna (meaning, "color") refers to the ancient and somewhat ideal fourfold division of the Hindu society: **(1)** the Brahmans, the priestly and learned class; **(2)** the Kshatriyas, the warriors and rulers; **(3)** the Vaisyas, farmers and merchants; and **(4)** the Sudras, peasants and laborers. Below the category of Sudras were the untouchables, or Panchamas (meaning "fifth division"), who performed the most menial tasks. Although there has been much confusion between the two, jati and Varna are different in origin as well as function. The various castes in any given region of India are hierarchically organized, with each caste corresponding roughly to one or the other of the Varna categories.

Q5. Describe the two theoretical perspective of caste.

Ans. The Interactional Approach: The interactional approach is the more prevalent one today. However, the uni-dimensional model has been found inadequate, specially the orthodox Marxist model with its economic reductionism, which seems hardly credible when the religious and political overtones of caste are reduced to epi-phenomena in the super-structure.

The classic multi-dimensional model of Weber has greater potentiality for a better understanding of caste and has been frequently used ever since Weber himself first applied it to caste. Beteille has applied the Weberian model in a careful case study of a south Indian village. Beteille concludes to a trend towards a shift from a closed to an open stratification system. Whereas fifty years ago the caste structure largely subsumed economic and political gradations, today with the emergence of caste-free occupations and power resources other than the ones tied to land, there is less status consistency between the three areas of caste, class and power, and a trend to the autonomisation of each.

The Sanskritisation that was the chief channel of mobility in pre-independent India can very easily be described in terms of this theory. But the socio-economic changes in post-independent India and particularly the new found status of 'citizen' and 'voter' that lower caste groups have activated makes political participation serve as a fundamental alternative towards mobility instead of Sanskritisation. Indeed the whole Buddhist movement among the navbudhs is rightly interpreted as a rejection of Sanskritisation. Lynch is emphatic "that political participation... is the path that mobility movements will increasingly follow in India."

The Attributional Approach: The interactional approach to caste draws attention to the structural aspect as opposed to the attributional one. However, for an institution like caste the 'ideology' supporting it of critical importance to a proper understanding of caste and the identity politics of today. In the Indian context Dumont has made an incisive statement against the use of a stratification model for caste in his *Hemo Hierarchicus* and has forced attention to the ideological approach once again. Attributional approach is based more on specific feature of caste including the ascriptive criteria.

In urging the relevance of the principle of hierarchy Dumont notes how alien it is to the modern mentality. Modern man's ideology is decidedly egalitarian and individualistic, diametrically opposite to a hierarchical and collectivist one. But whereas equality is an ideal to be socially realised, hierarchy is a reality that is a societal given. For, if a society is functionally differentiated it must also be value integrated to be viable. This inevitably introduces a rank order and the principle of hierarchy with it. Thus, Dumont observes: "man does not only think, he acts. He has not only ideas, but values. To adopt a value is to introduce hierarchy."

A hierarchy, then, integrates a society by reference to its values. Dumont defines hierarchy "as the principle by which the elements of a whole are ranked in relation to the whole." However, this ranking is not in terms of 'a scale of power' but of 'a gradation of statuses'. For hierarchy expresses, not the material unity of a society brought about by generalized medium of exchange like power, or money, or prestige (this is precisely how the stratification model derives), but it essentially expresses its conceptual or symbolic unity, one that includes that the social order in a cosmic one. In others words, the social order is perceived as but the ritual expression of the cosmic one.

Religious Hierarchy: The symbolic unity is elaborated in the hierarchical relation, "a relation between larger and smaller, or more precisely between that which encompasses and that which is encompassed." For Dumont: in every society one aspect of social life receives a primary value stress and simultaneously is made to encompass all others and express them as far as it can. In the context of the caste system which is a religious hierarchy, this would mean that functions in which the religious aspect is minimal are *encompassed* within a system that is decisively shaped by religious functions. This religious hierarchy is ritually expressed in the opposition between the 'pure' and the 'impure'. It is this fundamental dichotomy that underlines the separateness and distinction between caste while including them all in a hierarchical whole.

Dumont's concept of hierarchy as applied of hierarchy as applied to caste, which he considers a case of 'pure hierarchy', is indeed challenging but not without its critics. Mckim Mariott finds a remarkable consensus about caste hierarchical rankings but he links it primarily to four dimensions of community structure and not to an ideology. He concludes his study thus:

"the ritual hierarchy itself in part grows out of, expresses, and tends to remain positively correlated with, and therefore indirectly influenced by economic, political, and other non-ritual hierarchies of interaction. Most castes appear ultimately to achieve positions in the ritual hierarchy which are in harmony with their relative possession of wealth and power."

Dumont is aware of such 'status consistency' but he still insists on the primacy of attribution over interaction as the factor in the ranking order. Thus, in reference to the untouchables he writes "that the overwhelming religious inferiority of these castes in effect expresses and encompasses their strict secular dependence on the dominant caste." (1972: 180) While there is social mobility, through the symbolic justification implied in the process of Sanskritisation, it is accommodated as positional, not structural change. This is in effect a reaffirmation of the hierarchical principle.

Dumont's Approach: The ideological emphasis of Dumont's approach is fairly successful in an analysis of a stable social situation where we would expect a consistent reciprocity between structure and culture. But in the context of social change there may arise inconsistencies and strains between these two elements as cultural lags develop in which either element could be the primary factor precipitating the change. A comprehensive explanation of change must include both elements, specially in the context of modernisation, since this implies both structure and cultural changes of far reaching consequences. Dumont's analysis while very insightful in its interpretation of the traditional caste system, needs to be complemented in its analysis of the changing caste situation today.

Q6. Outline the attributional and interactional approaches to the explanation of caste. [Dec 08, Q. 10][June 08, Q. 11][Dec 07, Q. 11]

Ans. The early insights of Marx Weber and Bougle to develop what has came to be known as the "attributional approach". Attributional approach discusses primarily the significant features of the caste system qua system and what distinguishes it from other forms of the social stratification.

Attributes are inherent inalienable qualities associated with the caste system. As such every caste must necessarily partake of these attributes.

G.S. Ghurye: Ghurye wrote in the 1930's and considered that each caste was separated from the other in a hierarchical order. This ordering sprang legitimately from its attributes of a caste. These were:

i) Segmental Division: Thus, membership to a caste group is acquired by birth and with it come the position in the rank order relative to other castes.

ii) Hierarchy: Following from the above society was arranged in rank orders, or relations of superiority or inferiority. Thus, Brahmis were accepted as highest in the hierarchy and untouchables at the very bottom.

iii) Caste Restrictions: These were placed on every caste which gave permission to its members only to interact with particular groups of people. This included its dress, speech, customs, and rituals from whom they could accept food. The system was geared to maintain purity of the ground members, hence of the caste group itself.

iv) Caste Pollution: In this idea the whole effort of a caste was to avoid contamination from pollution objects (those involved unclean occupations, or of the lowest caste). This shunning of pollution is reflected in the residential separation of the caste groups.

v) Traditional Occupation: Ghurye felt that every caste had a traditional occupation the clean castes had clean occupations whereas the unclean and impure caste had defiling ones.

vi) Endogamy: This trait of the castes was very distinct and essential to keeping it together as a group that maintained its own distinct character. Essentially it maintained that one could only marry within ones caste.

Thus, through six attributes Ghurye sought to define the process by which a caste group maintained its caste identity. By preserving the various attributes of segmental division, hierarchy, caste restrictions, caste pollution, traditional occupation, and marriage within a particular caste circle, the caste group maintained its own separate (through interrelated) identity which it sought to perpetuate over generations.

J.H. Hutton: Hutton had described the caste structure in his book Caste in *India.* Hutton held that the central feature of the caste system was endogamy. Around this fact are built up the various restrictions and taboos. Interaction must not violate these restrictions placed on the various castes. Another important feature of the caste system as seen by Hutton was the taboo on taking cooked food from any caste but one's own. Such restrictions raised questions in themselves:

i) Who cooks the food?

ii) What type of pot was the food cooked in?

iii) Is the food "Kaccha" uncooked or (cooked in water) or "pakka" (fried in oil". The latter is acceptable from other castes as well.

iv) There is a hierarchy of food and vegetarian food is ranked higher than non vegetarian food. Brahmins are usually vegetarian but not everywhere. In Bengal and Kashmir Brahmins eat non-vegetarian food as well.

These restrictions reflect the process of the formation of caste identity. They are reflective of separation and hierarchy between the caste groups. Thus, non-acceptance of food reflects superiority of rank. The whole idea of maintaining 'purity' and reducing 'pollution' is also found to permeate the interactions.

In parts of the South India for instance the fear of pollution gets translated into physical distance being maintained between the superior and inferior caste. Again the castes low in rank order has to avoid village temples and wells and maintain a physical distance in their interaction with higher caste members. Thus, Hutton explains caste interactions with the notion of attributes of a caste, primarily in terms of endogamy, purity and impurity and restrictions on commensality.

M.N. Srinivas: Before proceeding further it may be mentioned that the scholars using the attributional approach stress the attributes of a caste. However, each of them lays emphasis on one or other of these attributes and how they affect interaction. In the cast of Srinivas writing in the 50's we find that he chooses to study the structure of relations arising between castes on the basis of these attributes. Thus, he introduces a dynamic aspect of caste identity very forcefully. This aspect becomes clearer in Srinivas's work on positional mobility known as 'Sanskritisation'. Sanskritisation is a process whereby a caste attempts to raise its rank within the caste hierarchy by adopting in practice, the attributes of the caste or castes above them, in the rank order. This is to say the 'low' attributes are gradually dropped and the 'high' attributes of the caste above them are imitated. This involves adoption of vegetarianism, clean occupations of so on.

Closely connected is the concept of dominant caste. The dominant caste in a village is conspicuous by its:

i) Sizeable numerical presence

ii) Ownership of land, and

iii) Political power.

Thus, a dominant caste has numerical significance as well as economic and political power. It is also interesting to note that the dominant caste need not be the highest ranking caste in the village caste hierarchy. The dominant caste commands the service of all other castes.

Interactional Approaches to Caste: Interaction approach takes into account how castes are actually ranked with respect to one another in a local empirical context.

Attributes of a caste be used as a approach to study caste. It would also have come clear to you that a set of attributes denotes its own interactional processes. Thus, we cannot say that attributes have no bearing or interaction. On the other hand we find that the interaction too has its attributional aspects. So, the questions comes down to which of these aspects is emphasized more than the other, and given primacy in analyzing the caste dynamics and identity formation. Let us study some of the pioneering works so for a interactional approaches to the study of caste are concerned.

F.G. Bailey: Bailey feels that caste dynamics and identity are united by the two principles of segregation and hierarchy. He feels that "Castes Stand in ritual and secular hierarchy expressed in the rules of interaction". The ritual system overlaps the political and economic system.

Bailey explained his viewpoint with reference to village Bisipara in Orissa; and showed how the caste situation in Bisipara become changed and more fluid after Independence when the Kshatriyas lost much of their land. This caused a downslide in their ritual ranking as well. There was a clearly discernable change in the interaction patterns which we have delineated above e.g. acceptance and non acceptance of food from other castes.

A. Mayer: Mayer studied Ramkheri village in Madhya Pradesh. To understand the effect on caste hierarchy, Mayer observed interactive between castes in term of:

i) Commensality of eating, drinking water and smoking,

ii) Food type exchanged whether is 'Kaccha' or 'pakka,'

iii) Context of eating, ritual or otherwise,

iv) Seating arrangements at eating,

v) Who provides food and who cooked it,
vi) The vessel in which water is given – metal or earthen.

Thus, the commensal hierarchy is based on the belief that any or all of the above factors can lead to greater or lesser pollution for a caste thus affecting its identity and ranking in the hierarchy order. Those at the top of the hierarchical order will ensure that only a caste or type of food and water vessel which will not pollute them is accepted or used by them. For example pakka food may be accepted from a lower caste but kachcha food will accepted only from within the same caste or subcaste.

M. Marriott: Marriott analyses caste hierarchy with reference to the local context. Marriott studied the arrangement of caste ranking in ritual interaction. Marriott confirmed that ritual hierarchy is itself linked to economic and political hierarchies. Usually economic and political ranks tend to coincide. That is to say both ritual and non-ritual hierarchies affect the ranking in the caste order though ritual hierarchies tend to play a greater role. In this way a consensus emerges regarding caste ranking and this is collectively upheld. It must be make clear here that this process is not as clear cut as it first seems. This is because the sociologist enters the field when this process of caste ranking in its full blown form and he or she does not observe the historical process and took place by deduces or infers about the same from the data that is available on hand. Marriot studied Kishan Garhi and Ram Nagla two village in the Aligarh District of U.P. in 1952. Marriott's study showed that there is consensus about caste ranking in these villages. The basis on which this is done is the observation of ritual interaction, in the village itself.

In the villages Marriot studied, we find that the important indicators or rank are:
i) Giving and receiving of food,
ii) Giving and receiving of honorific gestures and practices, and
iii) Thus, Brahmins are ranked high since they officiate at the most exclusive and important rituals. They simultaneously receive all services from the other castes. Again Brahmins accept only "pakka" food from another group of high castes. Thus, a caste can be considered high if Brahmins accept 'pakka' food from them and low if Brahmins accepting 'kaccha' food from them. There were ten such 'high' castes in Kishan Garhi and four such 'high' caste in Ram Nagla. The lowest caste does not receive any service from other castes, but has to provide its services to all other castes and had made it a practice to accept 'Kaccha' food from them as well.

Food and services, and how they are offered and accepted are therefore major indicators of caste ranking. However, Marriott observed that there were rules also about:
i) smoking together,
ii) the arrangement of the housing complex,

iii) details and bodily contact, and

iv) feasting and the order in which the food is served.

In Kishan Garhi political and economic dominance matched the ritual hierarchy. Let us see how ritual status and economic power (land ownership) overlap:

Rank and land Ownership in Krishan Garhi

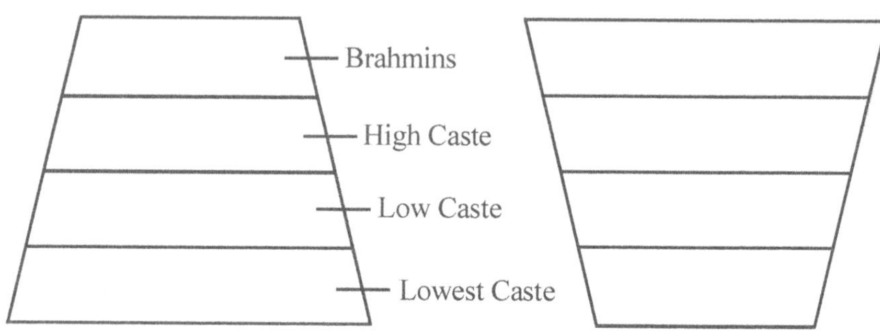

Chart: 5.1

Thus, there is a tendency among castes to transform their political and economic status into ritual status.

However inconsistencies can and do exist. This gives room for social mobility. Again, though it is true that the local interaction is important, but a reference to other village can also help determined local rank. However, by and large the ritual hierarchy tends to be consistent with political and economic dominance. Interaction sustains a given ranking order which can be witnessed in the various facts that have been mentioned.

L. Dumont: Dumont added a new dimension to the studies of caste in an interactional perspective. His study of caste emphasizes relations between castes rather than attributes. Attributes can only be explained with reference to the relationship between castes. According to Dumont the local context has a role in caste ranking and identity, but this is a response to the ideology of hierarchy which extends over the entire caste system. Thus, for Dumont caste is a set of relationship of economic, political and kinship systems, sustained by mainly religious values. For Dumont caste is a special type of inequality and hierarchy is the essential values underlying the caste system, and it is this value that integrates Hindu society.

The various aspects of the caste, says Dumont are based on principle of opposition between the pure and impure underlying them. 'Pure' is superior to the 'impure' and has to be kept separate. Thus, the caste system appears to be rational to those because of the opposition between the pure and the impure. Dumont also feels that hierarchy in the caste system indicates ritual status without accepting the influences of wealth or power authority. Thus, hierarchy is the principle through which the elements are ranked in relation to the whole. Ranking is basically religious in nature. In Indian society Status (Brahmins) has always been separated from power (King). To go further, power has been subordinated to 'status'. The king is subordinate to the priest, but both are dependent on each other. Thus, hierarchy is something ritualistic in nature and supported by religion. Only when power in subordinated to status, can this type of pure hierarchy develop. The Brahmins who represents purity is superior and at the top of the whole system. But the Brahmin along with the king opposes all the other categories of the Varna system.

For Dumont the Jajmani system of economic interaction is a ritual expression rather than an economic arrangement. Jajmani system is the religious expression of inter dependence where interdependence itself is derived from religion. Similarly, commensal regulations emphasize hierarchy rather then separation. However, the question of purity does not arise on all such occasions of commensality. Thus, the washerman is a 'purifier' and can enter the house freely. But he cannot attend a marriage party with similar caste.

Q7. Discuss the religious and sociological explanations of caste.

Ans. Various explanations of the origins of the caste have been forwarded, and early explanations often veer around the notion of 'attributes' or 'inalienable characteristic' of caste. Since we will be examining some of the explanations it would be better if we provide some idea of these characteristics. These are provided by religious theories and by secular sociological explanations. Let us now turn to the religious theories at first.

Religious Explanations: Religious explanations of caste origins in Hinduism refer to first of all the theory of 'divine origin' of caste. The idea in this theory is developed from verses in the Rig Veda right up to the Bhagavad Gita in contemporary times. It must be added that this is a Brahmanical version and not shared by many other communities.

The varna scheme is a four fold scheme. It is further pointed out with reference to the theory of divine origin that over time each of the varnas developed into jatis or caste groups with specific attributes. The first three groups made up a category of the "twice born" and were initiated into the caste by the sacred thread ceremony (yagyapavita). Each of the groups began specializing in particular type of profession and was restrained from performing the work of any other caste. Hierarchy was manifested both in attributional and interactional modes.

A second type of religious explanation is based on the guna theory, which is to be found in the religious literature including the Bhagavad Gita. This theory talks of the inherent qualities that characterize human beings. These three gunas are as below:

i) 'sattva', or the quality of truth, Knowledge, goodness, virtue and alertness; **ii)** 'rajas' or the quality of activity, courage, bravery, force, power and passion; **iii)** 'tamas' or the quality of gloominess, dullness, stupidity and indolence.

It is easy to see how the above qualities were associated hierarchically with the Brahmins being considered 'Sattvic'; the Kshatriyas and Vaisyas being considered below the Brahmins, and being rajasic. Finally on the lowest rung of the ladder were the 'tamasic' Shudras.

Sociological Explanations: Unlike religious explanations the early sociological explanations of caste moved toward socially recognizable reality. Let us consider this briefly in the work of i) Karl Marx ii) Max Weber and iii) Celestin Bougle.

i) For Marx, the relationships of social groups to land and its ownership determined the groups position in society. Thus, for him in the Indian village these were:

ii) Castes working on land, and

iii) Artisans and service classes.

The castes working on land produced a surplus which according to Marx, they gave to the artisan castes. These in turn gave the former a part of the traditional craft. Thus, both castes produced for their own needs and for exchange, and harmony prevailed. This "village republic" model has since been criticized as utopic.

In the case of Max Weber, caste was considered to be a 'status groups' whose group members were recognize by s

and economic position. These entailed a particular life-style, which in itself was curtailed by certain restrictions on interaction, including the kind of work which could be done. The relationship between castes was also determined by the ritual opposition between the states of 'purity' and 'pollution' which could be associated with persons or objects. Thus, castes were placed in a hierarchy according to their level of purity. Thus, the Brahmins level of purity was highest as they followed 'clean' occupations such as priesthood. It was important too that the 'purity' be maintained through avoidance of those who were impure. For this reason, Weber argued that caste was an extreme form of stratification.

For Bougle who wrote after Weber a caste was recognized by its place in the hierarchy and by the occupation its members followed. Castes were constrained and other social restrictions that were imposed upon them. Thus, hierarchy and separation between groups were the attributes that helped maintain the status of a caste in the hierarchy order and determined interactional patterns.

Q8. Outline briefly the system of Jajmani exchanges. [Dec 08, Q. 16]

Ans. William H Wiser introduced the term Jajmani system in the vocabulary of Indian sociology through his book "The Hindu Jajmani system" where he described in detail how different caste group interact with each other in the production and exchange of goods and services. In different parts of India different terms are used to describe this economic interaction among the castes for example in Maharashtra the term Balutadar is used. However in sociological literature jajmani system has come to be accepted as a general term to describe the economic interaction between the castes at the village level. This system is also a ritual system concerned with the aspects of purity and pollution as with economic aspects. It functions so that the highest caste remains pure while the lowest castes absorb pollution from them. Villages are composed of number of jatis each having its occupational speciality. Jajmani system is essentially an agriculture based system of production and distribution of goods and services. Through jajmani relations these occupational jatis get linked with the land owning dominant caste. The jajmani system operates around the families belonging to the land owning dominant caste the numbers of which are called jajmans. The land owning caste occupies a privileged position in the jajmani relations. The interaction between occupational castes and the land owning castes take place within the framework of non-reciprocal and asymmetrical type of relations. The land owning castes maintain a paternalistic attitude of superiority towards their occupational castes that are called Kamins in North India. The term Kamin means one who works for somebody or serves him. In terms of Karl Polanyi's classification of exchange system -Jajmani exchange can be termed as redistributive system of exchange. The Functionalist view of jajmani system regards it as the basis of self-sufficiency, unity, harmony and stability in the village community. However the Marxist scholars hold a very different opinion. They regard the jajmani system as essentially exploitative, characterized by a latent conflict of interest which could not crystallize due to the prevalent social setup. Thus, if in future the conditions of the lower caste improve an open conflict between the lower and upper caste is inevitable. Oscar Lewis who studied Rampur village near Delhi and Biedelmn has been critical of the Jajmani system which they regard as exploitative. According to them the members of occupational jatis are largely landless labourers and have no resources to wage a struggle against the dominant caste out of the compulsion of the need for survival. They succumb to all injustice perpetuated by the landowning dominant caste who enjoy both economic and political power. Scholars like Berreman, Harold Gould and Pauline Kolenda etc. accept that there is an element of truth in both the functionalist and Marxist views of the jajmani system. They believe that consensus and harmony as well as conflict and exploitation are prevalent in the village society. According to Dumont jajmani system makes use of hereditary personal relationships to express the division of labour. This system is a ritual expression rather than just an economic arrangement. S.C. Dube refers to the system as corresponding to the presentation and counter presentation by which castes as a whole are bound together in a village which is more or less universal in nature. Leach believes that the system maintains and regulates the division of labour and economic interdependence of castes.

Q9. Explain the meaning of caste system and its features.

Ans. The **Indian caste system** describes the social stratification and social restrictions in the Indian subcontinent, in which social classes are defined by thousands of endogamous hereditary groups, often termed as *jâtis* or castes. Within a jâti, there exist exogamous groups known as gotras, the lineage or clan of an individual, although in a handful of sub-castes like Shakadvipi, endogamy within a gotra is permitted and alternative mechanisms of restricting endogamy are used (e.g. banning endogamy within a surname). Although generally identified with Hinduism, the caste system was also observed among followers of other religions in the Indian subcontinent, including some groups of Muslims and Christians. The Indian Constitution has outlawed caste-based discrimination, in keeping with the socialist, secular, democratic principles that founded the nation. Caste barriers have mostly broken down in large cities, though they persist in rural areas of the country, where 72% of India's population resides. Nevertheless, the caste system, in various forms, continues to survive in modern India strengthened by a combination of social perceptions and divisive politics.

Features of Caste system: Hierarchically divide the society. A sense of highness and lowness or superiority and inferiority is associated with this gradation or ranking. The Brahmins are placed at the top of the hierarchy and are regarded as pure or supreme. The degraded caste or the untouchables have occupied the other end of the hierarchy. The status of an individual is determined by his birth and not by selection nor by accomplishments. Each caste has its own customs, traditions practices and rituals. It has its own informal rules, regulations and procedures. The caste panchayats or the caste councils regulate the conduct of members. The caste system has imposed certain restrictions on the food habitats of the members these differ from caste to caste. In North India Brahmin would accept pakka food only from some castes lower than his own. But he would not accept kachcha food prepared with the use of water at the hands of no other caste except his own. As a matter of rule and practice no individual would accept kachcha food prepared by an inferior casteman. The caste system put restriction on the range of social relations also. The idea of pollution means a touch of lower caste man would pollute or defile a man of higher caste. Even his shadow is considered enough to pollute a higher caste man. The lower caste people suffered from certain socio-religious disabilities. The impure castes are made to live on the outskirts of the city and they are not allowed to draw water from the public wells. In earlier times entrance to temples and other places of religious importance were forbidden to them. Educational facilities, legal rights and political representation were denied to them for a very long time. If the lower castes suffer from certain disabilities some higher caste like the Brahmins enjoys certain privileges like conducting prayers in the temples etc. There is gradation of occupations also. Some occupations are considered superior and sacred while certain others degrading and inferior. For a long time occupations were very much associated with the caste system. Each caste had its own specific occupations which were almost hereditary. There was no scope for individual talent, aptitude, enterprise or abilities. The caste system imposes restrictions on marriage also. Caste is an endogamous group. Each caste is subdivided into certain sub castes which are again endogamous. Inter caste marriages are still looked down upon in the traditional Indian society.

Q10. Describe the concepts of Sanskritisation, differences, and mobility. [Dec 06, Q. 9(a)]

Ans. Sanskritisation is a particular form of social change found in India. The term was popularized by Indian sociologist M N Srinivas, to denote the process by which castes placed lower in the caste hierarchy seek upward mobility by emulating the rituals and practices of the upper or dominant castes. It is a process similar to passing in anthropological terms. Srinivas defined sanskritisation as a process by which "*a 'low' or middle Hindu caste, or tribal or other group, changes its customs, ritual ideology, and way of life in the direction of a high and frequently 'twice-born' caste. Generally such changes are followed by a claim to a higher position in the caste hierarchy than that traditionally conceded to the claimant class by the local community.*" One clear example of sanskritisation is the adoption, in emulation of the practice of twice-born castes, of vegetarianism by people belonging to the so-called "low castes" who are traditionally not averse to non-vegetarian food. According to M.N. Srinivas, Sanskritisation is not just the adoption of new customs and habits, but also includes exposure to new ideas and values appearing in Sanskrit literature. He says the words *Karma, dharma, papa, maya, samsara and moksha* are the most common Sanskrit theological ideas which become common in the talk of people who are sanskritised. This phenomenon has also been observed in Nepal among the Khas, Newar and Magar people over the century Srinivas first propounded this theory in his D.Phil. thesis at Oxford University. The thesis was later brought out as a book titled "Religion and Society among the Coorgs of South India." Published in 1952, the book was an ethnographical study of the Coorg community of Karnataka, India. Srinivas writes in the book: "The caste system is far from a rigid system in which the position of each component caste is fixed for all time. Movement has always been possible, and especially in the middle regions of the hierarchy. A caste was able, in a generation or two, to rise to a higher position in the hierarchy by adopting vegetarianism and teetotalism, and by Sanskritising its ritual and pantheon. In short, it took over, as far as possible, the customs, rites, and beliefs of the Brahmins, and adoption of the Brahmanic way of life by a low caste seems to have been frequent, though theoretically forbidden. This process has been called 'Sanskritisation' in this book, in preference to 'Brahminisation', as certain Vedic rites are confined to the Brahmins and the two other 'twice-born' castes."

The book challenged the then prevalent idea that caste was a rigid and unchanging institution. The concept of Sanskritisation addressed the actual complexity and fluidity of caste relations. It brought into academic focus the dynamics of the renegotiation of status by various castes and communities in India.

Difference: The concept of difference has been developed by Dipankar Gupta to present a picture of the caste system which is totally different from the one that we find in many books including Dumont's *Homo Hierarchicus.* Gupta claims that empirically as well as logically it is wrong to say that a single all inclusive hierarchy based on the principle of the opposition of purity and pollution can be a defining feature of the caste system. To quote him, "Any notion of hierarchy is arbitrary and valid from the perspective of certain individual castes. To state that pure hierarchy is one that is universally believed in, or one which legitimizes the position of those, who participate in the caste system, is misleading. The separation between castes is not only on matters which connote the opposition between purity and pollution. Distinctions and diacritical notches which are not even remotely suggestive of purity and pollution are observed as strictly. Adversely, distinctions relating to purity and pollution do not systematically affect caste status. The cultivating Amot caste solemnize their Goraiya festival with the sacrifice of a pig and yet Brahmans take water from them" Gupta points out.

Therefore, Gupta opines that 'difference' and 'ritualisation of multiple social practices' constitute the essence of the caste system. To quote him, "we will define the caste system as a form of differentiation wherein the constituent units of the system justify endogamy on the basis of putative biological differences which are semaphored by the ritualisation of multiple social practices". In order to make the meaning of the phrase 'ritualisation of multiple social practices' clear, Gupta writes, "By rituals we mean all those social practices that are followed because they are supposed to be inherently good irrespective of Weber's 'means-ends' rationality".

Marginalised Communities and Stratification

Q1. Outline the constitutional provisions for the upliftment of the Dalits. [June 08, Q. 10]

Ans. The Constitution of India has played important role in the overall upliftment of the Scheduled Castes. In Part IV of the Constitution, certain fundamental rights are guaranteed to the citizens. Article 15(2) states that no citizen shall, on grounds only of religion, race, caste, sex, place of birth be discriminated with regard to **(a)** access to shop, public restaurants, hotel and public entertainment; or **(b)** the use of wells, tank, bathing ghats, roads, and places of public resorts. Under Article 15(4), the State is permitted to make any special provision for advancement of any socially and educationally backward classes of citizens or for the Scheduled Castes and the Scheduled Tribes.
In the field of education, there is reservation of seats in admission of the Scheduled Caste and tribe students in schools, colleges and university. Also, there is a provision of scholarship for the students belonging to SCs and STs Categories. All these constitutional provisions have helped the members of various scheduled castes groups to make progress in every sphere of life. Since independence, the ethos of Indian society has also vastly changed. The education as a means of achieving upward social mobility has proved to be very useful to the Dalits and there is conscious effort on their part to get their children educated. Educational institutions provide indispensable avenues of mobility to a large number of individuals from Dalit community. Without education all the constitutional safeguards including reservation in services would be infractous. The government policy of reservation in employment has played an important role for Dalits. The policy broadly envisages representation of Dalits in proportion of their population in all the government services as well as the institution which receive grants from the government.

Q2. Discuss about the socio-religious movement.

Ans. The socio-religious movements in Bengal during the British period are considered some of the most important and influential events in the history of

India. Most of the socio-religious movements in Bengal were led by the English educated Indian elite people clustered in Calcutta. They mostly opposed the evil rituals practised in Hinduism and other religions and tried to eliminate the malevolent rituals to offer religion the desired contour. The major socio-religious movements in Bengal related to Hinduism included the Brahmo Samaj movement, Arya Samaj movement, Ramkrishna Mission, Theosophical movement, etc. On the other hand, the religious movements relating to Islam included the Ahmadiyya movement, Faraizi movement, etc.

The Brahmo Samaj movement was one of the most prominent socio-religious movements in Bengal during the British period. The movement was led by the eminent educationalist and social reformer, Raja Ram Mohan Roy, who strongly opposed the evil rituals of Hinduism like Sati. He also propagated the idea of worshipping only one God, who is omnipresent. He also denied worshiping the God under any name or designation or title. The Arya Samaj movement was another prominent socio-religious movement in Bengal. This movement was started and led by Dayananda Saraswati and one of the most important features of this movement was the Shuddhi movement. This was a ritual developed by the Aryas to readmit the lower caste Hindus, who were converted into Islam or Christianity. The Arya Samaj also actively opposed the evil rituals that were practised in Hinduism and supported the cause of women education. The Samaj established educational institutions for providing education to the women at various levels as well. Ramakrishna Mission played an important part in the socio religious movement in Bengal. The Mission was established by Swami Vivekananda, who followed and publicized the visions and ideas of Ramkrishna Paramhansa Dev. Vivekananda emphasized mainly on social service and on fulfillment and reorientation of Ramakrishna's wishes. He was true to the traditions of Hinduism and established the Ramkrishna Math that still works for serving the humanity. The Theosophical movement was also an important socio-religious movement in Bengal during the British period. The movement was mainly inspired from outside India and was politically ambiguous. There were also a few socio-religious movements in Bengal during the British period, which dealt with the problems of Islam. The Socio-religious movements among Bengali Muslims drew upon the dynamics of that society for their motivation. The Ahmadiyya movement and Faraizi movement were the two most influential movements among the Islam-related religious movements. The Ahmadiyya movement was formed in Punjab and was started by Mirza Ghulam Ahmad. He started to proclaim a mission as Masih Mawud Mtgaddid (restorer) and Mahdi (guide) and he also endowed himself with powers of prophet hood. He directed his campaign against some well-known Sunni Ulama of the Deoband and Ahl-I, Hadith movements that were increasingly influential among Sunnis in the region. He also opposed the increasing influence of the Christian missionaries in the region. The supporters of Ahmadiyya movement described them as a distinct religious community and also claimed that they were the only upholders of 'true Islam'. The Faraizi movement was a prominent religious reform movement and was founded by Haji Shariatullah during the nineteenth century. The Faraizis were those who had the only objective of implementing and imposing the mandatory religious duties ordained by Allah. Hazi Shariatullah believed that the Faraizis should imply to assimilate every religious duty ordained by the Holy Quran and also by the Sunnah of the Prophet. Besides Hazi Shariatullah, Dudu Miyan and Naya Miyan were the two other prominent leaders of the Faraizi movement. The socio religious movements made huge impacts on the Indian society and also became successful to eradicate some of the evil rituals that were practised in various religions during that period. The movements were also an integral part of Bengal renaissance during the eighteenth and nineteenth century.

Q3. Describe the backward classes' movement in India.

[June 09, Q. 3][Dec 07, Q. 6]

Ans. The Self-Respect Movement was founded in 1925 by E.V. Ramasami Naicker (also known as Periyar) in Tamil Nadu, India. The movement has the aim of achieving a society where backward castes have equal human rights, and encouraging backward castes to have self-respect in the context of a caste based society that considered them to be a lower end of the hierarchy. The movement was extremely influential not just in Tamil Nadu, but also overseas in countries with large Tamil populations, such as Malaysia and Singapore. Among Singapore Indians, groups like the Tamil Reform Association, and leaders like Thamizhavel G. Sarangapani were prominent in promoting the principals of the Self-Respect Movement among the local Tamil population through schools and publications. A number of political parties in Tamil Nadu, such as DMK and AIADMK owe their origins to the Self-respect movement, the latter a 1972 breakaway from the DMK. Both parties are populist with a generally social democratic orientation. The movement has been in political power in Tamil Nadu since 1967, when the DMK under C. N. Annadurai defeated the ruling Congress Party. The incumbent (as of 2006) Chief Minister is M. Karunanidhi of the DMK.

Anti-Brahmanism: Tamil Brahmins (Iyers and Iyengars) were frequently held responsible by followers of Periyar for direct or indirect oppression of lower-caste people on the canard of "Brahmin oppression" and resulted in attacks on Brahmins and which among other reasons started a wave of mass-migration of the Brahmin population. Periyar in regards to a DK member's attempt to assassinate Rajagopalachari "expressed his abhorrence of violence as a means of settling political differences". Eventually, the anti-Brahmanism subsided with the replacement of the DMK party by the AIADMK.

Self-Respect Marriages: One of the major sociological changes introduced through the self respect movement was the self-respect marriage system, where by marriages were conducted without being officiated by a Brahmin priest. Periyar had regarded the then conventional marriages were mere financial arrangements and often caused great debt through dowry. Self-Respect marriages encouraged inter-caste marriages and arranged marriages to be replaced by love marriages. It was argued by the proponents of self-respect marriage that the then conventional marriages were officiated by Brahmins, who has to be paid for and also the marriage ceremony was in Sanskrit which most people did not understand, and hence were ritual and practices based on blind adherence.

The rise of the non-Brahmins under the leadership of crusaders against social injustice mainly from the intermediate castes represents a landmark development. It was reflective of a determined resistance to perpetuation of the traditionally legitimized inequality. Jyoti Rao Govind Rao Phule made the first attempt to form a Bahujan Samaj in Maharashtra to challenge the supremacy of the Brahmins who constituted the privileged few dominating the socio-economic political contours of the state. Phule himself a Shudra questioned the dominance of Brahmins in the colonial dispensation. His opposition to the caste system found articulation in his efforts to raise a new social order based on truth reason and equality. He initiated a movement to discard the services of Brahmins in the religious ceremonies of the non-Brahmins as he regarded them to be the unwanted middlemen between the people and the God.

The non-Brahmanical movement was accorded institutionalisation in the programmes of the Satya Shodhak Samaj founded by Phule. He considered Brahminism as cunning and self-seeking and condemned it as intolerable imposition to ensure the perpetuation of the high in the caste hierarchy. The "dominant agricultural castes' that formed the core and support of this movement subsequently ushered were very pro Congress. Phule's interpretation of lower caste exploitation ignored the economic and political contexts. Exploitation was interpreted in terms of cultural and ethnicity. Phule however stressed the need for return to pre-Brahmin religious tradition. Organisation and education were considered essential for attainment of such goals.

Praja Mitra Mandal: Karnataka: In Karnataka the caste associations of the dominant landed interest federated themselves under the auspices of the Praja Mitra Mandali expressing opposition to dominance of the Brahmins. Under the pressure of the forces that thus emerged steps to ensure adequate representation of the non-Brahmins in the public service ensured. Successful mobilisation of the backward classes contributed effectively in weakening the hold of the Brahmins in politics bureaucracy and professions. The prejapaksha that emerged as the replacement for the Praja Mitra after the latter's disintegration led to the further strengthening of the position of the intermediate castes in general and the lingayats and the Vokallingas in particular. The two castes emerged as the lead castes in the states politics after independence. Between the two, the Lingayats consolidated themselves more effectively in the power structure. Such permutation of power that constituted the other backward classes as its locus after independence oriented itself more seriously to take measures wedded to benefit the owner cultivator's interests. Legislations were enacted to facilitate transfer of land from the landed castes of Brahmins to the actual tillers of such land belonging mainly to the intermediate castes. The Brahmins of Karnataka were thus forced out of the village to find livelihood in the white collar jobs. The power equilibrium thus rose disintegrated subsequently in the wake of the emergence of the smaller backward castes who opposed the dominance of the powerfull in the intermediate caste. The excluded among the other backward classes resisted such dominance and organized themselves to emerge as strong contender for power.

Movements in the South: Andhra and Kerela: The Brahmins were opposed also in Andhra Pradesh. Their location as elite in the traditional as well as emerging secular stratification system left many at the margin of the opportunity structure. Perpetuation of the old and appropriation of the new by them found stiff resistance from those benefited through commercial revolution in agriculture. Castes inferior to the traditional Brahmin elite soon questioned their supremacy. People from those castes in support with other castes lower to them in the traditional stratification system turned themselves against the Congress demand for the Home rule suspecting it to be a ploy seeking to facilitate the perpetuation of the old order. The apprehensions of Brahmins preeminence led these non-Brahmin sections to oppose Visalandhra movement that had the aim of a separate state of the Telgu-speaking people of the Madras Presidency. The dominance of a few prosperous non-Brahmin peasant castes unwilling to favour castes lower to them prompted the latter on occasions to assert for their interest. The Munnuru Dapa movement and the Padmasali movement are examples of such assertion in the pre-independence phase. Individual backward classes associations federated themselves after independence to claim reservations. Such sponsored mobility of the deprived notwithstanding, in the bureaucracy the Brahmin dominance is not over and the dominant peasant castes on account of their economic advantage and political manipulations are poised to preserve their overriding influence.

OBCs in U.P.: The intermediate castes or the OBC, did not emerge that assertive in non-peninsular India. Brahminism perpetuated itself in the sanskritik heartland of India the Uttar Pradesh drawing sustenance from the traditional embedded. In the pre-independence Uttar Pradesh protest against the dominance of the upper caste tended to be mild. Castes associations floated during this period in addition to foster inter-caste solidarity and inter-caste fraternity among the proximately placed intermediate castes were oriented to seek occasional redressal against the excesses of the upper castes. Thus, in the annual conferences of the Yadava Mahasabha opposition used to be whipped against the upper castes. These upper castes were seen as exploiting and blocking their progress. The well off among the middle range castes found themselves favourably inclined to sanskritisation as the strategy for status elevation. Competition within the stratum for superior location the stratification system worked against the solidarity needed to produce an effective uprising. Situations however remained unfavourable to the rise of the other backward classes. They failed to mobilize themselves for effective gains. Consequently, the intermediate castes remained appendage to permutations dominated by the upper castes even in the year immediately after independence. With the ushering of the famous Green Revolution and the subsequent emergence of the other backward classes as a political force under the leadership of Charan Singh the equilibrium of power favouring the status quo was disturbed. Fraternity thus fostered remains the locus for initiatives oriented to claims of equality with the upper castes. Success eludes such aspirations in absence of cohesion and mobilisation.

OBCs in Bihar: In Bihar the educated elite from the other backward castes sought to federate themselves to claim elevation in their traditional social status by taking resort to sanskritisation. The Kurmis and the Yadavas especially those who turned out to be prosperous and conscious formed caste association to usher reform from within and to exert pressure outward for improvement in their condition. Attempts to unite the powerful among the middle range caste were also made under the auspices of the Triveni Sangh that was sought to emerge as a federation of the Yadavas the kurmis and the koeris. Such initiatives on their part tended to be least effective as they lacked support of the upper caste leaders who constituted the locus of power. The leadership mobilizing masses during the freedom struggle thought it prudent to ignore them in order to serve the interests of their own caste who would have been loosers in the event of such relief to this sections of the society.

Even the Kisan sabhas in Bihar ignored its proclaimed intent to help tenant from the cultivating intermediate castes as the upper caste leadership in such stirrings were opposed to it. Parochial outlook of such outfits ignored this. Independence and some of the measures of land reform triggered fall outs conducive to the rise of the middle range castes. Landlords from the upper castes lost their dominance as Zamindari was abolished. Privileged among the middle range caste asserted for their increased representation in the bureaucracy and professions. Socio-economic development appeared facilitative to their social elevation, economic prosperity and political development. Sanskritisation however soon ceased to be the strategy for their mobility. Claims for rank

precedence in the traditional stratification system did not find articulation as an effective concern. Protest against conditions of relative deprivation emerged to be the dominant theme in the ideology of the other backward classes movement.
Education and Values: Exposure to egalitarian values and attainment of higher levels of education provoked awareness of the negative discrepancy between the legitimate expectation and actuality. This realisation of their dominant political status made them capable of initiating a process of struggle to ensure distribution of resources in a highly egalitarian manner. Appropriation of resources through bureaucratic manipulation that favoured the privileged upper castes received stiff opposition. The rise of the middle range castes in its wake has sounded the death knell of permutations favouring dominance of the traditionally high. The emergence of these forces reflects an endorsement to the strategy of allocation of resources, opportunity and honour in favour of the intermediate caste. However such sections among the middle range castes as are not so favourable placed in resource endowments tend to lag behind. Once important surrogate to upper caste dominated parties the dominant owner cultivators placed in the middle of the traditional stratification system constitute the locus of power.

Q4. Explain the relation between sanskritisation and social mobility.
Ans. Prof. M.N. Srinivas introduced the term Sanskritisation to Indian Sociology. The term refers to a process whereby people of lower castes collectively try to adopt upper caste practices and beliefs to acquire higher status. It indicates a process of cultural mobility that is taking place in the traditional social system of India. M.N Srinivas in his study of the Coorg in Karnataka found that lower castes in order to raise their position in the caste hierarchy adopted some customs and practices of the Brahmins and gave up some of their own which were considered to be impure by the higher castes. For example they gave up meat eating, drinking liquor and animal sacrifice to their deities. They imitated Brahmins in matters of dress, food and rituals. By this they could claim higher positions in the hierarchy of castes within a generation. The reference group in this process is not always Brahmins, but may be the dominant caste of the locality. Sanskritisation has occurred usually in groups who have enjoyed political and economic power, but were not ranked high in ritual ranking. According to Yogendra Singh the process of Sanskritisation is an endogenous source of social change. Mackim Marriot observes that sanskritic rites are often added on to non-sanskritic rites without replacing them. Harold Gould writes, often the motive force behind sanskritisation is not of cultural imitation per se but an expression of challenge and revolt against the socioeconomic deprivations.
Social mobility: Individuals are recognized in society through the statuses they occupy and the roles they enact. The society as well as individuals is

dynamic. Men are normally engaged in endless endeavor to enhance their statuses in society, move from lower position to higher position, secure superior job from an inferior one. For various reasons people of the higher status and position may be forced to come down to a lower status and position. Thus, people in society continue to move up and down the status scale. This movement is called social mobility.

The study of social mobility is an important aspect of social stratification. Infact it is an inseparable aspect of social stratification system because the nature, form, range and degree of social mobility depends on the very nature of stratification system. Stratification system refers to the process of placing individuals in different layers or strata. According to Wallace social mobility is the movement of a person or persons from one social status to another. W.P Scott has defined sociology as the movement of an individual or group from one social class or social stratum to another.

Q5. Discuss about the tribal population.

Ans. According to 1991 census tribal population of 54,74,881, which forms 12.44 percent of the total population of the state. The population has grown at a rapid rate for the last eighty years and at an almost flooding rate during the last three decades. During 1901 the total population in the state was 103 lakhs, which rose to 564 lakhs in 2001. During the decades 1961-71 and 1971-81 the growth rate of tribal population in Rajasthan was 35.33 percent and 34.46 percent respectively. There is a slight decrease (0.87 percent) in the growth rate of tribal population in Rajasthan. The growth rate of tribal population was 31 percent during 1981-91. It is higher than the growth rate of total population of the state.

Regional Concentration: Similarly, the regional concentration is of great diversity. About 55 percent of the tribals live in central, 28 percent in Western, 12 percent in North-East and 4 percent in Southern India, and only 1 percent elsewhere in country. But it is interesting to note that, with minor exceptions, there is a continuous belt or tribal habitat from Thane district of Maharasthra to Tengnoupal district of Manipur. Also, the tribals are mostly found in the meeting points of dominant Lingua States. In the 1960s, one-third of the tribals lived in the districts where they were in majority. Infact, over sixty percent lived in the districts where they composed of 30 percent of more of the total population. Even now, the situation may not be very much different.

Role of Growth: It is a fact that the tribal population has been growing faster at a higher rate than the general population. During the 1981-91 decade, the general population grew at the rate of 2.1 percent a year and the tribal population grew at the rate of 2.6 per cent a year. The growth is, however, much higher in the North-East, i.e., at the rate of 4.6 percent per year as against 2.5 percent in Central Indian belt and barely 1.5 percent in southern tribal region. The growth in the North-East must have to consider immigration from outside the country, and elsewhere particularly in the Central and the Western Indian tribal belt the inclusion of new or non-tribal communities in the list of the Scheduled Tribes owing to political compulsions.

The average, however, do not completely comprehend the gamut of differentiations in the tribal milieu. There is enormous heterogeneity not only in terms of the numerical strength, rate of demographic expansion, regional concentration, gender composition, literacy, urbanisation but also occupation, ecology, linguistic affiliation, racial composition, kinship systems, history of movements and vast number of other variables.

Q6. Briefly discuss about the tribal social movement.

Ans. The 18 century, the tribal people appeared to be rather passive to their own centralized power as well as Hindu and Muslim rules. The only exception was certain regions and tribes under the Maratha rulers. The tribal rulers rarely extorted more than acceptable for the reproduction of the system. In a sense, legitimisation of their power was decentralized.

It was colonialism, for the first time which forced them into the centralized repressive state. Consequently, the dispersed and relatively unorganized tribes and their divisions got united and rose in revolts of course at the local level. During the 19th century, most of the numerically strong and settled tribal communities like Santal, Oraon, Kol, Koya, Bhil, Saora, etc. fought against colonialism and feudalism as was perceived in their immediate context. Apart from related to land alienation, forest reservation, forced and indentured labour, oppressive, taxation, loss of culture and religion, and replacement of their traditional power. The anti-colonial perspective, however, was not well articulated precisely because the British interests were pursued through the local and regional powers. The intra-tribal contradictional were overshadowed by the onslaught of non-tribals, and the ethnic bonds and common heritage spared their own exploiting members from attack. With the rise of the nationalist movement in the early 20th century, anti-colonial perspective percolated to the tribal struggles of Kandha, Koya, Oraon, Munda, Saora, Warli, Gond, and others.

Tribal Movements Since Independence: However, since independence, the tribal movements have become more diverse. Despite their heterogeneity at large, the common grievances of tribals is their dispossession and indignity, and aspirations form a common platform with some subjected non-tribals and thereby, consolidate pan-regional loyalties and consciousness. Yet, almost all tribal movements organized so far have been intrinsically associated with the ethnic or nationality question. Small wonder, the current tribal movements in terms of socio-cultural mobility towards the twice-born cultural complexes have become insignificant. Instead, the reverse trend is becoming more and more conspicuous.

The organized struggle mostly appears among the relatively large population with some level of literacy, awareness of national democratic process and internal socio-economic differentiation. Evidence suggest that the tribals that are more differentiated provide greater resistance to subjugation and the elite structure serve as the rallying point for struggles. Their struggles or movement are concentrated expressions of the socio-economic, political and cultural expressions of the tribal people at large.

Motive Forces of Struggle: The tribal struggles are essentially rooted in three interrelated motive forces namely, the epistemology of individualism, statistideology and capitalist model of development. The movements are, therefore, for recognition of collective rights over the survival resources and internal self-determination in the legitimate cultural, linguistic spheres as well as a dynamic strategy for sustainable development. Unfortunately, however, the militant nationalist struggles of the tribals their political autonomy in the North-East and the radical agrarian struggles against the obnoxious methods of surplus appropriation in parts of the obnoxious methods of surplus appropriation in parts of central India tribal belt are simply treated as a law and order issue and dealt in military terms. The demands for political autonomy and extension of the 6th Schedule to tribal areas are perfectly legitimate and constitutional deserving appropriate democratic handling of the issues.

Q7. Describe the position of tribal's in the emergence social stratification.

Ans. It is interesting to note that in the 18th century writings on India, the term caste has often been used synonymously with tribe, and later in cognate manner as in the phrase castes and tribes. Even the Indian Constitution (Art. 341(1) holds that a tribe may include in the category of scheduled castes. Infact, 1951 Census temporarily accommodated over a million tribals in the Other Backward Classes category.

Be that alone, the little attention that has been paid to tribal transition in social science research is largely seen as a shift from tribal to caste. Indeed, some sociologists have had interactions with the Hindus, Muslims and other, and in the process of which, changes have appeared in the cultural as well as structural complexes of the tribals, castes and others. But the historical and contextual evidence rarely supports the thesis of the trend of transformation of tribes into castes as such. For a couple of decades, emulation of the dominant culture through Sanskritisation swayed the tribal people. But as these attempts hardly improved their status of material conditions of life, most have retrieved their unique ethnic identity. Historically, they were many but existentially they are tending to be one in the contemporary period.

Recent Studies: Some recent studies have observed features among a few numerically important tribes. But the characterisation of tribal peasant society varied from more or less undifferentiated communities of peasants to stratified groups and further as a class society. Again, the motive force of change – exogenous, endogenous or both remain still an unexplored arena in tribal research. Among these who have rejected the tribal peasantry as a single interest group, most have analysed differentiation as stratification, i.e., categories of wealth, income and status through which families move up and down. Income distribution, assets control, occupational structure, etc. may provide description of the social strata but not the social relations and how the system operates it also cannot identify the motive forces of change. Besides, any two researchers following the same approach would arrive at different classification of the same population. Most often, these strata are commonly called as classes – upper, middle and lower, rich and poor, and so on. But these descriptive divisions may at best provide a series of approximations illustrating partial aspects of social class.

The Marxist Conception: The Marxist conception of class, on the other hand, is analytical and contrasts sharply with the synthetic gradation scheme so prevalent in current literature on social stratification. To put it simply, the differentiation of the peasantry in the materialist sense is tied to the conditions under which the surplus is generated, appropriated and consumed or reinvested. But the operationalisation of the concept of class in the backward economic structures, where the boundary tends to be rather ambiguous, besets with a number of problems. Control of means of production and participation in the labour process do not sufficiently indicate the class identity and structure, for most tribals experience the world primarily in the idiom of tribe.

Needless to mention that the land ownership among the tribals is very unequal. However, in the present time nearly 55 percent of landowners own less than 5 acres each whereas 11 percent control over 15 acres each. A study in Gujarat found that 25 percent of the tribal households controlled only 3.6 percent of the total land whereas less than one-tenth of the households control a – third of the land resources. The inequality in land control is equally explicit with respect to individual village, and each and every tribe. In short, the tribal world is entwined with the larger capitalistic sector. Ruling classes of both have at once contradictions and alliances, and hold the key to economic progress of stagnation.

Tribes as Peasant Societies: There are distinction between tribe and peasantry but at the existential level all the major tribes are actually peasant societies existing within the broad political economy of the State. Their existence and motion and perhaps be better understood in terms of a class the State. Their existence and motion and perhaps be better understood in terms of a class analysis of these societies and the level of articulation of the different modes of production within their ethnic structures. As the ethnic consciousness and practices continue, class practices have not yet become dominant at political level.

Q8. Explain the status of women in India. **[June 07, Q. 4]**

Ans. The status of women in India has been subject to many great changes over the past few millennia. From a largely unknown status in ancient times through the low points of the medieval period, to the promotion of equal rights by many reformers, the history of women in India has been eventful. Women in India now participate in all activities such as education, politics, media, art and culture, service sectors, science and technology, etc. The Constitution of India guarantees to all Indian women equality (Article 14), no discrimination by the State (Article 15(1)), equality of opportunity (Article 16), and equal pay for equal work (Article 39(d)). In addition, it allows special provisions to be made by the State in favour of women and children (Article 15(3)), renounces practices derogatory to the dignity of women (Article 51(A) (e)), and also allows for provisions to be made by the State for securing just and humane conditions of work and for maternity relief. The feminist activism in India picked up momentum during later 1970s. One of the first national level issues that brought the women's groups together was the Mathura rape case. The acquittal of policemen accused of raping a young girl in Mathura in a police station, led to a wide-scale protests in 1979–1980. The protests were widely covered in the national media, and forced the Government to amend the Evidence Act, the Criminal Procedure Code and the Indian Penal Code and introduce the category of custodial rape. Female activists united over issues such as female infanticide, gender bias, women health, and female literacy. Since alcoholism is often associated with violence against women in India, many women groups launched anti-liquor campaigns in Andhra Pradesh, Himachal Pradesh, Haryana, Orissa, Madhya Pradesh and other states. Many Indian Muslim women have questioned the fundamental leaders' interpretation of women's rights under the Shariat law and have criticized the triple talaq system. In 1990s, grants from foreign donor agencies enabled the formation of new women-oriented NGOs. Self-help groups and NGOs such as Self Employed Women's Association (SEWA) have played a major role in women's rights in India. Many women have emerged as leaders of local movements. For example, Medha Patkar of the Narmada Bachao Andolan. The Government of India declared 2001 as the Year of Women's Empowerment (Swashakti). The National Policy for the Empowerment of Women came was passed in 2001. In 2006, the case of a Muslim rape victim called Imrana was highlighted in the media. Imrana was raped by her father-in-law. The pronouncement of some Muslim clerics that Imrana should marry her father-in-law led to widespread protests and finally Imrana's father-in-law was given a prison term of 10 years, The verdict was welcomed by many women's groups and the All India Muslim Personal Law Board.

Women's Marginal Position: Women's marginal position can be inferred from the high incidents of female foeticide and female infanticide. Demographers show us how in the age specific death rates more females than males die at every age level up to the age of 35 years. Young girls suffer from malnutrition more than boys. This continues until adulthood and passes on to the next generation. Maternal mortality rate in India is depressingly high. It is a customary practice in Indian families that a female child gets less nourishing diet, and if she falls sick then she doesn't receive the required care. Even medical treatment is postponed. During her teenage, her special nutritional needs are constantly ignored. This state of malnutrition pushes her close to complications and mortality during pregnancy and child birth. While boys grow to their full potentials, girls hardly grow as much. They are forced into early marriage and subsequent subordination to the continued patriarchy and discrimination in the husband's home.

Measures for Raising the Status of Women: In the post independent India, there are two important foundations which have brought about significant changes in overcoming the marginalisation of women both within and outside the family. These foundations are as follows:

i) The constitutional guarantee to formal equality.

ii) State sponsored social welfare activities.

Let us briefly discuss these measures to find out their relevance to the uplifting of women's life.

i) The Constitution guarantees gender equality. Article 14 ensures equality before Law and Article 15 prohibits any discrimination. Article 16(1) guarantees equality of opportunity for all citizens in matters relating to employment or appointment to any office of the state. There is a provision for free and compulsory education for all children upto the age of 14, right to an adequate means of livelihood for men and women equally, equal pay for equal work and maternity relief. The adult franchise employs women as voters. The enactment of Hindu Law guarantees women the right to divorce and remarriage. The Inheritance Act provides equal shares to women in the property.

ii) State sponsored social welfare : In 1953 the government of India established a Central Social Welfare Board for promoting women's welfare and development and those of other under privileged groups. The Social Welfare Board encouraged the growth of a large number of women's organisations and promoted emergence of a huge number of women's organisations and promoted emergence of a huge number of social and political women workers.

It is equally important to mention that the Feminist of Women's Liberation Movement of the late 1960's and early 1970's in the United States and Europe played a decisive role in creating awareness about marginalized and discriminatory status of women in societies across the world. The contribution of these movements lay in the fact that they raised fundamental questions and demands regarding women's degraded life. The movement also created new visibility of women's experiences and highlighted their specific problems and concerns. The global effort for raising the status of women also received strong support from the United Nations. Assistant The year 1975 was declared by the UNO as the International Women's Year and 1975-85 as the United Nation's Decade for women. It was declared that "discrimination against women violated the principle of equality or rights and aspect for human dignity ......" The discrimination was regarded as an obstacle to the participation of women, on equal terms with men, in the political, social economic and cultural life of their countries. It was pointed out that discrimination hampered the growth of the society and the family, and made more difficult the full development of the potentialities of women. It was understood that the full and complete development of a country required the maximum participation of women on equal terms with men in all fields.

Policies for Women's Welfare: In the light of the international consciousness, Indian government adopted progressive policies for women's welfare and encouraged women studies. A notable development in the country was the appointment of the Committee on the Status of Women in India by the government in 1971. The Committee focused on the social trends and responses to the principle of equality with a view to suggest measures for their implementation. The Committee submitted its report and titled Towards Equality' (1974). The report brought to light the causes of women's subordination and explained their exploitation in terms of caste, class and gender inequality. For the first time in post independent India there was an upsurge of studies on women's status and life circumstances. It was noted by various scholars that certain aspects of women's degradation follow from certain negative consequences of the process of development itself. The disabilities and the inequalities imposed on women were seen in the total context of society where other sections of the population also suffered in their own way under the oppression of an exploitative system. These studies changed the orientation of the people towards viewing the place of women in the context of development process. Rather than viewing women as targets of welfare policies they have now come to be viewed as critical category for development. This redefinition of women found expression in the Sixth Year Plan (1980-85) which carried, for the first time in India's history of planning, a separate chapter on women and development. This shift asserts the principle of equality and pointed out that India's future would be incomplete without women's participation in the process of development. It also recognized as never before that social and economic transformation badly affected women. The Sixth Five Year Plan brought out three strategies as essential for women's development from the margin to the core of society. These are there: **(1)** economic independence, **(2)** educational development, and **(3)** access to health care and family planning.

Women and Ecological Degradation: Many studies on rural societies tell us that a girl child is usually a helping hand to her mother in doing household chores. When the mother's work becomes heavier due to poverty, migration and environment degradation, the first sufferer of the increase work load of the mother is her daughter. One big casualty of the degradation of basic survival resources is the girl's education. It is possible to say that when the poverty level of the family goes down, the girl child is the first to be withdrawn from the school. We shall outline for you a story of a village called Syuta (not the real name) situated in the Himalayan region. The story of Syuta shows how the erosion of basic survival resources increases the work load of the mother. This lead to the daughter dropping out of the school even when access to the school is easy. Syuta is a Himalayan village situated near the Alaknanda River at a height of about 1600 meters in Chamoli district of Uttar Pradesh.

The burden of work falls mainly on women, who form a majority of the village's labour force. Women start working at a much younger age than men. They begin to play an active role in the household's economic activity even before they are fifteen years of age. Not all men work but all women in the village are cultivators. Women not only long hours at home but their burden in the village's agricultural economy is also inadequately shared by men. It is the woman who breaks up the hard earth, makes it ready for the plough, sows the seed and then reaps it. She also pounds the paddy to remove it's husk, carries manure from cattle shed to distant fields, does all the house work and takes care of animal. She also collects and carries huge load of grass and fuel from the forest. The burden of work and hardship of women's in everyday life is reflected sharply in their ill health and often early and untimely death. There is a clear difference in the lifespan of Syuta's men and women. While nine of the men in the village were above 55, only three women had reached this age. Whether the woman is young, old or pregnant, she gets no rest on whatever is the day of the week.

Q9. Discuss the status of children in India. **[June 07, Q. 5]**

Ans. As India races towards achieving super powerdom, its children are still far behind in terms of healthcare, education and other facilities. Children especially girls are faced with lack of educational opportunities, malnourishment, infant mortality and early marriages. According to the latest data collated by the National Health Survey 2005-06 the all India average for malnourished children is 47%. Every second child under 5 years is malnourished. Even the prosperous states like Gujarat and Kerala there is rise in the number of malnourished children. Both states saw an increase of 2% between 1991-2001. Other states for instance Madhya Pradesh registered a rise from 54% in 1991 to 60% in 2001.

Nearly 3/4ths of all infants between 6-35 months of age are anemic in the 19 states for which NFHS -3 data are available. Among all the children upto 3 years age over 1/3 are stunted and more than $1/6^{th}$ are wasted. Two out of five children are underweight. This state of the youngest Indians points towards pervasive malnutrition. For most of these infants, malnutrition would have started in the womb itself. This is apparent from the data on married and pregnant women. An astounding 54% of pregnant women and nearly the same proportion of married women were found anemic. Infact the Body Mass Index (ratio of weight to height- a measure of nutritional availability) of nearly $1/3^{rd}$ of all women was below normal.

What is alarming that the situation is worsening or at best not improving over the years? Comparison with NHFS-2 carried out five years ago shows that the proportion of wasted children has increased while underweight children are only marginally less. Similarly, the proportion of anemic infants has marginally increased. The number of pregnant women who are anemic has jumped from about 49% to over 54% in these five years in these 19 states. The prevalence of anemia among infants has declined in several states but it has not improves or even worsened in AP, Assam, Karnataka, Kerala, Meghalaya, Orissa, Punjab and UP. In no state has the proportion fallen below 50%. UP, Rajasthan, Punjab, Haryana, Karnataka, Gujarat and Assam all have shockingly high proportions of anemic infants-80% or above.

Incidentally nearly a third of married men in the eastern states of W.Bengal, Orissa, Assam and Meghalaya and in highly advanced Gujarat is anemic and have lower than normal BMI. Chattisgarh has the highest number of underweight children closely followed by Gujarat and Uttar Pradesh. However while the numbers have declined in the former, they are increasing in the latter two over the past five years. Another indicator is high infant mortality rate where India is bettered by Pakistan, China, Brazil and even Nigeria. The all-India average is 58 infant deaths for every 1000 live births and states like Uttar Pradesh (73), Rajasthan (65), Arunachal Pradesh (61) and Gujarat (50) top the list.

An immunisation level is one of the indicators which show serious concern. The NFHS shows that only in six of the 19 states for which data has been made public are more than 60% of children fully immunized. In 8 states the proportion of fully immunized children is less than half. Not only do children have fewer chances of surviving and are underfed they also lack educational opportunities. Literacy rate among girls from scheduled castes and scheduled tribes is 42% and 35% respectively, much lower than Muslim girls who have a literacy rate of 50%. In general too only 30 of 100 girls who enter school complete their primary education. The worst offenders in lack of educational opportunities for girls are Bihar (33%), Arunachal Pradesh (33.4%), Sikkim (37.2%) and Rajasthan (38.2%) as opposed to an all India average of 55.6%. Meghalaya is an exception where female literates are actually much more than their male counterparts. Early marriages are far from being eradicated. In Rajasthan, 41% girls get married between 15-19 years of age while in Punjab; the proportion of girls being married before 18 has risen from 12% to 19% in seven years, between 1998-99 to 2005-06.

Table: 6.1

Table -1:	**Immunization**
State	**Kids below 2yrs fully immunized**
UP	22.9
Rajasthan	26.5
Arunchal Pradesh	28.4
Assam	31.6
Meghalaya	32.8
Gujarat	45.2
Andhra Pradesh	46.0
Chattisgarh	48.7
Orissa	51.8
Karnataka	55.0

Table: 6.2 Anemia

	Anemic infants		Anemic pregnant women	
States	**NFHS-3**	**NFHS-2**	**NFHS-3**	**NFHS-2**
Assam	76.7	63.2	72.0	62.3
Karnataka	82.7	70.6	59.5	48.6
Kerala	55.7	43.9	33.1	20.3
Arunchal Pradesh	66.3	54.5	49.2	49.2
Uttar Pradesh	85.1	73.8	51.6	45.8
AP	79.0	72.3	56.4	41.8
Gujarat	80.1	74.5	60.8	47.4
Orissa	74.2	72.3	68.1	60.5
Meghalaya	68.7	67.6	56.1	58.6
Punjab	80.2	80.0	41.6	37.1

Some of the harsh facts:

· Every second child under 5 years is malnourished.
· 1 in 4 adolescent girls between 15-19 years is married.
· 30 of 100 girls who enter school do not complete primary –level education
· 50% of new AIDS infections are between 15-24 years.
· Worst offenders are Bihar , Arunachal Pradesh, Sikkim and Rajasthan.

Q10. What is meant by marginalized group?

Ans. In sociology, marginalisation is the social process of becoming or being made marginal "the marginalisation of the underclass"; "marginalisation of literature" and many other are some examples. Marginalisation involves people being denied degrees of power. Marginalisation has the potential to result in severe material deprivation, and in its most extreme form can exterminate groups. Material deprivation is the most common result of marginalisation when looking at how unfairly material resources are dispersed in society. Along with material deprivation, marginalized individuals are also excluded from services, programs, and policies (Young, 2000). Marginalisation can be understood within three levels: individual, community, and global-structural / policies. Although examples are listed within these three specific levels, one must recognize the intersecting nature of marginalisation and its capacity to overlap within each. Many communities experience marginalisation, with particular focus in this section on Aboriginal communities and women. Marginalisation of Aboriginal communities is a product of colonisation. As a result of colonialism, Aboriginal communities lost their land, were forced into destitute areas, lost their sources of income, and were excluded from the labour market. Additionally, Aboriginal communities lost their culture and values through forced assimilation and lost their rights in society. Today various communities continue to be marginalized from society due to the development of practices, policies and programs that "met the needs of white people and not the needs of the marginalized groups themselves" also connects marginalisation to minority communities when describing the concept of whiteness as maintaining and enforcing dominant norms and discourse. A second example of marginalisation at the community level is the marginalisation of women. Moosa-Mitha discusses the feminist movement as a direct reaction to the marginalisation of white women in society. Women were excluded from the labor force and their work in the home was not valued. Feminists argued that men and women should equally participate in the labor force, the public and private sector, and in the home. They also focused on labour laws to increase access to employment, as well as recognize child rearing as a valuable form of labour. Today women are still marginalized from executive positions and continue to earn less than men in upper management positions.

Q11. Write about the changing status of marginalized groups.

[June 09, Q. 10]

Ans. Changing Status of Scheduled Castes: Following are the marginalized groups in India:

(1) Scheduled Castes, **(2)** Scheduled Tribes, **(3)** Women, **(4)** Children, **(5)** Aged. Today the marginalized groups are gradually coping with their situation with the help of self-help groups and government.

The social mobility among scheduled castes can be understood better in the light of some empirical data. For example, the literacy rate of the scheduled castes has increased from 10 per cent in 1961 to nearly 37 per cent in 1991. Their enrolments in schools have doubled between 1981 and 1991. The number of scheduled caste employees in the government offices and administration have increased from 2,12,000 in 1956 to nearly 6,00,000 in 1992. The number of scheduled castes employed in public sector organisations have increased from 40,000 in 1970 to 3,69,000 in 1992. In rural areas, the percentage of the poor among the scheduled castes has declined from 58 per cent in 1983-84 to

50 per cent in 1987-88.

Another indication of social change and social mobility among the scheduled castes in the rural and urban societies can be inferred from the incidents of caste tensions and caste conflicts. Most of the violence against the scheduled castes took place due to their occupations. Some of the jobs prescribed by the discriminatory caste customs have been to perform the age-old degraded occupations such as disposing off dead cattle, midwifery and beggary or forced labour without wage. Increasingly, the scheduled castes have refused to obey the authority of the non scheduled castes regarding restrictions on the use of public places such as village tanks, wells, streets, temples, etc. The provision of adult franchise has also brought about political awakening and self respect among the scheduled castes. In economic matters, a scheduled caste person cannot be easily made bonded labour on nominal or no wage. Similarly, it is no longer easy to dispossess them of their land and houses. These refusals and non-conformities have created situations of caste conflicts and caste tensions.

The dominant castes that have traditionally thrived on the exploitative relationship with the scheduled castes are provoked into violence when the scheduled castes question the existing relationship. The violence against scheduled castes may be seen in the incident of forcible snatching of properties, rape and selling of scheduled caste women, burning and killing of the scheduled caste people. The caste conflict as an expression of social mobility among the scheduled castes can easily be observed in rural areas. This is less so in urban areas due to greater degree of modernisation and social development through education, secular employment, and economic and technological change.

The improvement in the marginal position of the scheduled castes cannot be adequately described without mentioning the contribution of various reformist leaders such as Mahatma Jotirao Phule, and Dr. B.R. Ambedkar. Ambedkar's ideology is primarily an ideology of social equality, liberty and fraternity, and his strategy to get it materialized is the protest against the social inequality in the caste system. He had launched protest movement for radically altering the society which routinely degraded and dehumanized the marginal castes. Furthermore, he stressed the rights of the untouchables caste to social equality. In Ambedkar's view, equality of the lower castes is to be seen in the socio-political, religious and opportunity contexts where it is opposed to excessive inequality in the same contexts. In other words, equality for Ambedkar is relative.

Changing Status of Scheduled Tribes: After 947, when the new Constitution was framed, the government's policy of isolation was changed. This was also in conformity with the promises made to tribals during the freedom movement. During the movement, Mahatma Gandhi and other national leaders were critical of the segregation of the tribes by the British rulers. The objective of the new tribal policy in the independent India was to integrate the tribals in the mainstream of the Indian society. The main thrust of the constitutional provisions for the scheduled tribes is: **(a)** to protect and promote tribal interest through legal and administrative provisions, and **(b)** to raise their economic condition so as to upgrade their quality of life.

After India's independence, the government recognized three urgent tasks with regard to the tribal development: **(a)** reducing the communication gap between the tribals and non-tribal communities so as to promote national integration, **(b)** protecting the life support system of the tribals so that they can grow collectively and live up to the national challenges, and **(c)** attending to the immediate needs of the tribal population so that their participation in the process of development is ensured.

To meet these objectives, three strategies were adopted in the Constitution: **(i)** The Fifth Schedule indicated measures for the administration of tribal areas, **(ii)** The Sixth Schedule was meant for tribal majority states. It provided for the establishment of Autonomous District Councils which could make laws for the management of land and forest, shifting cultivation, appointments of chiefs and headmen, inheritance of property, marriage and divorce, social customs and anything related to village administration. And **(iii)** Article 275 of the Constitution provides financial resources to the state for promoting the welfare of scheduled tribes and development of the administration of the scheduled area. Article 46 provides for the promotion of the educational and economic interests of the tribal people and their further protection against all forms of social injustices and exploitation.

The actual course of economic development gives a mixed picture of tribal marginalisation as well as social mobility. A large number of development projects – industrial, mining, irrigation projects lead to forcible eviction of the tribals from their land. In the world view of development, the acquisition of the tribal land is supposed to serve the national interest. The displacement of the tribals from their land is considered as a major cost for which the tribals could always be compensated.

The most notable development among the tribals that helps them in overcoming their marginalisation is in the area of education. The level of literacy among the tribals has gone up by 32 per cent during the decade 1971-81. The enrolment of the tribal children in primary schools has also gone up, although there is a high dropout rate as well. Education has also led to the emergence of a small minority which has become a part of the administrative machinery of their government. Through education tribals are exposed to the outside world which helps them to articulate their demands and mobilize favourable public opinion.

Changing Status of Women: In the light of the international consciousness,

Indian government adopted progressive policies for women's welfare and encouraged women studies. A notable development in the country was the appointment of the Committee on the Status of Women in India by the government in 1971. The Committee focused on the social trends and responses to the principle of equality with a view to suggest measures for their implementation. The Committee submitted its report and titled Towards Equality' (1974). The report brought to light the causes of women's subordination and explained their exploitation in terms of caste, class and gender inequality. For the first time in post independent India there was an upsurge of studies on women's status and life circumstances. It was noted by various scholars that certain aspects of women's degradation follow from certain negative consequences of the process of development itself. The disabilities and the inequalities imposed on women were seen in the total context of society where other sections of the population also suffered in their own way under the oppression of an exploitative system. These studies changed the orientation of the people towards viewing the place of women in the context of development process. Rather than viewing women as targets of welfare policies they have now come to be viewed as critical category for development. This redefinition of women found expression in the Sixth Year Plan (1980-85) which carried, for the first time in India's history of planning, a separate chapter on women and development. This shift asserts the principle of equality and pointed out that India's future would be incomplete without women's participation in the process of development. It also recognized as never before that social and economic transformation badly affected women. The Sixth Five Year Plan brought out three strategies as essential for women's development from the margin to the core of society. These are there: **(1)** economic independence, **(2)** educational development, and **(3)** access to health care and family planning.

7 Class in Indian Society

Q1. Outline the agrarian class structure in India. [Dec 08, Q. 1]

Or

Discuss the classical Notion of undifferentiated Present society. [June 09, Q. 6]

Ans. Social structure can be described through institutions based on birth, the family, lineage, sub-caste and caste. An alternate way of describing the structure is through class and here there are two views **(i)** class is a better spring board for describing structure and **(ii)** both caste and class are necessary to describe the structure. K.L. Sharma (1980) elaborates the second position, "caste incorporates the element of class and class has a cultural (caste) style, hence the two systems cannot be easily separated even analytically". In the modern period, the British land revenue system gave rise to a more or less similar agrarian class structure in villages in India. They were the three classes of the landowners *(zamindars)*, the tenants and the agricultural labourers. The landowners *(zamindars)* were tax gatherers and non-cultivating owners of land. They belonged to the upper caste groups. The agricultural labourers were placed in a position of bondsmen and hereditarily attached labourers. They belonged to the lower caste groups. The impact of land reforms and rural development programmes introduced after independence has been significant. Land reforms led to the eviction of smaller tenants on a large scale. But the intermediate castes of peasants, e.g., the Ahir, Kurmi etc. in Bihar and Uttar Pradesh benefited. Power of the feudal landed families started declining all over the country. The onset of the Green Revolution in the 1960s led to the emergence of commercially oriented landlords. Rich farmers belonging generally to upper and intermediate castes prospered. But the fortune of the poor peasantry and the agricultural labourers did not improve. This has led to accentuation of class conflicts and tensions. Agrarian unrest in India has now become a common feature in various parts of the country. P.C. Joshi (1971) has summarised in the following manner the trends in the agrarian class structure and relationships. **(i)** It led to the decline of feudal and customary types of tenancies. It was replaced by a more exploitative and insecure lease arrangement. **(ii)** It gave rise to a new commercial based rich peasant class who were part owners and part tenants. They had resource and enterprise to carry out commercial agriculture. **(iii)** It led to the decline of feudal landlord class and another class of commercial farmers emerged for whom agriculture was a business. They used the non-customary type of tenancy. The process of social mobility has been seen in two directions. In his study of six villages in Rajasthan, K.L. Sharma (1980) observed that in some villages, not only the agricultural labourers but quite a few of the ex-landlords have slide down in class status, almost getting proletarianised. On the contrary, the neo-rich peasantry has emerged as the new rural bourgeoisie replacing the older landlords. Ramkrishna Mukherjee (1957) in his work *Dynamics of a Rural Society* dealt with the changes in the agrarian structure suggesting that a number of classes (categories) were reduced, and that small cultivators were becoming landless workers. Further, Kotovsky (1964) has noted the process of increasing proletarianisation of the peasantry in villages. According to him, "with the agriculture developing along capitalist lines the process of ruination and proletarianisation of the bulk of the peasantry is growing more intensely all the time". This is substantiated by the fact that in the two decades between 1961 and 1981 the share of cultivators came down from 52.3 percent to 41.5 percent while during the same period the share of agricultural labourers increased from 17.2 percent to 25.2 percent of the total labour force. During the two decades the proportion of peasants operating less than two hectare increased from 40 percent to 55 percent of the total. By the year 2001 the share of cultivators to the total work force further declined to 31.7 percent and the share of agricultural labourers became 26.7 percent (Census Report (provisional), 2001). The increase in proportion (and certainly numbers) of agricultural labourers has gone along with a general increase in wage labourers in the rural economy. The process of social mobility and transformation in rural India has been explained by sociologists by the terms embourgeoisement and proletarianisation. Embourgeoisement refers to the phenomenon of upward mobility of the intermediate class peasantry i.e., their emergence as new landlords. Proletarianisation describes the process of downward mobility, i.e., depeasantisation of small and marginal peasants and a few landlords and their entry into the rank of the rural landless agricultural labourers.

Q2. Explain the features of class in industrial societies. [June 07, Q. 7]
Ans. Industrial Society: It is important to distinguish the descriptive from the analytical uses of this term. At a descriptive level, an industrial society is simply one displaying the characteristic features of industrialism, as listed under that heading. However, the term is also used in the abstract to denote

the thesis that a definite type of society exists whose culture, institutions, and development are determined by its industrial production process. As such, theories of industrial society constitute a species of technological determinism, or scientific evolutionism. It is claimed that the logic of applied science, or of the technical processes based on scientific expertise and values, makes necessary certain fundamental and irreversible modifications to the traditional culture and institutions of a society. This view is expressed in the writings of Claude-Henri de Saint-Simon and by many nineteenth century social theorists, including Auguste Comte, Herbert Spencer, and Émile Durkheim. But the most influential example in classical sociology is to be found in Max Weber's interpretation of the modernisation of the Western world as progressive rationalisation, and the disenchantment of the traditional magical and supernatural systems of beliefs and values which once gave meaning to human life. For Weber's critics, however, a profound metaphysical pathos—a deeply pessimistic but unsubstantiated moral philosophy—underlies his claim that bureaucracy is inescapable in modern industrial society and politics.

Features of capitalist society: The initial usage of the term *capitalism* in its modern sense has been attributed to Louis Blanc in 1850 and Pierre-Joseph Proudhon in 1861. Marx and Engels referred to the *capitalistic system* (*kapitalistisches System*) and to the capitalist mode of production (*kapitalistische Produktionsform*) in *Das Kapital* (1867). The use of the word "capitalism" in reference to an economic system appears twice in Volume I of *Das Kapital*, p. 124 (German edition), and in *Theories of Surplus Value*, tome II, p. 493 (German edition). Marx did not extensively use the term. Marx's notion of the capitalist mode of production is characterised as a system of primarily private ownership of the means of production in a mainly market economy, with a legal framework on commerce and a physical infrastructure provided by the state. Engels made more frequent use of the term *capitalism*; volumes II and III of *Das Kapital*, both edited by Engels after Marx's death, contain the word "capitalism" four and three times, respectively. The three combined volumes of *Das Kapital* (1867, 1885, 1894) contain the word *capitalist* more than 2,600 times. An 1877 work entitled *Better Times* and an 1884 article in the *Pall Mall Gazette* also used the term *capitalism*. A later use of the term *capitalism* to describe the production system was by the German economist Werner Sombart, in his 1902 book *The Jews and Modern Capitalism* (*Die Juden und das Wirtschaftsleben*). Sombart's close friend and colleague, Max Weber, also used *capitalism* in his 1904 book *The Protestant Ethic and the Spirit of Capitalism*

Socialist society is a membership organisation that is affiliated with the Labour Party in the UK. The best-known socialist society is the Fabian Society, founded in 1884, some years before the creation of the Labour Party itself (in which the Society participated). The Society's membership is relatively small (around

7000), but in Labour circles, it exerts much influence. The Co-operative Party is not strictly a "socialist society" in the context of the Labour Party. It is in fact a separate political party with an electoral agreement with the Labour Party. It acts as a socialist society for the most part although it has certain additional rights. *Affiliation* means that the socialist societies - like a number of British trade unions - pay an affiliation fee to the Labour Party, and the affiliates' members become affiliated members of the Labour Party (a different status from full member), unless they specifically choose otherwise. In return the societies receive a formal role in Labour decision-making, and the affiliated members can take part in all-member ballots in certain circumstances. For example, they can participate in the election of Labour Party leaders. Socialist societies also elect a delegate (currently Dianne Hayter) to the Labour National Executive Committee and can affiliate at a local level to Constituency Labour Parties. A second seat was allotted to the Black Socialist Society in early 2007, when its membership rose above 2,500.

Classes in Capitalist Societies: Most scholars use economic factors as the basic criteria for differentiating classes. Adam Smith was the first person who spoke of society being divided into groups based on economic criteria and he calls them order and according to him, there are three kinds of orders.

i) Those who live by rent (Rentiers)

ii) Those who live by wage (Wage earners)

iii) Those who live by profit (The capitalist)

According to Aristotle, there are three classes in Society The Upper class, Middle class and Poor class. According to him, out of these three classes, the Middle class is least ambitious and good for the development of any society. The upper class wants to earn profit and maintain its position. The poor class is too poor, their ambition being to improve their position. Thus, between the two ambitious classes, the Middle class is the best.

According to Bergel, Classes represent different sub-cultures which are related to each other and are derived from different roots. According to him, existence of class implies that there is idea of Social distance.

Q3. Write a short note on mode of production.

Ans. In the writings of Karl Marx and the Marxist theory of historical materialism, a mode of production is a specific combination of: productive forces: these include human labour power and the means of production (e.g. tools, equipment, buildings and technologies, materials, and improved land). Social and technical relations of production: these include the property, power and control relations governing society's productive assets, often codified in law, cooperative work relations and forms of association, relations between people and the objects of their work, and the relations between social classes.

Marx regarded productive ability and participation in social relations as two essential characteristics of human beings and that the particular modality of these relations in capitalist production are inherently in conflict with the increasing development of human productive capacities.

Q4. Outline the Max Weber views on Pre-industrial societies.

Ans. The concept of "pre-industrial society" is widely used across the social sciences and it is preferred over similar concepts that are ideologically loaded. Pre-industrial society can be said to be "value free" as opposed to others (see objectivity). For example, it is commonly used and interchanged with the term: "traditional society", a term coined by Emile Durkheim in *The Division of Labor in Society*. One objection to this term is that tradition implies "stagnation". Durkheim himself used it to describe the logic by which community norms were governed. Karl Marx, who gave the theoretical foundations to the concept, used the term "pre-capitalist society". However, it is not a neutral term since it implies that a transition to capitalism was a progressive or inevitable development (in Marx's view, necessary for a transition to communism). His followers (i.e. Louis Althusser) used "pre-industrial society" interchangeably with that of Marx. Other synonyms are "agrarian society" and "pre-modern society". All of these concepts are related as they derive from Marx and Hegel's ideas. Nonetheless, each of these are not strictly "synonyms". Each has their own ideological and intellectual lineage, and deserves independent treatment. There are several ideas that gave way to the term: "Pre-industrial society". The Marxist and Hegelian idea that history progresses forward; always towards the improvement of the spirit (as in Hegel) and/or the social conditions (as in Marx). The Marxist idea that history progresses in stages of development. Although this notion of gradual movement was implied by Marx (*The Grundrisse*); it was explicitly developed by Friedrich Engels in 'his 'Dialectics of Nature *and in* The Origins of the Family, Private Property, and the State. In classic Marxist theory, there is the idea that the progression of human history is determined by its modes of production. (economic determinism, dialectics, historical materialism).

The *Pre-industrial stages* proper are:

· 1st stage. Primitive communism (no private property)

· 2nd stage. Slavery (rise of private property)

· 3rd stage. Feudalism (consolidation of authority)

The *Industrial or Modern stages* are: Capitalism, Socialism (a transitional stage) and Communism. Contemporary political theory claims that capitalism, avoiding socialism and communism, has already transcended the industrial stage. Daniel Bell called the current stage as the "post-industrial society"; others (in example Foucault) call the actual stage as "post-modern."

Q5. Describe the main characteristics of the middle classes in India.
[Dec 07, Q. 7]

Ans. Middle classes in India as of 2005, 85.7% of the population lives on less than $2.50 (PPP) a day, down from 92.5% in 1981. This compares with 80.5% in Sub-Saharan Africa. 75.6% of the population lives on less than $2 a day (PPP), which is around 20 rupees or $0.5 a day in nominal terms. It was down from 86.6% and compares with 73.0% in Sub-Saharan Africa. A 24.3% of the population earned less than $1 (PPP, around $0.25 in nominal terms) a day in 2005, down from 42.1% in 1981. 41.6% of its population is living below the new international poverty line of $1.25 (PPP) per day, down from 59.8% in 1981.

The single most common indicator used to quantify standard of living is the per capita purchasing power parity (PPP) adjusted gross domestic product (GDP). In 2007, the per capita PPP-adjusted GDP for India was US$2,659. These figures can be compared to $5,292 for neighbouring China. With one of the fastest growing economies in the world, clocked at an average growth rate of 8% between 2004-2005, India is fast on way to become a large and globally important consumer economy. The Indian middle class, estimated to be 300 million people by Indian standard (but much lower by European or North American standard), is fast becoming used to Western culture If current trends continue, Indian per capita purchasing power parity will grow to be approximately one third that of the developed world by the middle of the 21st century . In 2006, 22 percent of Indians lived under the poverty line. India aims to eradicate poverty by 2020. The standard of living in India shows large disparity. For example, rural areas of India exist with very basic (or even non-existent) medical facilities, while cities boast of world class medical establishments. Similarly, The very latest machinery may be used in some construction projects, but many construction workers work without mechanisation in most projects. A 24.3% of the population earned less than $1 (PPP, around $0.25 in nominal terms) a day in 2005, down from 42.1% in 1981. 41.6% of its population is living below the new international poverty line of $1.25 (PPP) per day, down from 59.8% in 1981. The World Bank further estimates that a third of the global poor now reside in India. On the other hand, the Planning Commission of India uses its own criteria and has estimated that 27.5% of the population was living below the poverty line in 2004–2005, down from 51.3% in 1977–1978, and 36% in 1993-1994. The source for this was the 61st round of the National Sample Survey (NSS) and the criterion used was monthly per capita consumption expenditure below Rs. 356.35 for rural areas and Rs. 538.60 for urban areas. 75% of the poor are in rural areas, most of them are daily wagers, self-employed householders and landless labourers. Although Indian economy has grown steadily over the last two decades, its growth has been uneven when comparing different social groups, economic groups, geographic regions, and rural and urban areas. Between 1999 and 2008, the annualized growth rates for Gujarat (8.8%), Haryana (8.7%), or Delhi (7.4%) were much higher than for Bihar (5.1%), Uttar Pradesh (4.4%), or Madhya Pradesh (3.5%). Poverty rates in rural Orissa (43%) and rural Bihar (41%) are higher than in the world's poorest countries such as Malawi. India has a higher rate of malnutrition among children under the age of three (46% in year 2007) than any other country in the world. Despite significant economic progress, ¼ of the nation's population earns less than the government-specified poverty threshold of $0.40/day. Official figures estimate that 27.5% of Indians lived below the national poverty line in 2004-2005. A 2007 report by the state-run National Commission for Enterprises in the Unorganized Sector (NCEUS) found that 25% of Indians, or 236 million people, lived on less than 20 rupees per day with most working in "informal labour sector with no job or social security, living in abject poverty." Since the early 1950s, successive governments have implemented various schemes, under planning, to alleviate poverty that have met with partial success. Programmes like *Food for work* and *National Rural Employment Programme* have attempted to use the unemployed to generate productive assets and build rural infrastructure. In August 2005, the Indian parliament passed the *Rural Employment Guarantee Bill*, the largest programme of this type, in terms of cost and coverage, which promises 100 days of minimum wage employment to every rural household in 200 of India's 600 districts. The question of whether economic reforms have reduced poverty or not has fuelled debates without generating any clear cut answers and has also put political pressure on further economic reforms, especially those involving downsizing of labour and cutting down agricultural subsidiary.

Q6. Compare middle class India with Western countries.

Ans. The 'middle class' is an over-used expression and difficult to pin down, since it is defined not just in terms of income, but also as values, cultural affinities, lifestyles, educational attainments and service sector employment. Using income, one way of defining middle class is in terms of how much of income is left over for discretionary expenditure, after paying for food and shelter. If more than one-third is left, that qualifies one for inclusion in the 'middle class'.

This is the way the Economist recently defined middle class, and quoted Surjit Bhalla's forthcoming work (The Middle Class Kingdoms of India and China) to the effect that a third wave of middle-class emergence is currently under way globally. The first was in nineteenth century Western Europe, the second was in the baby boomer (1950-80) generation in developed countries, and the third is the consequence of income growth in countries like India and China. When India opened up in the early 1990s, the middle class was often cited to sell the attractiveness of India's domestic market. Figures of 300 million were bandied about, but producers realised to their chagrin that this market was elusive and did not, in fact, exist. Depending on the product, the market might very well be 30 million.

In part, the problem arises from using income as the criterion in defining middle class, ignoring heterogeneity beyond income categories. But let's ignore that story, which has been told very well by Rama Bijapurkar.

For two different reasons, 30 million is now approaching 300 million. One, income distributions are positively skewed. Therefore, once the thick part of a distribution passes above the threshold, suddenly there is a disproportionately high increase in the numbers of the 'middle class'.

Two, a disproportionate distribution of income growth can raise the numbers of the middle class. When income growth occurs, the share of the middle class in the total population increases to more than 50%. The Economist quotes NCAER to tell us that the middle-class share in India's population will increase from 5% in 2005 to 20% in 2015 and more than 40% in 2025.

But there is yet another feature of being middle class that we need to flag—one which has been apparent in every country that has developed. The middle class no longer wants subsidies and hand-holding from the state, and is content to pay taxes, so that cross-subsidisation to poorer sections can happen. The middle class gives up demanding from the government. That hasn't happened in India yet, and the middle class is still described as the "common man".

Q7. Write a note about the growth of middle classes after independence.

Ans. India's independence from the colonial rule marked the beginning of a new phase in its history. The independent Indian State was committed, in principle, to democratic institutions of secularism, freedom, justice and equality for all the citizens, irrespective of caste, creed or religion and at all levels – social, economic and political. To achieve these ends, India embarked upon the path of planned development. Plans were chalked out for the development of agricultural, industrial and the tertiary sectors of the economy. There was an overall attempt to expend the economy in all directions. The government of India introduced various programmes and schemes for different sectors of the economy. The execution of these programmes required the services of a large number of trained personnel.

Apart from the increase in a number of those employed in the government sectors, urban industrial and tertiary sectors also experienced an expansion. Though compared to many other countries of the Third World, the growth rate of the Indian economy was slower, in absolute terms the industrial sector grew many folds. Growth in the tertiary sector was more rapid. Increase in population, particularly the urban population, led to a growth in the serving industry. Banks, insurance companies, hospitals, hotels press, advertisement agencies all grew at an unprecedented rate, giving employment to a large number trained professionals.

The next stage of expansion was in the rural areas. Various development programmes introduced by the Indian State after independent led to significant agricultural growth in the regions that experienced Green Revolution. Success of the Green Revolution technology increased productivity of land and made the landowning sections of the Indian countryside substantially richer. Economic development also led to a change in the aspirations of the rural peoples. Those who could afford it started sending their children not only to English medium schools but also to colleges and universities for higher studies. Consumption patterns also began to change. 'Material goods hitherto considered unnecessary for the simple lifestyle of a farmer, began to be sought. And lifestyle as yet remote and shunned were emulated' (Varma, 1998:95). A new class has emerged in rural India that partly had its interests in urban occupations. The process of agrarian transformation added another segment to the already existing middle classes. In ideological terms, this "new" segment of the middle classes was quite different from traditional middle classes. Unlike the old urban middle classes, this new, "rural middle class" was local and regional in character. The members of the rural middle class tended perceive their interests in regional rather than in the nationalist framework. Politically, this class has been on forefront of the movements for regional autonomy. Another new segment of the middle class that emerged during the post-independence period came from the dalit caste groups. Government policies of positive discrimination and reservations for members of the ex-untouchables/Schedule castes enabled some of them to get educated and employed in the urban occupations, mostly in the servicing and government sectors. Over the years, a new dalit middle class has thus also emerged on the scene.

Q8. What is class conflict?

Ans. Class conflict refers to the underlying tensions or antagonisms which exist in society due to conflicting interests that arise from different social positions. Class conflict is thought to play a pivotal role in history of class societies (such as capitalism and feudalism) by Marxists who refer to its overt manifestations as class war, a struggle whose resolution in favor of the working class is viewed by them as inevitable under capitalism. Class conflict can take many different shapes. Direct violence, such as wars fought for resources and cheap labor; indirect violence, such as deaths from poverty, starvation or unsafe working conditions; coercion, such as the threat of losing a job or pulling an important investment; or ideology, either intentionally (as with books and articles promoting anti-capitalism) or unintentionally (as with the promotion of consumerism through advertising). It can be open, as with a lockout aimed at destroying a labor union, or hidden, as with an informal slowdown in production protesting low wages or unfair labor practices.

Definition of Classes and Class Conflict: Class conflict is a term long-used mostly by socialists, Communists and many anarchists define a 'class' by its relationship to the 'means of production' such as factories, land, and machinery. From this point of view, the social control of production and labour is a contest between classes, and the division of these resources necessarily involves conflict and inflicts harm.

Q9. Briefly describe the views of Dahrendorf's and Lewis Coser of class conflict.

Ans. Views on Dahrendorf's: The ideas of Marx spawned a rich literature; much of it is polemical and political, but some authors have tried to avoid the historical or empirical errors Marx committed, to learn from changes since his time, and to apply the spirit of his sociology to contemporary industrial society. The best of these efforts is Ralf Dahrendorf's *Class and Class Conflict in Industrial Society* (1959). Dahrendorf recognizes two approaches to society, which he calls the Utopian and the Rationalist. The first emphasizes equilibrium of values, consensus, and stability; the second revolves around dissension and conflict, the latter being the mover of structural change. Both are social perspectives; neither is completely false, but each views a separate face of society. Unfortunately, he feels, the consensus view has dominated contemporary sociology, especially in the United States, and he sets out to create some balance between the two views by developing and illustrating the theoretical power of a class-conflict perspective. He begins as he must with a review of Marx's writings, a clarification of his model, a discussion of the sociopolitical changes since Marx. A review of subsequent theoretical works bearing on class is followed by a sociological critique of Marx. These necessary scholarly chores completed, Dahrendorf presents his own view of class. He sees Marx's defining characteristic of class (as property ownership) as a special case of a more general authoritative relationship. Society grants the holders of social positions power to exercise coercive control over others. And property ownership, the legitimate right to coercively exclude others from one's property, is such power. This control is a matter of authority, which Dahrendorf defines, according to Weber, as the probability that a command with specific content will be obeyed by certain people. Authority is associated with a role or position and differs from power, which Dahrendorf claims is individual. Authority is a matter of formal legitimacy backed by sanctions. It is a relation existing between people in imperatively coordinated groups, thus originating in social structure. Authority, however, is dichotomous; there is always an authoritative hierarchy on one side and those who are excluded on the other. Within any imperative group are those who are super ordinate and those who are subordinate. There is an arrangement of social roles comprising expectations of domination or subjugation. Those who assume opposing roles have structurally generated contradictory interests, to preserve or to change the status quo. Incumbents of authoritative roles benefit from the status-quo, which grants them their power. Those toward whom this authoritative power is exercised, and who suffer from it, however, are naturally opposed to this state of affairs. Super ordinates and subordinates thus form separate quasi-groups of shared latent interests. On the surface, members of these groups and their behavior may vary considerably, but they form a pool from which conflict groups can recruit members. With leadership, ideology, and the political (freedom) and social conditions of organisation being present, latent interests become manifested through political organisations and conflict. They are latent or manifest conflict groups arising from the authority structure of imperative coordinated organisations. Class conflict then arises from and is related to this structure. The structural source of group conflict lies in authoritative domination and subjugation; the object of such conflict is the status quo; and the consequence is to change (not necessarily through revolution) social structure. It should be stressed that Dahrendorf's theory is not limited to "capitalist" societies. Since authoritative roles are the differentia between classes, classes and class conflict also exist in communist or socialist societies. Classes exist insofar as there are those who dominate by virtue of legitimate positions (such as the Soviet factory manager, party chief, commune head, or army general) and those who are habitually in subordinate positions (the citizen, worker, peasant).

The Views of Lewis Coser: Lewis Coser regards conflict as functional for society. He says that social reality is a product of inter-related parts. Imbalances between parts, give rise to inter-group and intra-group conflicts which is an important elements of social interaction. Coser feels that conflict frequently helps to reform existing norms or it contributes to the emergence of new values in society. In saying this he goes to the extent of saying that a balance of power is a factor in social relationship.

Q10. What is conflict theory?

Ans. Conflict theory is a social theory which emphasizes a person's or group's ability to exercise influence and control over others, thereby affecting social order. It posits that individuals and groups struggle to maximize their benefits, inevitably contributing to social changes such as innovations in politics and outright revolutions. Conflict theory examines class conflict, such as that between the proletariat and bourgeoisie, and contrasts ideologies such as capitalism and socialism. It proposes that continual struggles exist among all different aspects of a particular society. These struggles do not always involve physical violence; they can be underlying efforts by each group or individual within a society to maximize its benefits. The theory has roots in the critical theory of Karl Marx and the interpretive sociology of Max Weber.

In conflict theory there are a few basic conflicts: One of the basic conflicts in conflict theory is that of class. There are low and high ranks in class, and that gives a certain group more power over another group which causes conflicts. For the most part, when an individual is part of a high ranked class they usually own a lot of property. That means that if you are of a lower class, then you don't own as much property. This usually causes conflict on who owns the most property and what property one does own. In Marx's original conception, ownership of property was the most essential determinant of the class structure. On the other hand Weber thought that property ownership was only one factor determining class structure. Also, in the words of Jurgen Habermas, the conflicts of different social structures and classes provide the many motives it takes to create and preserve many patterns of culture. Another basic conflict in conflict theory is that of race and ethnicity. Much like in the class system, groups in this system are ranked by their prestige and power. This means that if a certain race or ethnicity has more education, prestige, and power then it is considered the better race or ethnicity which creates conflict. Another kind of conflict is that of gender. This type of conflict can be noticeable by the implication of a type of culture that is for men and a type of culture that is for women. Regions are another kind of conflict. This type of conflict is brought about by all of the different assumptions that people from one region have about people that are from another region. The regions could range from one country to another or one state/province to another. Lastly, there is the conflict of religion. The conflict of religion is itself quite stratified; even though there is a group of people belonging to each religion they are divided much like the social structure of classes. All of these groups seek to gain power and use it to reshape society the way they see it best. It seems that this is the determining factor in the ruling class.

8 Social Mobility

Q1. Explain the types and forms of social mobility. [June 09, Q. 5]

Ans. Horizontal and Vertical Social Mobility: A distinction is made between horizontal and vertical social mobility. The former refers to change of occupational position or role of an individual or a group without involving any change in its position in the social hierarchy, the latter refers essentially to changes in the position of an individual or a group along the social hierarchy. When a rural laborer comes to the city and becomes an industrial worker or a manager takes a position in another company there are no significant changes in their position in the hierarchy. Those are the examples of horizontal mobility. Horizontal mobility is a change in position without the change in status. It indicates a change in position within the range of the same status.

It is a movement from one status to its equivalent. But if an industrial worker becomes a businessman or lawyer he has radically changed his position in the stratification system. This is an example of vertical mobility. Vertical mobility refers to a movement of an individual or people or groups from one status to another. It involves change within the lifetime of an individual to a higher or lower status than the person had to begin with.

Forms of Vertical Social Mobility: The vertical mobility can take place in two ways individuals and groups may improve their position in the hierarchy by moving upwards or their position might worsen and they may fall down the hierarchy. When individuals get into seats of political position; acquire money and exert influence over others because of their new status they are said to have achieved individual mobility. Like individuals even groups also attain high social mobility. When a dalit from a village becomes an important official it is a case of upward mobility. On the other hand an aristocrat or a member of an upper class may be dispossessed of his wealth and he is forced to enter a manual occupation. This is an example of downward mobility.

Q2. Describe the dimension and implications of social mobility.
[June 07, Q. 3]

Ans. Inter-Generational Social Mobility: Time factor is an important element in social mobility. On the basis of the time factor involved in social mobility there is another type of inter-generational mobility. It is a change in status from that which a child began within the parents, household to that of the child upon reaching adulthood. It refers to a change in the status of family members from one generation to the next. For example a farmer's son becoming an officer. It is important because the amount of this mobility in a society tells us to what extent inequalities are passed on from one generation to the next. If there is very little inter-generational mobility, inequality is clearly deeply built into the society for people' life chances are being determined at the moment of birth. When there is a mobility people are clearly able to achieve new statuses through their own efforts, regardless of the circumstances of their birth.

Intra-Generational Mobility: Mobility taking place in personal terms within the lifespan of the same person is called intra-generational mobility. It refers to the advancement in one's social level during the course of one's lifetime. It may also be understood as a change in social status which occurs within a person's adult career. For example a person working as a supervisor in a factory becoming its assistant manager after getting promotion.

Structural Mobility: Structural mobility is a kind of vertical mobility. Structural mobility refers to mobility which is brought about by changes in stratification hierarchy itself. It is a vertical movement of a specific group, class or occupation relative to others in the stratification system. It is a type of forced mobility for it takes place because of the structural changes and not because of individual attempts. For example historical circumstances or labor market changes may lead to the rise of decline of an occupational group within the social hierarchy. An influx of immigrants may also alter class alignments -especially if the new arrivals are disproportionately highly skilled or unskilled.

Upward and Downward Mobility: Upward social mobility is a change in a person's social status resulting in that person receiving a higher position in their status system. Likewise, downward mobility results in a lower position. A prime example of an opportunity for upward mobility nowadays is athletics. There is an increased number of minorities seeking careers as professional athletes which can either lead to improved social status or could potentially harm them due to neglecting other aspects of their life (ex. education). Transformative assets would also allow one to achieve a higher status in society, as they increase wealth and provide for more opportunity. A transformative asset could be a trust fund set up by family that allows you to own a nice home in a nice neighborhood, instead of an apartment in a down trodden community. This type of move would allow the person to develop a new circle of friends of the same economic status.

Range of Mobility: When people move up or down the social scale, they may travel through one or many strata. The social distance thus covered is denoted by the term 'range'. It could be movement covering a short social distance, i.e., short-range shift. Also, a big slide across a numbers of strata (up or down) is also possible. This is a caste of long-range mobility. For example, when Blau and Duncan collected information on a national sample of 20,000 males, they concluded that there is much vertical mobility in the United States. Interestingly, nearly all of this is between occupational positions quite close to one another. 'Long-Range' mobility is rare. On the contrary, Frank Parkin stresses on instances of 'long-range' mobility.

Possibilities of Mobility: Studies of social mobility invariably leads one to the question of openness and closeness of a society. Mobility is not possible it a society is rigid enough to allow any movement within its graded structure. On the other hand, mobility is facilitated if a society exhibits flexible character.

Very little vertical mobility is possible in a closed society. Pre-modern Colombia and India more or less approximate such type. In contrast, an open society allows for greater vertical social mobility. However, even in open societies people cannot move from one stratum to another without resistance. Every society has established criteria – which might be proper manners, family lineage, education, or racial affiliation etc., which must satisfied before people can move to a higher social level.

Most open societies tend to be highly industrialized. As societies industrialize, new skills are demanded and occupations are created that were pervasively unnecessary. New occupations mean more opportunities for a wide section of people. Additionally, urbanisation contributes to vertical social mobility because ascriptive criteria become less important in the anonymity of the city. People become achievement oriented, competitive, and status-striving. In industrial societies, most often government also undertakes welfare programmes which foster mobility.

What makes mobility a reality is a change in occupation structure, enlarging the range and proportion of middle – and upper-level occupations while reducing the proportions of lower ones. Mobility created by changes in the occupational structure of the society is called **structural mobility** (sometimes also called forced mobility).

Many schools pointed out that the overall impact of capitalist path of industrialisation has resulted in widespread downward mobility. While-collar occupations do not provide sufficient scope for vast sections of population for upward mobility. Marxist theory inspired scholars have showed that there is systematic 'degrading', rather than upgrading, of labour under the compulsion of late capitalism. The consequence has been large-scale downward mobility of collective kind.

Comparative Social Mobility: Once social mobility as concept is clarified and we are acquainted with the theoretical implications, it would be useful to take note of actual empirical studies of social mobility. The finding and inferences of such studies covering diverse societies would help us to relate the concept and forms of social mobility with real determinate social situation. We can indicate the most representative's studies.

Gerhard Lenski computed a manual-non manual index based on data from a variety of sources. His study shows the United States as first with a mobility rate of 34%, but five other European countries are close behind: Sweden, 32%, Great Britain, 31%, Denmark, 30%, Norway, 30% and France, 29%. So we can observe that the mobility rate is fairly similar in industrial societies.

Frank Parkin made a subtle, yet a substantive study to throw new light on social mobility. He sought out data from erstwhile communist run societies of Eastern Europe and attempted some comparison:

i) the dominant class of managers and professionals, like such classes in capitalist societies, is able to transmit competitive advantage to their own children, and

ii) the privileged classes assure high position for their children, there is nevertheless much social mobility for peasants and manual workers in these societies.

Parkin cited a study of Hungary to show that 77% of managerial, administrative, and professional positions were filled by men and women of peasant and worker origin, and that 53% of doctors, scientist and engineers were from such families.

The increase in white-collar position as a consequence of industrial expansion had provided in Eastern Europe a level of mobility for those lower in occupational rank that exceeds that in the United States and Europe. This fact instilled higher aspirations among the working classes.

These studies indicate that social mobility – its possibilities and implications, are all being connected to specific social contexts.

There are various dimensions in any study of social mobility. If change of social position is diagnosed over the life-span of an individual, it is a case of intra-generational mobility. If the change occurs across two or more generations, then it is called intergenerational mobility.

The change of social position may be across short long 'social distance.' Range of mobility takes care of this phenomenon.

As against popular belief, downward mobility is also widespread in modern industrial societies. In modern industrial societies it is mainly the 'achievement' oriented criteria that determine upward mobility. Most modern societies are believed to be more 'open' to facilitate social mobility. Nevertheless, every society has its own criteria and mobility attempts are also resisted differently.

Q3. Write a short note on the liberal theory and Lip set and Zetterberg Theory of industrialism.

Or

Describe the Modern Analyses of social mobility.

Ans. The Liberal Theory: This theory is the most intuitive one associated with the industrialisation and modernisation, and the most optimistic as well. It posits that the rate of social mobility increases - further, the rate of the increase should increase over time as well - as society is freed from the constraint of highly stratified feudal structure based on ascriptive stratification. Because of the expansion of bureaucratic and managerial jobs, it is also postulated that upward mobility should be more common than the downward mobility.

Lip set and Zetterberg Theory: Modification of the above theory, altering the former in some key respects. It posits that the overall pattern of social mobility is much the same in industrial countries of the West. However, unlike the former theory it does not maintain that the rate of economic expansion and mobility rates are correlated. Rather, it posits the much more restricted "threshold effect" that once certain level of industrialisation is achieved then the social mobility rate tends to be relative high.

Q4. What is social mobility? Discuss with appropriate example.

[Dec 08, Q. 8]

Ans. Social mobility is the degree to which an individual's family or group's social status can change throughout the course of their life through a system of social hierarchy or stratification. Subsequently, it is also the degree to which an individual's or group's descendants move up and down the class system. The individual or family can move up or down the social classes based on achievements or factors beyond their control. It is a sociological concept.

Q5. Explain the mobility in caste.

Ans. The relative ranking of other castes was fluid or differed from one place to another prior to the arrival of the British. Sociologists such as Bernard Buber and Marriott McKim describe how the perception of the caste system as a static and textual stratification has given way to the perception of the caste system as a more processual, empirical and contextual stratification. Other sociologists such as Y.B Damle have applied theoretical models to explain mobility and flexibility in the caste system in India. According to these scholars, groups of lower-caste individuals could seek to elevate the status of their caste by attempting to emulate the practices of higher castes. Flexibility in caste laws permitted very low-caste religious clerics such as Valmiki to compose the Ramayana, which became a central work of Hindu scripture. According to some psychologists, mobility across broad caste lines may have been "minimal", though sub-castes (jatis) may change their social status over the generations by fission, re-location, and adoption of new rituals. Sociologist M. N. Srinivas has also debated the question of rigidity in Caste. In an ethnographic study of the Coorgs of Karnataka, he observed considerable flexibility and mobility in their caste hierarchies. He asserts that the caste system is far from a rigid system in which the position of each component caste is fixed for all time. Movement has always been possible, and especially in the middle regions of the hierarchy. It was always possible for groups born into a lower caste to "rise to a higher position by adopting vegetarianism and teetotalism" i.e adopt the customs of the higher castes. While theoretically "forbidden", the process was not uncommon in practice. The concept of sanskritisation, or the adoption of upper-caste norms by the lower castes, addressed the actual complexity and fluidity of caste relations.

Historical examples of mobility in the Indian Caste System among Hindus have been researched. There is also precedent of certain Shudra families within the temples of the Sri Vaishnava sect in South India elevating their caste. The distinctions, particularly between the Brahmins and the other castes, were in theory sharper, but in practice it now appears that social restrictions were not so rigid. Brahmins often lived off the land and founded dynasties like Sunga Empire, Hindu Shahi Dynasty, Bhumihar Brahmins, Tyagi Brahmins and Konkanastha Brahmins. Most of the groups claiming Kshatriya status had only recently acquired it. The conscious reference to being Kshatriya, a characteristic among Rajputs, is a noticeable feature in post-Gupta politics. The fact that many of these dynasties were of obscure origin suggests some social mobility: a person of any caste, having once acquired political power, could also acquire a genealogy connecting him with the traditional lineages and conferring Kshatriya status. A number of new castes, such as the Kayasthas (scribes) and Khatris (traders), are mentioned in the sources of this period. According to the Brahmanic sources, they originated from inter caste marriages, but this is clearly an attempt at rationalizing their rank in the hierarchy. Many of these new castes played a major role in society. The hierarchy of castes did not have a uniform distribution throughout the country. Khatri appears to be unquestionably a Prioritized form of the Sanskrit Kshatriya.

Level of Mobility: Mobility has taken place at the level of individual, family and group. Sharma has made a careful analysis of these levels of mobility.

i) Mobility of an Individual within a family: Some individuals even though of low caste, may have better status and prestige compared to other members of their family. This may be on account of one's personality traits such as integrity, honesty, acquisition of education and other achievements. Similarly, an individual of higher may lose his position on account of misdeeds and slothful habits. This may result in downward mobility for the individual. The individual mobility is therefore a consequence of the individual's capabilities or lack of it and hence does not influence the prestige of the caste and is least corporate in nature.

ii) Mobility of a minority of families within a caste: This kind of mobility is linked to socio-economic and political aspects of the families. The improvement in status could be result of acquisition of land and education which is further reiterated by emulating the practices of higher caste with regard to dress, lifestyle and ritual. Mobility of this type is not cooperative in nature and can be viewed as **'horizontal mobility'** rather than **'vertical mobility'** which bridges the gap between status distinctions. Burton Stein points out that this trend was predominate in medieval period.

iii) Mobility of a majority of family or group: This kind of mobility is 'corporate' in nature. It involves collective state at prestige, honour, status and is therefore marked by changes in socio-cultural practices regarding purity and pollution. Certain castes improve their positions by discarding practices regarding impure and degrading. Sanskritisation was the chief process which helped these castes to move up in hierarchy and legitimize their claim to the upward mobility.

Q6. Explain the relation between Sanskritisation and Westernisation.

Ans. Sanskritisation: Prof M.N. Srinivas introduced the term sanskritisation to Indian Sociology. The term refers to a process whereby people of lower castes collectively try to adopt upper caste practices and beliefs to acquire higher status. It indicates a process of cultural mobility that is taking place in the traditional social system of India. M.N Srinivas in his study of the Coorg in Karnataka found that lower castes in order to raise their position in the caste hierarchy adopted some customs and practices of the Brahmins and gave up some of their own which were considered to be impure by the higher castes. For example, they gave up meat eating, drinking liquor and animal sacrifice to their deities. They imitated Brahmins in matters of dress, food and rituals. By this they could claim higher positions in the hierarchy of castes within a generation. The reference group in this process is not always Brahmins but may be the dominant caste of the locality. Sanskritisation has occurred usually in groups who have enjoyed political and economic power but were not ranked high in ritual ranking. According to Yogendra Singh the process of sanskritisation is an endogenous source of social change .Mackim Marriot observes that sanskritic rites are often added on to non-sanskritic rites without replacing them. Harold Gould writes, often the motive force behind sanskritisation is not of cultural imitation per se but an expression of challenge and revolt against the socioeconomic deprivations.

Westernisation: Westernisation or **occidentalisation** is a process whereby societies come under or adopt the Western culture in such matters as industry, technology, law, politics, economics, lifestyle, diet, language, alphabet, religion, philosophy, or values. Westernisation has been a pervasive and accelerating influence across the world in the last few centuries. It is usually a two-sided process, in which western influences and interests themselves are joined by a wish of at least parts of the affected society to change towards a more westernized society, in the hope of attaining western life or some aspects of it. Westernisation can also be related to the process of acculturation and/or enculturation. Acculturation refers to the changes that occur within a society or culture when two different groups come into direct continuous contact. After the contact, changes in cultural patterns within either or both cultures are evident. In popular speech, Westernisation can also refer to the effects of Western expansion and colonialism on native societies. For example, natives who have adopted European languages and characteristic Western customs are called acculturated or westernized. Westernisation may be forced or voluntary depending on the situation of the contact.

Different degrees of domination, destruction, resistance, survival, adaptation, and modification of the native culture may follow inter-ethnic contact. In a situation where the native culture experiences destruction as a result of a more powerful outsider, a "shock phase" often is a result from the encounter. This shock phase is especially characteristic during interactions involving expansionist or colonialist eras. During the shock phase, civil repression using military force may lead to a cultural collapse, or ethnocide, which is a culture's physical extinction. According to Conrad Phillip, the westerners "will attempt to remake the native culture within their own image, ignoring the fact that the models of culture that they have created are inappropriate for settings outside of western civilisation"

Q7. Describe the social class and social mobility.

Ans. Significance of Class Mobility: Classes are a very significant and pervasive dimension of stratification and the analysis of mobility along class lines is of crucial significance not only as an end in itself but also on account of its ramifications on other social processes. The extent of mobility has been used as a measure of the "openness" of industrial society and high mobility rates are an indication of the society being characterized by achievement rather than ascription and that it is meritocratic where individuals reap regards on the basis of their personal qualities rather than through inherited wealth and positions. Class mobility is a crucial for the understanding of class formation. Also, study of class mobility can provide indications of life chances of the members of society i.e. the impact of one's class or origin on life chances. Besides this, the responses and reactions of those undergoing mobility are important for analyzing social stability and expansion. Together with these the extent of social mobility has been used as measure of "openness" of industrial society and high mobility rates are in indication of society being characterized by achievement rather than ascription.

Class Mobility and Class Formation: The most crucial aspect of class formation. A large number of scholars have shown keen interest in this area of study. Karl Marx was concerned about the relationship between class formation and action on the hand and the extend of mobility between class positions on the other. He was of the view that proletarianisation was inimical to the process of class formation. Also in advanced capitalist societies, the expansion of middle class in based on recruitment from proletariat. Marx also recognized that a certain degree of immobility is seen as an indispensable prerequisite for the emergence of class consciousness. Similarly, Weber too emphasized on the significance of social mobility for class formation. Weber recognized immobility as a chief determinant for social and cultural identity of a class.

Westergaard and Resler reiterate the crucial part played in shaping of class structure as a recognize the importance of mobility and lack of it as a factor influencing peoples responses to their class situation, class consciousness and class organisation. Like Westergaard and Resler, Giddens too visualizes mobility as process of central importance to class formation. But for Giddens, its importance lies not only in the development of class consciousness and organisation as classes for themselves, it also extends back as recognizable social phenomena i.e. as 'classes in themselves'. Giddens is of the opinion that greater the restrictions on mobility i.e. greater the immobility, greater the chances for formation of distinct identifiable classes in terms of reproduction of life chances, cohesion and class solidarity. Similarly, in a society with constant flux and greater mobility rate, class distinctions are blurred. Mobility is a basic source of class 'structuration' i.e. it is the rate and pattern of mobility that will determine the extent to which classes may be recognized as collectivities of individual or families occupying similar locations. Secondly, the extent of mobility may be taken as significant indicator for prevailing modes of class action. Parkin has argued that class conflict is to an important degree expressed in the formation of strategies of exclusion adopted by advantaged groups. Mobility rates and patterns serve to reveal the effectiveness of exclusion and potential success for solidarism.

Industrialisation and Mobility: In the analysis of mobility processes and patterns that term class in not used strictly in the sense used by Marx or by Weber. Rather class is viewed in terms of occupational groupings because occupation is an aspect of one's merit, education and qualifications and it determines one's status, prestige and salary which is turn influences the consumption pattern and life chances.

Industrialisation has introduced a lot of changes not only in the economy sphere but in all realms of society. Industrial societies are referred to as 'open' societies where the opportunities for mobility are available in plenty. The high rates of mobility in industrial societies are attributed to rapid economic change which necessitates occupational geographical and social mobility to make optimum and efficient use of available talent. It is on this account that Lipset and Zettergerg feel that industrialism creates uniform mobility patterns. Duncan and Blua emphasise on a number of factors generated by industrialisation that have a bearing on mobility patterns. They are of the opinion that industrialisation is connected with growing rationalism which accounts for universalistic criteria for selection and upgrading occupational division of labour, weakening of Kinship and neighbourhood ties.

The emphasis on achievement as a criteria for selection in industrialisation has generated both upward and downward mobility. While it is clear that upward mobility is the result of the reorganisation given to merit, downward mobility is the result of lack of inheritable positions of the elites.

Industrialisation affects the occupational patterns. In every industrialized or industrializing society there is an increase the proportion for professional official managerial and white – collar positions and decline in the proportion of unskilled labour jobs which create a surge of upward mobility. More and more people are required to manage, for administration and for distribution of goods and services.

Education and Mobility: The impetus on achievement and qualifications as determinants of one's merit has resulted in the increasing emphasis on education and training to obtain them. Education has attained a key role in facilitating mobility especially in the industrial societies. The increasing specialisation and division of labour presuppose the existence of qualified personnel who can handle specialized tasks. These specialists whether in the field of industry laws, or medicine are trained and educated in specialized branches of knowledge. These educational and training facilities are open to all in the industrial societies. In the traditional set up, it was imparted to a very small number of people in the guilds which then restricted mobility. Education has been used as a route to attain upward mobility. Educational attainment is a major determinant of career mobility and deeply affects the patterns of inter-generational and intra-generational mobility.

Intergenerational and Intragenerational Mobility: It refers to mobility or shift (upward or downward) vis-à-vis one's parents' class. If a son or daughter of a supervisor becomes an unskilled labour it would **be downward mobility** and if the same person's son or daughter becomes a manager it would amount to **upward mobility.**

One of the first major studies on inter-generational mobility was conducted in England and Wales by Dabid Glass in 1949. It was found that intergenerational mobility was quite high and about two-third of the persons interviewed were in a different occupational category from that of their father. Most of the mobility was short range i.e. people were found in categories close to their father. Upward mobility was more common than downward mobility and was mostly concentrated in the middle levels of the class structure.

Another significant study was conducted in Western Europe and U.S. It was found that cross-class mobility was about 30% for all western industrial societies and that most of the mobility was short range. They found that inter-generational mobility links the effect of family background on the occupational and social placement of individuals. Educational qualifications have a bearing on mobility patterns. Those with higher qualifications were found in non-manual occupations. Also, with similar educational attainments, some of manual workers entered in manual jobs while those of non-manual workers entered manual jobs. Only college education enabled some manual workers to enter in non-manual jobs. According to Lipset and Bendix, poverty, lack of education, lack of exposure is other factors that affect mobility.

Later studies by Hauzer and Hout have confirmed that short range mobility is greater than long range and that mobility is more likely in the middle of socio-economic hierarchy than at its peak. Intra-generational Mobility i.e. where the individual changes social position during his/her career. For example a clerk may be promoted to managerial cadre during his/her career. It has been found that work like mobility is generally less than inter-generational mobility its degree on the first job. Work life mobility decreases with age i.e. it does not increase much after the age of 35 years. Although it is not rule, yet work life mobility is largely upward. It has been found that intra-generational mobility is also linked to educational qualifications and more specific the educational qualifications and more specific the educational training less the scope for mobility. According to Lipset and Bendix self employment is one of the few means of the acquiring higher positions and mobility among manual workers.

Q8. Write a note on the Secularisation.

Ans. Secularisation or **secularisation** generally refers to people of the transformation by which a society migrates from close identification with religious institutions to a more separated relationship. It is also the name given to a general belief about history, namely that the development of society progresses toward modernisation and lessening dependence on religion as religion loses its position of authority. Secularisation has many levels of meaning, both as a theory and a historical process. Social theorists such as Karl Marx, Sigmund Freud, Max Weber, and Émile Durkheim, postulated that the modernisation of society would include a decline in levels of religiosity. Study of this process seeks to determine the manner in which, or extent to which religious creeds, practices and institutions are losing their social significance (if at all). The term also has additional meanings, primarily historical. Applied to church property, secularisation involves the abandonment of goods by the church where it is sold to purchasers after the government seizes the property, which most commonly happens after reasonable negotiations and arrangements are made. In Catholic theology, the term can also denote the permission or authorisation given for an individual (typically clergy, who become secular clergy) to live outside his or her religious colony (monastery), either for a fixed or permanent period. Six uses of the term secularisation in the scientific literature, the first five are more along the lines of 'definitions' while the sixth is more of a 'clarification of use':

1. When discussing **macro social structures**, secularisation can refer to *differentiation*: a process in which the various aspects of society, economic, political, legal, and moral, become increasingly specialized and distinct from one another.

2. When discussing **individual institutions**, secularisation can denote the transformation of a religious into a secular institution. Examples would be the evolution of institutions such as Harvard University from a predominantly religious institution into a secular institution (with a divinity school now housing the religious element illustrating differentiation).

3. When discussing **activities**, secularisation refers to the transfer of activities from religious to secular institutions, such as a shift in provision of social services from churches to the government.

4. When discussing **mentalities**, secularisation refers to the transition from *ultimate* concerns to *proximate* concerns. E.g., individuals in the West are now more likely to moderate their behavior in response to more immediately applicable consequences rather than out of concern for *post-mortem* consequences. This is a personal religious decline or movement toward a secular lifestyle.

5. When discussing **populations**, secularisation refers to broad patterns of societal decline in levels of religiosity as opposed to the individual-level secularisation of (4) above. This understanding of secularisation is also distinct from (1) above in that it refers specifically to religious decline rather than societal differentiation.

6. When discussing **religion**, secularisation can only be used unambiguously to refer to religion in a generic sense. For example, a reference to Christianity is not clear unless one specifies exactly which denominations of Christianity are being discussed.

Q9. Discuss the major factors of social mobility. [Dec 07, Q. 8]

Or

Describe the importance of social environment.

Ans. The factors that Sorokin deemed relevant, the changes that take place in the social environment is the most important. Indirectly in fact, this can influence the demographic factor (for e.g. advances in medicine lengthening life expectancy), as well the talents of individuals (expansion of educational opportunities may allow the discovery of talent, for e.g.) a major factor for mobility is thus social change. Changes of various kinds, economic social, political, legal, technological, and other, have an effect on social mobility. These macro processes of change affect not only mobility, but other aspects of society as well. One of important economic changes that have been unidentified by sociologists as having an impact on social mobility is industrialisation.

Industrialisation and Mobility: Much of the theorizing on mobility has been concerned with the relationship of industrialisation with social mobility. One of the leading arguments in this field, associated with Lipset and Bendix is that industrialisation leads to an increase in mobility over pre industrial rates, and that once all societies have reached a certain level of industrialisation, there is similarly in their rates of social mobility. A different but related thesis is the Convergence thesis, which has been propounded by Kerr and others, that all industrial societies converge towards a common pattern of mobility among other things, like overall patterns of stratification.

Let us discuss first the theory of Lipset and Bendix. In a famous comparative study of a number of European countries and the USA, they sought to test two main hypotheses. First, that once all societies have reached a certain level of industrialisation, they experience higher rates of mobility than pre-industrial societies. Second, the common perception that the USA offers significantly greater opportunities for mobility than the countries of Europe. Their data confirmed the first hypothesis but not the second. Lipset and Bendix, list five main points, the factors of social mobility in industrial societies. These are:

i) Changes in the number of available vacancies,

ii) Different rates of fertility,

iii) Change in the rank accorded to occupations,

iv) Changes in the number of inheritable status positions, and

v) Changes in legal restrictions pertaining to potential opportunities.

Available Vacancies: It is commonly agreed that with industrialisation, there is a shift in the occupational structure from Agriculture, to Industry, and later on, the Services. With the shift to industry, there is a sudden spurt in economy activity, an increase in the numbers of positions available in society. This has been well documented in numerous cases. The migration of people to cities from rural areas in order to work at the new factory jobs is one form of mobility. This has both geographical aspects, as well as a vertical aspect, as usually, city jobs are ranked higher in prestige hierarchies than rural ones. Other examples can also be cited. New white collar positions also come into existence, as for example in the computer profession. All of these result in the expansion in the number of available vacancies. In this way then industrialisation acts as a major factor generating social mobility.

Legal Restrictions: Changes in the political and legal framework can also be an important source of social mobility. The traditional caste order in India assigned individuals to traditional occupations, and certain occupations such as the learned occupations were legally or customarily forbidden to people of low birth. The democratisation of political system, with the concept of all citizens having equal rights under the law, removed barriers to social mobility. At the same time, the introduction of measures such as universal franchise, Panchayati Raj, etc. enabled persons hitherto denied political rights to enter into the political arena, Anand Chakravarti's study of village Devisar in Rajasthan, shows how changes in the wider political system were used for social mobility. Other examples abound.

Related to this is the fact that with industrialisation and its demand for skills hitherto not known, it is unlikely that position will come to be occupied on the basis of traditional specialisations. Thus, there is a reduction in the number of inheritable positions, and far larger increase in the number of positions filled through criteria of achievement. In this the education system plays a major role. It is not the place of this section to discuss the relation of education to stratification, which is done elsewhere in your course, but this is directly related to the increase in non ascriptive positions.

Related to this is the fact that with industrialisation and its demand for skills hitherto not known, it is unlikely that position will come to be occupied on the basis of traditional specialisations. Thus, there is a reduction in the number of inheritable positions, and far large increase in the number of positions filled through criteria of achievement. In this the education system play a major role. It is not place of this section to discuss the relation of education to stratification, which is done elsewhere in your course, but this is directly related to the increase in non ascriptive positions.

Rank and Position: Mobility can also occur without any change in an individual's position, if the ranking of positions changes. For example, in the

USA, one study shows that government positions have enhanced their prestige in the fifties compared to the twenties. Therefore government servants have experienced upward mobility without changing their jobs. This could, of course, lead to downward mobility as well. Due to reranking some occupations would come to be less important in the society and economy than formerly, and thus those occupying that position would be demoted.

The Convergence Hypothesis: A well known and much debated hypothesis regarding the relationship of industrialisation and stratification is the Convergence Hypothesis. This was most clearly articulated by Kerr and others who stated that in today's world, the fact of industrialisation was a common denominator which would impel all industrialized societies towards a common future society which they called pluralistic industrialist society. These societies would have common patterns of stratification as well as commonly patterns of mobility. Mobility would be high, as the demands of industrialisation would necessitate the free and easy mobility of persons from one position to another. This was a functionalist argument in one sense. They also implied that there would be a continuous increase in mobility rates over time.

The argument of Kerr and others has been comprehensively criticized by Goldthorpe. He cities the work of Miller, who, using more data than Lipset and Bendix, shows that in fact there is a lack of convergence between the rates of mobility of industrial societies. This shows that perhaps it is not industrialisation per se, but also other factors, such as cultural factors, the education system etc., which also have a bearing on social mobility. Goldthorpe himself holds the view that it is the political and ideological differences that are important between the socialist, which Kerr and Company include under one umbrella.

There is a superficial similarly, between the argument of Kerr and that of Lipset and Bendix, but in fact the latter's argument simply states that after a certain level of industrialisation, there is a rise in mobility rates. A continuous increase is not predicted, nor also a convergence. We may also note here that Sorokin did not predict either a continuous increase in mobility rates over time, nor did he predict a fall. He infact believed that industrialized societies are not completely open, nor are pre-industrial ones completely closed. If at all, he held to a cyclical view of the rates of mobility, which would rise and fall.

Q10. Show how the demographic factor has an effect on social mobility. [June 08, Q. 13]

Ans. Statistical socio-economic characteristics or variables of a population, such as age, sex, education level, income level, marital status, occupation, religion, birth rate, death rate, average size of a family, average age at marriage.

A census is a collection of the demographic factors associated with every member of a population.

In general, it has been observed that the birth rate of higher groups is lower than that of lower groups. Even though the death rates of the lower groups are higher, the net reproduction rate is such that there is usually some room at the top for members of lower groups. Perray, for e.g., found that out of 215 noble lineages in a certain region of France in 12000 only 149 were left a century later. In general, he found the life span of such lineages to be only 3 to 4 generations. They were then replaced by lineages of non noble birth, or by collateral lineages. Similarly, Alex Inkeles, in his study of stratification in the Soviet Union in the middle of this century, attributes the very high rates of mobility there partly to the loss of lives in the war, necessitating a high degree of mobility. The other important reason, of course is rapid industrialisation.

This is true not only in terms of higher and lower groups, but also in terms of urban and rural populations. The latter usually have higher net reproduction rates. Despite this, urban populations have been growing much more rapidly than rural ones. This is due largely to migration, rather than due to a natural increase in population.

There a concomitant of this has been the emergence of old age homes, hospitals for looking after terminally ill patients, etc. From the mobility angle, this means that new kind of vacancies are created which must then be filled.

Thus, the demographic factor definitely has a bearing on social mobility, but is itself not a purely biological phenomenon, as social factors in general have a bearing on demography. Mandelbaum and others have for example written on how cultural factors such as son preference have affected population structures.

Q11. Define Embourgeoisement. What is its relation to social mobility? [June 09, Q. 4][June 08, Q. 7]

Or

Discuss about the Political consequences of social mobility.

Ans. Embourgeoisement is the process of migration of individuals into the bourgeoisie as a result of their own efforts or collective action, such as that taken by unions in the US and elsewhere in the 1930 through 1960s that established middle class status for factory workers and others that would not have been considered middle class by their employments, allowing increasing numbers of what might traditionally be classified as working class people to assume the lifestyle and individualistic values of the so-called middle classes and hence reject commitment to collective social and economic goals. The opposite process is "proletarianisation". Charles E. Hurst describes this change to be a result of the post-industrialisation of society, in which there are far fewer manual labor jobs, which is the main classification of blue-collar work.

With post-industrialisation, former upper-level blue-collar workers are moving to white-collar work because of the decreased availability and prestige of manual labor jobs. Even when their actual jobs do not change, their lifestyles based on their job situation often change into a lifestyle that according to Mayer and Buckley, more closely resembles the lower-middle class than the rest of the lower blue-collar workers. The result of this idea of embourgeoisement is that more people are incorporated into the middle-class. As a result, there is decreased class consciousness and declining working class solidarity. This in turn could lead to less group action among the lower class if trying to get more rights or changes within their job field.

Heterogeneity of the Working Class: Unlike Marx's prediction of increasing homogeneity of working class with the progress of technology, some sociologists have been seen a definite reversal of the trend. In advanced and advancing industrial societies, due to progress in science and technology, in its application to industry, are influencing the very character and content of the working class. According to Ralf Dahrendorf, the working class has become increasingly heterogeneous or dissimilar. Due to changes in technology, complex machines are being introduced, which require well-trained and qualified workers to work on them, to maintain them and do repairs on them when necessary. Not just simple minders(a woman who looks after babies in her own home while their parents are working) of machines of yesteryears but technically trained and hence highly skilled workmen are required. (Even agriculture no longer is a hard, back-breaking task, irrespective of weather conditions. Increasing mechanisation of agriculture has transformed its character, and nature of work done. Now it is counted as one of the industries constituting an economy of the society). Therefore according to Ralf Dahrendorf, on the basis of nature of work required in various industries, workers can be divided into three distinct levels-unskilled, semi-skilled and skilled workers. This classification of workers is accompanied by differences in economic rewards (i.e., wages) and prestige accorded to each of them. Thus, skilled workers enjoy higher wages, more fringe benefits, greater job security and so higher prestige than the other two category of workers. Dahrendorf believes that in the twentieth century, due to mobility among workers, it has become meaningless to speak of working class, rather there has been a 'decomposition of labour' into various divisions.

Many sociologists like K. Roberts, F.M. Martin and others have negated this aspect of heterogeneity of the working class as a consequence of social mobility in the industrial societies of today. Rather, they have suggested, through the findings of various researchers, that the manual workers share similar market situation and similar life-chances. The workers are also aware of their shared class identity due to common class interests. Therefore, they can be distinguished from other classes in the society but their distinct sub-culture. Hence, to speak of heterogeneity of working class as an impact of social mobility is a fallacy. The working class do form a social class, and has not disintegrated into distinct categories.

The Enlarged and Fragmented Middle Classes: Though the middle class was never a cohesive social group in its origin, yet it was too small in numbers to actually make its presence felt in a decisive manner in the economy and polity of a society. In the earlier days it usually comprised of the lowermost officials of the state, the petty tradesmen, or the exceptionally few peasants who owned a free plot of land. But in the nineteenth century, with the expansion of commercial interests of various nations and the State playing an increasingly active role in governance, led to a demand for educationally and technically qualified personnel who could be mobile geographically as well aspirationally. Thus, the on-going process of expansion of the middle class since the mid-nineteenth century onwards has once again proved the fallacy of Marx's prediction that the middle strata would disappear (be proletaranized). Instead, Max Weber, A. Giddens, Frank Parkin etc. see the rise and expansion of the 'middle class', inherent in the very logic of industrial economy. Each has given a classification of classes. According to Weber, the white-collar middle class expands rather than contracts as capitalism develops, because the capitalist enterprises and the bureaucratic organisation of modern nation state requires the services of large number of administrative staff. As capitalism advances, the enterprises undergo vast changes-there is separation of ownership and control-leading to increase in number and role of manager and administrators. Therefore for Weber middle class would comprise of 'property less white-collar workers' whose market situation and life chances depend upon skills and services offered by them. Secondly, 'the pretty bourgeoisie' i.e., the small property owners who due to competition from large capitalists take to white-collar professions. Anthony Giddens identifies three major classes in advanced capitalist society, of which the middle class is based on the possession of educational and technical qualifications.

· Higher professionals, managerial and administrative-comprising of judges, barristers, lawyers, doctors, architects, planners, university lectures, accountants, scientists and engineers.

· Lower professionals, managerial and administrative-comprising of school teachers, nurses, social workers, librarians etc.

· Routine white-collar and minor supervisory-comprising of clerks, foremen etc.

Each sub-division occupies different positions not only in the occupational reward system, but are also accorded differential prestige and the corresponding status in the social scale of a particular society.

Not only are these accorded differential prestige and status, but they perceive their market situation and life-chances to be non-analogous. Therefore from a study of 'images of class', Robets, Cook Clarke and Semenoff came to the conclusion that the middle class is itself increasingly divided into a number of different strata, each with a distinctive view of its place in the stratification system. So to speak of a common class identification of the middle white-collar middle class needs to be discounted. The diversity of class images, market situations, life chances and interest within the white-collar group suggests that the middle class is becoming increasingly fragmented (Kenneth Robberts). Hence, to speak of a single social group as a middle class is debate, rather it is more meaningful to conceptualize it as a plurality of 'middle-classes'.

Rate of Social Mobility and Class Solidarity: Rate of Social mobility is the amount of movement from one strata to another in a particular society. In the contemporary society characterized by industrial economy, the rate of social mobility is considerably higher than the earlier societies. The reason behind this high rate of social mobility is the criteria of achievement based on merit, ability, talent, ambition and hard work, which determines a person position in the society. Class solidarity is the degree of cohesiveness of a particular class in the society. Therefore, the rate of social mobility has important consequences for class solidarity. According to many sociologists, the rate of social mobility is indirectly proportional to social solidarity i.e., if the rate of social mobility is low, class solidarity and cohesion will be high and vice versa. So for Anthony Giddens, if the rate of social mobility is low, most individuals will remain in their class of origin. This will lead to common life experiences over generations, formation of distinctive class subcultures, and aspirations to identify with the next higher class. Thus, sounding a death knell for class solidarity.

Even Marx believed that a high rate of social mobility would tend to weaken class solidarity. Classes would become increasingly heterogeneous as their members cease to share similar backgrounds. Distinctive class sub-cultures would disintegrate as norms, attitudes and values would change not only over generations but within a single generation for a particular class. Therefore, for Marx, the potential for class consciousness and the intensity of class conflict would be considerably reduced. Whereas, according to Ralf-Dahrendorf, due to high rate of social mobility in the contemporary industrial societies, the nature of class conflict has changed. Since, nowadays societies give primacy to the criteria to achievements, and he has become open, there is an increased competition among individuals of the same class for higher positions in the occupational reward structure. Therefore there is a reduction in class solidarity and intensity of class conflict.

Simultaneously, even Goldthorpe and Llewellyn have discounted class solidarity amongst the middle class. Due to heterogeneity of social background of its members, it thus lacks cohesion i.e., low classiness, and the image of middle class as a single social group is negated, akin to Kenneth Robert's image of 'fragmented' middle class.

The Image of Social Order: The effect of social mobility on social order has been the theme of many writers since Durkheim wrote about the concept of 'anomie', meaning, disruptive impact of unlimited aims and aspirations of people in a society unable to fulfill all these demands. Durkheim recognized that social mobility might have negative consequences, both for the society as well as the individual, in his classic study 'Suicide'. According to him, earlier societies maintained strict restraints on its stratification system such that an individual living in a particular society knew the legitimate limit of his aspirations. But when the stratification system is no longer subjective to these restraints, both – sudden growth of power and wealth, and economic disasters lead to situations which are potentially disastrous for the moral order of the society. Therefore, not only during periods of upheavals, like that of economic depression (as there would be declassification) but also, during a rapid rise in fortune or power (as there would be no ceiling on ambitions) have dissociative impact on the social integration of a system, leading to suicides by individuals due to undermining of personal integration. Thus, exhibiting anomic tendencies.

In similar vein, Lipset and Bendix and Germani have emphasized that social mobility have different consequences in different social structures. Social mobility is more likely to be disruptive in its effects in traditional societies, which have an 'ascriptive' system of stratification, with high degree of status rigidity and hence inadequate preparation for mobility. This is based on the assumption that the constraints of 'class of origin' in a traditional society, leave the individual isolated and anxious about his social status and identity. While in an 'industrial' society, marked by openness of its stratification system. Social mobility is a normal process fovourable for the maintenance of the system.

Even P.A. Sorokin, talking about 'Social and Cultural Mobility' (1927) too wrote about the disruptive consequences of social mobility. He believed that social mobility contributes to instability of the social order, cultural fluidity, diminishing solidarity. It may also lead to exhaustion of elite's and therefore decay of nations. It facilitates atomisation and superficiality in personality, skepticism, cynicism and misoneism. According to Sorokin social mobility plays a vital role in diminishing intimacy, sensitivity, increases mental strain and accompanying diseases. Increase in isolation, loneliness, restlessness may lead to a hunt for transitory sensual pleasures, which further leads to disintegration of morals in the society. Sorokin also attempted to balance out the negative impact of social mobility by putting forward positive influences of social mobility for the society as well as the individual. In this regard he talked about 'better and more adequate distribution of individuals' such that the best men at the top reduce narrow-mindedness and occupationally hazardous idiosyncratic behaviour; it facilitates economic prosperity and a rapid social progress, thereby enhancing the positive consequences of social mobility for the social order.

The means-in the sphere of work, the inherent virtue of work has lost all its meaning and given way to 'open portrayal of being successful' through consumption of power and property, has become the most important criteria of social mobility. This has led to denigration of work and thereby dignity of all tasks but few which are high income generating ones. This 'denial of work' has negative consequences for social integration. Further, rapid social mobility leads to imbalance of institutions like family, kin groups, religion, political and educational institutions, which are now measured against the yardstick of income and wealth generation. This has effect on the changing definitions and parameters of these institutions now based solely on their utility value. Thus, seriously endangering the major functions traditionally performed by them. In addition, not only are the various social institutions being undermined by the encroaching impact of social mobility, even the human element in terms of the older generations, steeped in the customs and traditions of the bygone era, are looks upon with vituperative contempt by the new-mobile segments of the population. This has been proved by the mushrooming of 'old age homes' not only in the so-called advanced Western societies, but nowadays even in the more tolerant societies of the East. Any society which wallows in its past indiscriminately or equally indiscriminately rejects it, will be the loser. Hence, a society should aim to achieve a balance between traditional and modernity to offset the negative impact of rapid social mobility. Further, Melvin Tumin laments the decline of 'social criticism' under the impact of 'a cult of gratitude' among significant sections of the mobile population. Even the intellectuals who are supposed to be upholders of creative criticism of the social order, responsibility for actively pursuing open and sharp debate for the maintenance of an open society, have not been spared by the vituperative impact of social mobility. Their ideas have now become commodities for sale in the aid of populist measures of the State. They derive their value from their marketability. There is a 'depreciation of taste and culture... when marketability become the criteria of aesthetic worth'. Consumption of art and culture is determined by elite fads and fashion. This process portends a doom for democratic tendencies in a pluralist society, as everything and everybody, even ideas give way to the advancing authority of capital and its social correlates. The ethnic groups become converted into status-competing hierarchies instead of being cultural groups. Thus, diminishing the possibility of genuine cultural pluralism in a diverse society. When such a dissociative image of social order is presented, then the individual is lost in the welter of rapidity of social change. Hence, engendering insecurity leading to alienation, extreme individualism, suicide and many similar processes disruptive in their consequences.

The portrayal of society order engendered by rapid social mobility as given above is extremely pessimistic. For some thinkers like Peter M. Blau this pessimism in its extreme is unfounded. He tries to give reasons for the changing social order in the dilemmas of acculturation faced by the socially mobile. Blau argues that a socially mobile individual faced dilemma in choosing between the values, attitudes, behaviour and friends of his class of origin, or the class of destination. It is this dilemma which leads to various observed consequences of social mobility like-social disintegration, insecurity or over conformity by the social mobile individuals. Therefore, Blau has not really challenged the dissociative image of social order, but though his 'acculturation hypothesis' tried to assign reasons for social change engendered by social mobility.

In contrast to the dismal picture of the social order portrayed by the exponents of 'dissociative hypothesis' (as explained above), Frank Parkin and C.J. Richardson in Britain, and H.L. Wilensky and H. Edwards in America examined class in capitalist society. Frank Parkin studying the effect of high rate of upward mobility came to the conclusion that, it acted as a 'political safety-valve'. Upward mobility provides opportunities for the fulfillment of aspirations of individuals to reach higher status and pay. As a result, it prevents frustrations from developing, which in the absence of upward mobility if intensified might threaten the social fabric. Usually, those who move out of working class are more preoccupied with acculturing themselves to the new norms and values of the higher class, rather than bothering about people left behind. Thus, weakening the intensity of class, rather than bothering about people left behind. Thus, weakening the intensity of class, rather than bothering about people left behind. Thus, weakening the intensity of class conflict between classes in a capitalist society. On the other hand, H.L. Wilensky and H. Edwards examined the consequences of 'downward mobility'. According to them people who actually move down in social hierarchy from middle class to working class, usually do not accept their lowly position, and so do not adapt themselves to the norms values of the working class. They always aspire to regain their lost status. Hence, engendering conservatism in their outlook. Thus, C.J. Richardson's study of social mobility in Britain, concludes that neither upward social mobility, nor downward social mobility arouse feeling of relative deprivation or dissatisfaction with their present lot, or has may disruptive consequences for the social order. Hence, both upward and downward mobility tend to reinforce status quo. Both tend to become even more conservative in their social and political outlook, one (the upwardly mobile) in the hope of restoration of their former status. Thus, none of them actually threaten the stability or integrity of a society.

Both the images of social order are based on actual and impressionistic studies of various societies. How far can they be wholly applied to a particular society, is debatable. But, we can safely presume that in reality a mixture of element from both the images obtain. The consequences of social mobility are neither wholly pessimistic, nor overly positive. Thus, the image of social order of present societies will lie in between the two poles of social order in a continuum.

Q12. Discuss about the political consequences of social mobility.
[June 09, Q. 4]

Ans. Political consequences of social mobility: Income inequality is one of the most important consequences of social class and mobility. Although class status is not a causal factor for income, there is consistent data that show those in higher classes have higher incomes than those in lower classes. This inequality still persists when controlling for occupation. The conditions at work vary greatly depending on class. Those in the upper-middle class and middle-class enjoy greater freedoms in their occupations. They generally are more respected, enjoy more diversity, and are able to exhibit some authority. Those in lower classes tend to feel more alienated and have lower work satisfaction overall. The physical conditions of the workplace differ greatly between classes. While middle-class workers may "suffer alienating conditions" or "lack of job satisfaction", blue-collar workers are the ones who have to worry about health hazards, injury, and even death. In the more social sphere, class has direct consequences on lifestyle. Lifestyle includes tastes, preferences, and a general style of living. These lifestyles could quite possibly affect educational attainment, and therefore status attainment. Class lifestyle also affects how one raises his or her children. For example, a working-class person is more likely to raise their child to be working class and middle-class children are more likely to be raised to be middle-class. This perpetuates the idea of class for future generations.

The order elites would make the newly-mobile aspirants loses faith in the fairness of the social process and make them question the openness or democratic ethos of their culture. Thus, rejected, they would create alternate' symbols of status like various ethnic associations (e.g. Dalit Associations in India), political parties (e.g. Samajwadi party or the Rashtriya Janata Dal) residential sites (e.g. Ambedkar Nagar) Colleges, schools, recreational facilities etc. this process would be further reflected in the voting behaviour of both the older elite and the nouveaux riches. The older elites trying to consolidate and reinforcing their traditional aspects of culture would become extremely conservative in their political outlook.

Therefore 'extreme rightism' is seen as a response to insecurity about social position. While on the other hand, the newly-mobile aspirants would support any faction of political party which opposes the older elite. Thus, the strains introduced by mobility aspirations will predispose individuals towards accepting more extreme political views.

More often than not, social mobility gives rise of 'status discrepancy' such that mobility in one' sphere need not necessarily lead to mobility all the other spheres. For instances, S.M. Lipset studying political behaviour in the province of Saskatchewan (Canada) found that leaders of the Socialist Party were either businessmen or professionals. Though they belonged to high occupational and income category, yet they were considered low in the social hierarchy, as they were largely of non-Anglo Saxon origin. Whereas, the Liberal and Conservative Parties were dominated by the middle class. Though lower in income and occupational category, they belonged to higher social class, as they were from Anglo-Saxon origin, (they formed 90% of the population). Even when the higher status, 'upper class' Anglo-Saxon population did not economically exploit the non-Anglo-Saxon group, yet they felt socially deprived of the privileges, which usually accompany high occupational and income category. Thus, the cleavage between the two groups was very sharp. The contradictions in their status positions were such that, the minority group (i.e., the non-Anglo-Saxon group) preferred to ideologically align themselves with the political party which was opposed to the 'upper class' (i.e., the Anglo-Saxon group). Thus, portraying extreme political views due to frustrated aspirations, brought about by status discrepancy.

In a similar vein, Robert Michels has analysed European Socialism before the First World War. The Jews had come to occupy a prominent position in the European socialist movement, because, even when legally free, they were still discriminated against socially all over Eastern Europe and Germany. Even though they were economically rich, no corresponding social or political advantages were ensured by the prevailing system. Only the socialist's utopia assuaged their feelings of hurt and rejection. This attitude of the Jews has been evident in the recent times also. For example, in Scandinavia, where there is relatively little anti-Semitism (i.e. Anti-Jewish feelings) and the Jews are progressively achieving a higher social class position, it is expected that they would not exhibit leftist political orientation to the same extent as earlier. Thus, discrepancy in status may lead to many permutation and combinations of social class statuses and their ideological alignments in the political sphere. Therefore one can see any of the following combinations actually operating depending upon the social, economic, statistical and political circumstances:

i) Political orientation to the left, when a group's social class position is lower then its occupational or economic position, in spite of the fact under normal circumstances, the group would have conservative outlook.

ii) Political orientation to the left, when a social group's deprived position normally orients it to take radical position against the economically and sociality dominant group.

iii) Political orientation to the right, when a group's social class position is higher then their occupational and economic position.

iv) Political orientation to the right, when for example, nouveaux riches are sometimes even more conservative than the older elite, as they seek to move up in the social hierarchy and be accepted by the order elite.

v) Political orientation to the extreme right, when a group's higher social class position if felt to be threatened by the incursion of emerging mobiles.

vi) Political orientation to the left, when a group's old but declining upper class status makes it more liberal in its outlook.

Mosca had even seen the emergence of a new social class-the middle class-in modern democracies, as a product of social mobility. He sees middle class as the intermediate strata from which the ruling elite usually recruit fresh talent to fill their vacant ranks. In this manner ambitious and talented individuals in the lower strata are able to fulfil their aspirations. Thus, as can be seen from above, the political consequence of social mobility is important in their implications for the processual development of society as a whole.

Question Papers

ESO-14: SOCIETY AND STRATIFICATION
June, 2007

***Note:** Answer **five** questions, **two** each from Sections A and B and **one** from Section C. All parts of Section C are **compulsory**.*

SECTION A

*Answer any **two** of the following questions.*

Q1. Describe caste as a system of social stratification. Your answer must include
(a) Demographic features of caste
(b) Social mobility
(c) Principles of hierarchy
Refer to Chapter-1, Q.No.-1

Q2. Describe the functionalist theory of stratification. You should include
(a) Parsons' approach
(b) Davis and Moore's theory
(c) A critique of the functionalist theory
Refer to Chapter-2, Q.No.-3 & Q.No.-4

Q3. Discuss the various dimensions of social mobility. Your answer should include
(a) Intra-generational and inter-generational mobility
(b) Horizontal mobility
(c) Downward and upward social mobility
Refer to Chapter-8, Q.No.-2

Q4. Explain the status of women in India. Your answer must include
(a) Women's marginal position
(b) Measures for raising the status of women
(c) Policies for women's welfare
Refer to Chapter-6, Q.No.-8

SECTION B

*Answer any **two** of the following questions.*

Q5. Discuss the status of children in India.
Refer to Chapter-6, Q.No.-9

Q6. Discuss the concepts of varna and jati, with suitable illustrations.
Refer to Chapter-5, Q.No.-1

Q7. Explain the features of class in industrial societies.
Refer to Chapter-7, Q.No.-2

Q8. Discuss the critique of Dumont's theory of caste.
Refer to Chapter-5, Q.No.-2

SECTION C

*Answer **all** parts of this question.*

Q9. (a) Match the following:

(i) Attributional theory	**1. Karl Marx**
(ii) Interactional theory	**2. G.S. Ghurye**
(iii) Functionalist theory	**3. Talcott Parsons**
(iv) Conflict theory	**4. M. Marriot**

Ans. (i) 2
(ii) 4
(iii) 3
(iv) 1

(b) How does Max Weber define the concept of class? Explain in about 50 words.
Refer to Chapter-2, Q.No.-1

ESO-14: SOCIETY AND STRATIFICATION
December, 2007

***Note:** Answer **five** questions, **two** each from Sections A and B and **one** from Section C. All parts of Section C are **compulsory**.*

SECTION A

*Answer any **two** of the following questions.*

Q1. Outline the dialectical approach to the study of social stratification. Your answer must include:
(a) General features of the dialectical approach
(b) Bourgeoisie and Proletariate
(c) Appraisal of dialectical approach
(d) Dehrendorf's critical appraisal
Refer to Chapter-1, Q.No.-4

Q2. Explain the role of social institutions in gender identity formation. Your answer must include:
(a) Caste
(b) Religion
(c) Marriage Regulations
Refer to Chapter-4, Q.No.-6

Q3. Critically discuss the functionalist theory of stratification. Your answer must include:
(a) Value Consensus and Stratification
(b) Contributions of Kingsley Davis and Wilbert Moore
Refer to June-2007, Q.No.-2 and Refer to Chapter-2, Q.No.-3

Q4. Discuss the synthesis between the functionalist and conflict approaches to the study of stratification. Your answer should include a discussion on
(a) Berghe's Synthesis
(b) Luhmann's Systems Theory
(c) Lenski's Power and Privilege
Refer to Chapter-2, Q.No.-7

SECTION B

*Answer any **two** of the following questions.*

Q5. Outline the attributional and interactional approaches to the explanation of caste.
Refer to Chapter-5, Q.No.-6

Q6. Describe the Backward Classes Movements in India. Substantiate your answer with examples.
Refer to Chapter-6, Q.No.-3

Q7. Describe the main characteristics of the middle classes in India.
Refer to Chapter-7, Q.No.-5

Q8. Discuss the major factors of social mobility.
Refer to Chapter-8, Q.No.-9

SECTION C

*Answer **all** parts of this question.*

Q9. (a) What do you understand by 'women's empowerment'? Give an example to indicate what you mean.
Refer to Chapter-4, Q.No.-8

(b) Define ethnicity in about 50 words.
Refer to Chapter-3, Q.No.-1

ESO-14: SOCIETY AND STRATIFICATION
June, 2008

Note: The question paper has ***three*** *sections. Attempt the questions as instructed in each section.*

SECTION I

Answer any ***two*** *of the following questions in about 500 words each.*

Q1. "Rituals and power are important dimensions of caste." Discuss.

Ans. According to Andre Beteille "Caste has been the fundamental institution of traditional India". Indeed it is so basic to Hindu society that M.N. Srinivas can say, "it is impossible to detach Hindustan from the caste system." But the non-Hindu communities in India are also pervaded by caste, for although Christians, Muslims and Sikhs were religiously opposed to such an ideal of "institutional inequality", they presented no viable alternative social organisation in the Indian context, and so ended up being acculturated into the caste system. One would naturally expect to find the fullest expression of this institution in Hindu society where it originated, but other communities on the sub-continent have closely related if more latent expressions of the same.

Caste is used in two different senses and these give rise to two divergent interpretations of its origin and meaning. Leave notes that "As an ethnographic category it refers exclusively to a system of social organisation peculiar to Hindu India, but as a sociological category it may denote almost any kind of class structure of exceptional rigidity." The first conceptualizes caste in socio-cultural terms and stresses its unique ritual aspects in Indian society; the second analyses caste in terms of power relations prevalent in the political economy of a society. The first approach has tended to stress the attributional or cultural dimension of caste and so restricts the term to the Indian context, as opposed to the second, which emphasizes the interactional or structural one, that can be generalized beyond.

Anthropology has been inclined to the first sense. Here caste is defined with a list of cultural traits that supposedly from a syndrome. Hutton enumerates seven such characteristics: endogamy, restrictions on commensality, hierarchical grading of castes, the concept of pollution related to food, sex and ritual, association with traditional occupations, hereditary ascription of caste status, the prestige of the Brahman.

However, this procedure has been rightly criticized by Dumont for such lists give us " a combination of distinct features, a *combination* which apparently springs from an historical accident." And so it does not get us beyond a purely historical explanation of caste. Going beyond this, then some anthropologists have attempted a 'structural analysis' to get to the 'deep structural' principle from which the traits derive.

Hocart was the first to single out the principle of hierarchy in relation to caste. He held it to be essentially a religious hierarchy deriving directly from religious ceremony.

Modifying this somewhat and elaborating it further, Dumont concludes to the opposition between the pure and the impure that is constitutive of this ritual hierarchy and the separation of the *jatis* the local sub-caste.

Sociology, on the other hand, in search for a more general and comparative scheme in which to conceptualise caste has interpreted the phenomena with the stratification model. Stratification systems are seen to lie on a continuum from close to open. Thus, Lynch considers that the "the differences between a real class system and a real caste system is based upon which end of the continuum, form mutually exclusive to cross-cutting status-sets, they approach." The classic Weberian model of class, status and power has provided a more adequate and more frequently used schema for a sociological understanding of caste. Here caste is interpreted as a special kind of status group based on the principle of a "clan charisma" that is inherited. The proliferation of castes is accounted for by "caste schism", that may derive from allows for the interaction of the different orders. Hence while caste differentiation is primarily religious, political power cooperates to legitimate it and economic interests help to sustain it. The fact that the caste phenomena are not reduced to a single dimension provides a take-off point for a multivariate analysis that has been used so extensively in stratification studies.

Q2. Discuss the concept of social movement with reference to tribes in India.

Refer to Chapter-3, Q.No.-4

Q3. What is meant by women's empowerment? Illustrate your answer with examples.

Refer to Chapter-4, Q.No.-8

Q4. Describe religious ethnicity in the context of Punjab.

Refer to Chapter-3, Q.No.-8

SECTION II

*Answer any **four** of the following questions in about 250 words each.*

Q5. Discuss Lenski and Berghe's attempt at synthesis of stratification theories.

Refer to Chapter-2, Q.No.-7

Q6. Discuss caste with reference to hierarchy and conflict.
Refer to Chapter-1, Q.No.-6

Q7. Define "embourgeoisement". What is its relation to social mobility?
Refer to Chapter-8, Q.No.-11

Q8. Give Marx's view on social stratification with reference to class.
Refer to Chapter-2, Q.No.-2

Q9. "Can ethnicity be the basis for social stratification?" Discuss.
Refer to Chapter-3, Q.No.-3

Q10. Outline the Constitutional provisions for the upliftment of the Dalits.
Refer to Chapter-6, Q.No.-1

Q11. How can caste identity be established according to the interactional approach?
Refer to Chapter-5, Q.No.-6

Q12. Show the role of purity and pollution in caste hierarchy.
Refer to Chapter-5, Q.No.-3

SECTION III

*Answer any **two** of the following questions in about 100 words each.*

Q13. Show how the demographic factor has an effect on social mobility.
Refer to Chapter-8, Q.No.-10

Q14. What is a "mode of production"?
Refer to Chapter-7, Q.No.-14

Q15. Write a note on gender and stratification.
Refer to Chapter-1, Q.No.-10

Q16. What is meant by marginalized group?
Refer to Chapter-7, Q.No.-10

ESO-14: SOCIETY AND STRATIFICATION
December, 2008

Note: *The question paper has three sections. Attempt the questions as instructed in each section.*

SECTION I

*Answer any **two** of the following questions in about 500 words each.*

Q1. Describe functionalist approach to social stratification.
Refer to Chapter-1, Q.No.-5

Q2. Give the views of Coser and Dahrendorf on social class.
Refer to Chapter-2, Q.No.-6

Q3. Discuss tribal social stratification systems in the context of North-East India.
Refer to Chapter-3, Q.No.-5

Q4. Examine the impact of economic development and technology on women workers.
Refer to Chapter-4

SECTION II

*Answer any **four** of the following questions in about 250 words each.*

Q5. In what ways are purity and pollution central to caste hierarchy?
Refer to June-2008, Q.No.-12

Q6. Write about the changing status of marginalized groups.
Refer to Chapter-7, Q.No.-10

Q7. Explain Durkheim's view on the division of labour.
Ans. Division of labour
One of the oldest concepts in the social sciences. It denotes any stable organisation, coordinating individuals, or groups carrying out different, but integrated activities. Its first and most celebrated use was in classical political

economy, the precursor to modern economics. According to Adam Smith, division of productive labour greatly increases the wealth-creating capacity of a society. Unrestrained by government or administrative rules, the free market encourages producers to specialize in activities where they have a natural advantage. By specializing they benefit from greater dexterity, more efficient use of materials and time, and from mechanisation. Simultaneously, the hidden hand of competition penalizes insufficiently specialized (by implication inefficient) producers, and encourages the prudent (rational) exchange of goods and services. For Emile Durkheim, the principal interest of the division of labour is its moral consequences, that is, its effect on the underlying solidarity of the society, which should restrain individual egoism, ruthlessness, and license. Although historians and anthropologists have subsequently questioned the idea that premodern societies lacked a division of labour, Durkheim argued that traditional societies are integrated by so-called mechanical solidarity, in which emphasis is placed on the values and cognitive symbols common to the clan or tribe. Individuals and institutions are thus relatively undifferentiated. Modern societies, he claimed, require the development of organic solidarity, in which beliefs and values emphasize individuality, encourage specialist talents in individuals, and the differentiation of activities in institutions. But although the economic division of labour may have initiated such a way of life, by itself the unregulated market loosens restraints on individual desires, undermines the establishment of social trust, and produces abnormal forms of the division of labour. This is the source of his celebrated concept of anomie, and of the forced division of labour associated with class and political conflict. Full organic solidarity will require appropriate education; legal restraint on inheritance and other unjust contracts; and intermediary institutions to integrate individuals into occupational and industrial life.

Q8. What is social mobility? Discuss with appropriate examples.
Refer to Chapter-8, Q.No.-4

Q9. Outline the agrarian class structure in India.
Refer to Chapter-7, Q.No.-1

Q10. Describe the attributional approach to the study of caste.
Refer to Chapter-5, Q.No.-6

Q11. Discuss the formation of gender identity in society.
Refer to Chapter-4, Q.No.-4

Q12. Write briefly on linguistic ethnicity and the state.
Refer to Chapter-3, Q.No.-10

SECTION III

*Answer any **two** of the following questions in about 100 words each.*

Q13. Write briefly about the salient features of Tribal Social Movements in North-East India.
Refer to Chapter-3, Q.No.-6

Q14. What does Coser mean by the function of conflict?
Refer to Chapter-2, Q.No.-5

Q15. Delineate the attributes of caste in society.
Refer to Dec-06, Q.No.-9(b)

Q16. Outline briefly the system of jajmani exchanges.
Refer to Chapter-5, Q.No.-8

ESO-14: SOCIETY AND STRATIFICATION
June, 2009

Note: *The question paper has* ***three*** *sections. Attempt the questions as instructed in each section.*

SECTION I

Answer any ***two*** *of the following questions in about 500 words each:*

Q1. Discuss the functionalist theory of satisfaction.
Refer to June-2007, Q.No.-2

Q2. How is gender identities formed? Explain.
Refer to Chapter-4, Q.No.-4

Q3.Discribe the politico-economic emergence of the Backward Classes Movements.
Refer to Chapter-6, Q.No.-3

Q4. What are the consequences of social mobility? Discuss.
Refer to Chapter-8, Q.No.-11 and Q.No.-12

Ans. Social-Psychological Consequences of Social Mobility

Inequality being the hallmark of stratification system, distributes rewards and privileges differentially amongst its inhabitants. Modern industrial societies usually organised around the democratic ethos undergo immense ideological pressures from all sides, as they are supposed to be upholders of 'opportunity for all'. It is this criteria of 'opportunity of all' which enjoins upon all the members of that society to aspire for a position in the 'sun' i.e. the higher-most, most sought after positions in the society. But, just as the most sought after goods are scarce and therefore valuable, similarly, the most sought after positions too are scarce and hence valuable. Not everybody can occupy them. It is after a long process of selection, starting from primary education till a person actually reaches the coveted position. Chances of his being rejected are built into the system. Therefore, the people who do not reach their desired goals usually suffer from mental strain, evoked by their denial of self-worth. In many cases it may also lead to rejection of the 'self' i.e., 'self-hatred'- acceptance of lower conception of self-worth. This according to Veblen, acts as a barrier to the possibility of self enhancement. This rejected image of self-worth is usually found in the individuals of lower-status minority groups, e.g. Jews. But, this self-hatred is difficult to maintain as self worth reasserts itself, and culminates into social action which may have ramifications for the society as a whole. The social consequences of a predominantly psychological phenomenon can usually be seen in the following three processes as put forward by S.M. Lipset and H.L.Zetterberg.

i) Some people may reject the dominant values of the upper classes. In such cases, rejection may take the form of lower-class religious values which morally deny the values accorded to wealth and power.

ii) Secondly, another form of rejection of dominant values and assertion of self-worth could take the form of rebellious 'Robin Hood' bands, or formal revolutionary, or social reform movements.

iii) Finally, individuals may make efforts to improve their status through legitimate or illegitimate means.

Thus, inequality inheres in itself an instability in the social order. This aspect of instability being such a pervasive phenomenon in the modern industrial society has negative consequences for the individual personality as well.

Hence, the social psychological consequences of social mobility may be disruptive in their impact, yet some people may find in their individual mobility an affirmation of self-worth, a positive culmination of their individual effort.

SECTION II

*Answer any **four** of the following questions in about 250 words each.*

Q5. Distinguish between horizontal and vertical social mobility.
Refer to Chapter-8, Q.No.-1

Q6. Distinguish the classical notion of undifferentiated peasant society.
Refer to Chapter-7, Q.No.-1

Q7. Describe the aspects of social stratification in the capitalist industrial society.
Refer to See Chapter-1

Q8. Discuss the interactional approach to caste system.
Refer to Dec-2007, Q.No.-5

Q9. Describe the economic and political factors of change and mobility in caste system.

Ans. Changes and mobility in the caste system brought about by various political and economic forces have been one of the main objects of study in Indian Sociology or Social anthropology. These studies reveal that the caste system has always interacted with and responded to political and economic forces of society.

i) Pre-modern period

During pre-modern period, i.e., before the establishment of the British rule in India, there were two most important factors in society which brought about considerable amount of mobility in the caste system: **(1)** fluidity of the political system; and **(2)** the availability of marginal land due to a static demographic situation. Because of the fluidity of the political system it was always possible for a Government official or a powerful family of a locally dominant caste to become politically powerful and, thereafter, acquire Kshatriya status by becoming a chief of king.

Because of the fluidity of the political system it was always possible for a king to raise members of a lower ranking caste to the status of Brahmins when he felt shortage of Brahmins for performing an important ceremony. This apart, a king used to raise or lower the ranks of casters as are ward or punishment. The second source of mobility in the caste system during pre-modern period was the availability of marginal land which could be brought under the plough. This sort of land was always available everywhere.

ii) Modern Period

In this period, new sources of mobility came into existence. Caste system underwent certain significant changes which added new structures and functions to it. Some most notable and significant economic and political policies listed by Srinivas are **(1)** the introduction of a single political role straddling the entire sub-continent; **(2)** the introduction of formal bureaucratic and military organisation; **(3)** the land survey and settlement work; **(4)** the introduction of tenurial reforms; **(5)** the introduction of private ownership to land which made it saleable; **(6)** making new economic opportunities in towns and cities available; **(7)** the introduction of the concept of equality of all citizens before the law; **(8)** providing right to everyone not to be imprisoned without resort due legal process; **(9)** introducing the freedom to practice as well as to propagate one's religion and culture, and culture, and **(10)** making suttee, human sacrifice and human slavery illegal.

iii) Dissociation between caste and occupation

The most notable change in the caste system is the dissociation between caste and occupation. It is greater in the towns that in the rural areas, and much greater in the big cities. Due to industrialisation and modernisation a number of new occupations have come into existence which can be considered "caste-free". One can easily notice people belonging to a caste getting involved into various traditionally forbidden occupations. Brahmins can be seen working in shoe factory. Similarly, Harijans can be seen performing administrative and academic jobs. Dissociation between caste and occupation has developed to such an extent that the phenomenon of caste can no longer be defined on the basis of its relation to a certain occupation.

iv) Disintegration of the Jajmani System

Related with this change in the caste system is the disintegration of the jajmani system. This phenomenon signifies a major change in the caste system because as Kolenda notes that purity pollution and hierarchy are all involved in the Jajmani system". Ideally the jajmani system constitutes three categories of people belonging to different castes. These categories are known as jajman, Kamin and Purohit. Kamins and Purohits provide services to jajmans. But they provide different services. Purohits perform rituals and worship deities for jajmans. Kamins perform manual work for jajmans like washing clothes, shaving, cutting and dressing hair, etc. In turn, jajmans pay Purohits in both cash and kind and Kamins in kind on a yearly basis which is fixed. Jajmans belong to all castes. Kamins belong to some specific castes. And Purohits are Brahmins.

It has been observed that jajmani system is disintegrating because of various reasons. Firstly, the families belonging to Kamin and Purohit castes who consider their traditional caste occupation less prestigious or non-prestigious and economically less beneficial have abandoned them at the earliest opportunity. They is neither all Brahmin families are Purohits nor all Kamin families are Kamins. There are also a lot of Jajman families who have decided not to avail the services of Kamins. This apart, there is a large variation so far as availing the services of Kamins is concerned. Secondly, as it has already been pointed out there is no caste-based division of labour. Families belonging to the low Kamin castes have taken up occupations which are traditionally supposed to be done by higher-twice born castes, and the other way round, too. There are also instances of non-Brahmin families acting as Purohit families. This phenomenon is more visible in those areas which have felt the impact of anti-Brahminical movements.

Because of such change the jajmani system to longer denotes a certain kind of relationship between castes but between families. Some of these families are labour buyers and some are wage earners. Their relationship is purely economic. Therefore, caste has ceased to be the primary component of the jajmani system even if it is said that the jajmani system still exists in one form or another.

v) Weakening of the Rules of Purity and Pollution

Increasing dissociation between caste and occupation and the concomitant process of disintegration of the jajmani system have accompanied with the weakening of he rules purity and pollution. It has been observed that people belonging to various caste hardly observe the rules of purity and pollution while selecting their occupations and interacting with fellow-beings and colleagues. In this respect, they assign profitability of an occupation their top most priority. For a caste it is no longer possible to deny basic conditions of decent living (size, shape and placement of a house, dress materials, style of living, etc.) to a person on the ground of birth in a particular caste. Disappearance of untouchability as a caste practice from the public sphere also denotes the weakening of the rules of purity and pollution.

vi) Breakdown in the Traditional Intercaste Power Relationship

The phenomenon of dominance of one caste over another is one of the most important factors in the maintenance of the caste system. Traditionally, economic and political dominance coincided with ritual dominance. Victims of dominant caste families used to be sheltered by other dominant caste families. This structural arrangement of the caste system has change to such an extent that it ceases to be a defining feature. The process started with the establishment of British rule. Yogendra Singh writes, "Instances of lower-subject-caste revolts against the upper-dominant-caste even during the Pre-Independence days have been many. In the villages Chanukhera in eastern U.P., the low castes (Chamars and Kahars) agitated against the Kshatriyas for better wages and freedom to participate in Congress movement for Independence, and to this with initial resistance the Kshatriyas finally had to acquiesce" (Singh 1977: 165). Bernard S. Cohn reports a similar case of challenge by a lower-subject-caste (Camars) to the dominance of Kshatriyas in Madhopur village.

F.G. Bailey in his study of Bisipara, a village in Khondamals in Orissa, provides a good example of a structural change in the power relationship of various caste which came in the wake of British rule. He observes that by trading in hides and liquor the 'untouchable' Boad distillers bought land equal to the upper-domanant warrior castes. Similarly, Ganjam distillers by trading in only liquor earned so much money to buy more land than any other caste in the village. These economic changes brought about changes in the political structure of the village altering the balance of inter-caste power relationship.

After Independence change in the configuration of power of castes gained momentum. William L. Rowe, in his study of Senapur, observed, "in the past a small group of economically and politically all powerful Kshatriya landlords quietly (for the most part) directed the society. Now with the social tie of landlord and tenant severed, a numerous and economically able caste community such as the Noniya (a lower caste) feels somewhat free to pursue its own ends independently. About the village Kishan Garhi McKim Marriott also points out a similar process of change.

With breakdown of intercaste power relationship the earlier aspiration of lower-subject castes for Sanskritisation has been replaced by a new honoured feeling of self identity within one's own caste or increased horizontal caste solidarity. The position of upper caste as reference group was challenged by differentiating ritual from the politico-economic aspects of caste system. In extreme cases as in D.M.K. or Arya Samaj movement the process of differentiation is absolutized by a conscious and total rejection of the caste ideology. Formation of a caste association with several new functions is a clear reflection of the caste ideology. Formation of a caste association with several new functions is a clear reflection of this phenomenon.

vii) Emergence of Caste Association

The nature of a caste association is different, in more than one sense, from caste as such Organisations like Kayastha Samaj, shatriya Sabha, Teli association, Vaishya Mahasabha, Jat Sabha, Kurmi Mahasabha, Koeri Mahasabha, Bhumihar-Brahmin Mahasabha are some of the examples of caste association. Emergence of various castes such as Mahars and Maratha in Maharashtra, Kmmas and Reddis in Andhra Pradesh and Lingayat and Okkaliga in Karnataka as political groups can also be cited as example of caste association. The main purpose of a caste association has always been to safeguard the interests of their members by building hostels, colleges, schools, houses on a co-operative basis, banks, and by founding journals and endowing scholarships. In their proceedings caste associations claimed backwardness in politico-economic field and a high status in cultural or ritual sphere. Therefore, after independence caste associations tended to become political pressure groups demanding for their members electoral tickets from the political parties, posts in the cabinet. Licences for undertaking various economic activities, concessions and privileges in education and appointment to government jobs, and a variety of other benefits.

viii) Process of Democratisation

The process of democratisation bestows political power and activity upon the groups which have numerical strength provided that strength could be politically mobilized, which is possible if the existential situation of the group as such as homogenous and uniform. These conditions are fulfilled more in the case of lower or subaltern castes. Emergence of lower caste based political parties such as B.S.P., I.P.F., S.P., D.M.K., etc. are some good examples. This apart, launching of movement for more say in the political processes by numerically more powerful low castes in the form of anti-Brahmin movements mark out increasing politicisation of caste.

There is a strong tendency among people to vote for a candidate of one's own caste. Political parties do not ignore this fact. They try their best to put up candidates belonging to the numerically largest castes of the constituency if other conditions remain same. That is why matching a candidate by another candidate of the same caste has been a common policy of political parties in elections.

This apart, caste consideration influence political process in other ways as well. A large group of the Maharastra Congress constituted by Brahmins formed Peasants and Workers party when they realised that Brahmin control over the Congress party, Kammas decided to control the communist party. That is why Kammas landlords were saved and protected by the Communits even in their violent struggle.

Politicisation of castes is so much that in order to be politically powerful distinct caste groups come together and act collectively. Their coming together sometimes take the form of a political party or a faction or a pressure group. B.S.P., S.P., R.J.D., and D.M.K. are some of the examples. In Gujrat Kshatriya Sabha Rajputs admitted a lower caste Kolis to the rank of Kshatriya in order to have a larger say in the power structure of Gujrat state.

Q10. Discuss the aspects of social mobility among the scheduled casters in India.

Refer to Chapter-6, Q.No.-11

Q11. Explain Davis and Moore's theory of social stratification.

Refer to Chapter-2, Q.No.-4

Q12. Discuss the caste-class nexus in India.

Refer to Chapter-1, Q.No.-7

SECTION III

*Answer any **two** of the following questions in about 100 words each.*

Q13. Describe the concepts of ethnicity.

Refer to Dec-2007, Q.No.-9(b)

Q14. Spell out the concept of 'Power elite'.

Ans. The concept of 'Power elite'

Power elite, in political and sociological theory, is a small group of people who control a disproportionate amount of wealth, privilege, and access to decision-making of global consequence. The term was coined by Charles Wright Mills in his 1956 book, *The Power Elite*, which describes the relationship between individuals at the pinnacles of political, military, and economic institutions, noting that these people share a common world view.

The power elite is described as consisting of members of the corporate community, academia, politicians, media editors, military service personnel, and high-profile journalists.

The power elite are the leadership of the upper class, able to shape the economy through their simultaneous access to both state and corporate power.
Unlike the ruling class, a social formation based on heritage and social ties, the power elite is characterized by the organisational structure through which its wealth is acquired. According to Mills, the power elite is "the managerial reorganisation of the propertied classes into the more or less unified stratum of the corporate rich." Domhoff further clarified the differences in the two terms: "The upper class as a whole does not do the ruling. Instead, class rule is manifested through the activities of a wide variety of organisations and institutions... Leaders within the upper class join with high-level employees in the organisations they control to make up what will be called the power elite."

Q15. What is the dialectical approach to social stratification?
Refer to Chapter-1, Q.No.-3

Q16. Explain the concept of the 'dominant caste'.
Ans. Andre Beteille observes that power has shifted from one dominant caste to another and it is shifted from the caste structure itself, and come to be located in more differentiated structures such as panchayats and political parties. Yet Beteille does not reflect upon the consequences of this shift. Can we study changes in caste structure without examining the consequent patterns of "distributive justice" or "equality/inequality"? If we cannot analyse the flexibility inherent in the norms of the an egalitarian system, it would be difficult to interpret the emergence of formal institutions and structures as indicators of a "shift" from caste to "caste-free" structures. Even if a caste as a whole is not "dominant" and the "dominant group" comprises families of several caste, it does not mean that the magnitude of inequality has substantially reduced.

ESO-14: SOCIETY AND STRATIFICATION
December, 2009

Note: *This question paper has* ***three*** *sections. Attempt the questions as instructed in each section.*

SECTION I

Answer any ***two*** *questions in about 500 words each.*

Q1. Describe the caste - class nexus in India.

Q2. Discuss the process of gender construction in India.

Q3. How does ethnicity become a basis of stratification in society?

Q4. Discuss the attributional approach to the understanding of caste system.

SECTION II

Answer any ***four*** *of the following questions in about 250 words each.*

Q5. Discuss the features of middle classes in India.

Q6. Describe the agrarian class structure in India.

Q7. Explain the different aspects of industrialization and social mobility.

Q8. Explain the relation between division of labour and class structure in Marxian analysis.

Q9. Discuss the divergent meanings of caste.

Q10. Discuss the relation between Sanskritization and social change.

Q11. Describe the impact of economic development on women.

Q12. Discuss Dahrendorf's theory of class and class conflict.

SECTION III

Answer any ***two*** *of the following questions in about 100 words each.*

Q13. Define the concept of social stratification.

Q14. Explain the process of embourgeoisement.

Q15. Discuss the relationship between education and mobility.

Q16. Outline the causes of language movements in India.

ESO-14: SOCIETY AND STRATIFICATION
June, 2010

Note: This question paper has ***three*** *sections. Attempt the questions as instructed in each section.*

SECTION I

Answer any ***two*** *of the following questions in about 500 words each:*

Q1. Discuss the approaches to the study of caste in India.

Q2. What is ethnicity? Explain the important elements of ethnicity.

Q3. Examine the changing status of women in rural India.

Q4. What is peasant movement? Discuss the features of peasant movements in independent India.

SECTION II

Answer any ***four*** *of the following questions in about 250 words each:*

Q5. Discuss the changing status of dalits in India.

Q6. Highlight the distinguishing features of Indian middle class.

Q7. Discuss the impact of development on tribal societies in India with suitable examples.

Q8. Explain the nature of working classes.

Q9. Explain the various dimensions of social mobility.

Q10. Examine the nature of stratification in socialist societies.

Q11. Discuss the process of secularization in India.

Q12. Explain the relationship between education and stratification.

SECTION III

Answer any ***two*** *of the following questions in about 100 words each:*

Q13. Delineate features of capitalist society.

Q14. Discuss the concept of scheduled tribes.

Q15. Discuss the concept of land reform.

Q16. Explain the concept of Sanskritization.

ESO-14: SOCIETY AND STRATIFICATION
December, 2010

Note: This question paper has ***three*** *sections. Attempt the questions as instructed in each section.*

SECTION I

Answer any ***two*** *of the following questions in about 500 words each.*

Q1. Discuss how education affects social stratification in modern society?

Q2. Explain the interactional approaches to the understanding of caste system.

Q3. Examine the process of gender socialization.

Q4. Discuss the contours of linguistic identities in India.

SECTION II

Answer any ***four*** *of the following questions in about 250 words each.*

Q5. Discuss class structure in industrial societies.

Q6. Compare and contrast feature of capitalist and socialist societies.

Q7. Describe with examples tribal movements in India.

Q8. Discuss the functions of social stratification.

Q9. Examine the constitutional measures for raising the status of women in India.

Q10. Discuss the role of the state for the socio-economic development of the tribals in India.

Q11. Explain the concept of class as applied in the study of agrarian societies.

Q12. Discuss Karl Marx approach to the study of social conflict.

SECTION III

Answer any ***two*** *of the following questions in about 100 words each.*

Q13. Discuss the concept of dominant caste.

Q14. Examine feudalism as a type of agrarian society.

Q15. Explain Karl Marx's concept of alienation.

Q16. Delineate the functions of social conflict.

ESO-14: SOCIETY AND STRATIFICATION
June, 2011

Note: This question paper has ***three*** *sections. Attempt the questions as instructed in each section.*

SECTION I

Answer any ***two*** *questions in about 500 words each.*

Q1. What do you understand by 'social stratification'? Explain Max Weber's theory of social stratification.

Q2. Explain how patriarchy contributes to gender inequality in society.

Q3. Discuss the concept of linguistic ethnicity with suitable examples.

Q4. Outline the major reasons for the rise of tribal movements in north-east India.

SECTION II

Answer any ***four*** *of the following questions in about 250 words each.*

Q5. Discuss F.G. Bailey's contribution to the study of caste in India.

Q6. What is the role of caste associations in modern India?

Q7. Discuss the social classes in urban India.

Q8. Critically discuss Louis Doumont's explanation of caste in terms of purity and pollution.

Q9. Discuss the agrarian class structure in India.

Q10. Explain the role of local elites in the socio-economic upliftment of tribal people.

Q11. What are the major constitutional provisions for the upliftment of scheduled casts?

Q12. Discuss how gender identities are constructed in the course of socialization process.

SECTION III

Answer any ***two*** *of the following questions in about 100 words each.*

Q13. What do you understand 'by class struggle'?

Q14. List the major reasons for declining sex ratio in India.

Q15. Distinguish between the old middle class and the new middle class.

Q16. Differentiate between gender and sex.

ESO-14: SOCIETY AND STRATIFICATION
December, 2011

*Note: This question paper has **three** sections. Attempt the questions as instructed in each section.*

SECTION I

*Answer any **two** questions in about 500 words each.*

Q1. Critically discuss Kinsley Davis and Wilbert Moore's contribution to the understanding of social stratification.

Q2. What are the basic features of minority groups? Give suitable examples.

Q3. What is social mobility? Do you think caste system in India permits social mobility? Discuss

Q4. Explain the concept of ethnicity and the manner in which it serves as a basis of stratification in society. Substantiate your answer with an example.

SECTION II

*Answer any **four** of the following questions in about 250 words each.*

Q5. Do you think conflict helps to establish and maintain group identities? Discuss.

Q6. Discuss Dahrendorf's critique of Karl Marx's theory of class conflict.

Q7. Explain how assertion of linguistic identity manifests as a movement. Substantiate your answer with a suitable example.

Q8. Does religion contribute to creating and maintaining unjust gender relations in India? Discuss.

Q9. What are the salient features of the caste system outlined by G.S. Ghurye?

Q10. What is M N Srinivas's major contribution to the understanding of caste system in India?

Q11. What is Jajmani system? Is the Jajmani system disintegrating in contemporary Indian society?

Q12. Explain the concept of the middle class. How does the historical context of development of middle class in western countries differ from that in India?

SECTION III

*Answer any **two** of the following questions in about 100 words each.*

Q13. What did Max Weber mean by 'life chances'?

Q14. What do you understand by 'class consciousness'?

Q15. What is a Jati?

Q16. What do you mean by women's work?

ESO-14: SOCIETY AND STRATIFICATION
June, 2012

***Note:** The question paper has **three** sections. Attempt the questions as instructed in each section.*

SECTION I

*Answer any **two** of the following questions in 500 words each.*

Q1. Discuss the changing status of women in rural India.

Q2. Discuss functionalist approach to the study of caste in India.

Q3. What do you understand by women's empowerment? Discuss with illustrations.

Q4. Discuss the social reality of caste.

SECTION II

*Answer any **four** of the following questions in the about 250 words each.*

Q5. What are the distinguishing features of capitalist industrialist society?

Q6. Describe the main features in Dumont's approach to caste analysis.

Q7. Discuss the education as a factor of social mobility.

Q8. Write a note on tribal elites in India.

Q9. Discuss the constitutional provisions for Scheduled Tribes and Scheduled Caste in India.

Q10. Discuss the changing features of caste in India.

Q11. Discus Marx's views on the division of labour.

Q12. Discuss briefly Marx and Weber's views on social classes.

SECTION III

*Answer any **two** of the following questions in about 100 words each.*

Q13. Explain the concept of class conflict.

Q14. What is the relationship between status and power?

Q15. Discuss the concept of ethnicity.

Q16. Describe Srinivas's notion of "dominant caste".

ESO-14: SOCIETY AND STRATIFICATION
December, 2012

Note: *This question paper has* ***three*** *sections. Attempt the questions as instructed in each section.*

SECTION I

Answer any ***two*** *of the following questions in about 500 words each.*

Q1. Describe ethnicity as a basis for stratification.

Q2. Analyse caste identity through the interactional approaches.

Q3. Discuss the internal differentiation with in scheduled tribes with examples.

Q4. Discuss social mobility and classes in India.

SECTION II

Answer any ***four*** *of the following questions in about 250 words each.*

Q5. Outline the features of middle classes in India.

Q6. Discuss Karl Marx's theory of class conflict.

Q7. Examine L. Dumort's approach to the study of caste.

Q8. "Status and power are not independent of each other". Discuss.

Q9. Discuss the main factors leading to the construction of gender identify.

Q10. Describe weber's main views on stratification.

Q11. Discuss aspects of caste and class in Urban India.

Q12. Bring out the views of Dahrendorf and Coser on class.

SECTION III

Answer any ***two*** *of the following questions in about 100 words each.*

Q13. What do you understand by linguistic ethnicity?

Q14. Bring out the main features of Jajmani system.

Q15. Discuss shanin's concept of peasant society.

Q16. Outline the main features of the capitalist society.

ESO-14: SOCIETY AND STRATIFICATION
June, 2013

Note: The question paper has ***three*** *sections. Attempt the questions as instructed in each section.*

SECTION I

Answer any ***two*** *questions in about 500 words each.*

Q1. Discuss the dialectical approach to understand social stratification.

Q2. Define the concept of class with special reference to L. Coser and R. Dahrendorf's.

Q3. Examine the significance of ethnicity as a basis of social stratification.

Q4. "Idea of hierarchy is fundamental to caste system". Discuss.

SECTION II

Answer any ***four*** *of the following questions in about 250 words each.*

Q5. Discuss gender as a basis of social stratification.

Q6. Discuss the dimensions of heterogeneity among working class in India.

Q7. Discuss the self respect movement and its impact on society.

Q8. Briefly describe dimensions of social stratification among the tribes in India.

Q9. Discuss the classical notion of undifferentiated peasant society.

Q10. Analyse the factors for the rise of middle class in India.

Q11. Define social mobility and discuss its types.

Q12. Explain the relation between caste and class.

SECTION III

Answer any ***two*** *of the following questions in about 100 words each.*

Q13. List the features of dominant castes.

Q14. Elaborate the concept of de-sanskritisation.

Q15. Who are the Scheduled Castes?

ESO-14: SOCIETY AND STRATIFICATION
December, 2013

*Note: The question paper has **three** sections. Attempt the questions as instructed in each section.*

SECTION I

*Answer any **two** questions in about 500 words each.*

Q1. Discuss the concept of a social stratification and its various forces.

Q2. Discuss social stratification system among ethnic groups in India.

Q3. Explain functionalist perspective on social stratification.

Q4. Describe social consequences of social mobility with suitable examples.

SECTION II

*Answer any **four** of the following questions in about 250 words each.*

Q5. Is Nationality linked with ethnicity? Explain.

Q6. Is caste different from class? Discuss.

Q7. Who are the "Other Backword Classes"? Explain.

Q8. Discuss briefly conflict theory of social stratification.

Q9. Describe the agrarain class structure in India.

Q10. Discuss the issues related to tribal movements in north-East-India with a suitable example.

Q11. What are the major constitutional provisions for the safegards of scheduled castes in India?

SECTION III

*Answer any **two** of the following questions in about 100 words each.*

Q12. Define the concept of power.

Q13. Discuss sanskritisation as a process of social mobility.

Q14. Elaborate the concept of Elite.

ESO-14: SOCIETY AND STRATIFICATION
June, 2014

Note: This question paper has ***three*** *sections. Attempt the questions as instructed in each section.*

SECTION I

Answer any ***two*** *questions in about 500 words each.*

Q1. Explain how gender serves as a basis of stratification in society?

Q2. Discuss Max Weber's view on social stratification.

Q3. Write a critique of Davis and Moore's theory of social stratification.

Q4. Explain the nature of social stratification among the Jaintias and Khasis.

SECTION II

Answer any ***four*** *of the following questions in about 250 words each.*

Q5. What are the basic functions of stratification in society?

Q6. Do caste and religion contribute to unequal gender in society? Discuss.

Q7. Explain the interactional approach to the understanding of caste with focus on the viewpoint of Marriott.

Q8. Distinguish between intergenerational and intragenerational social mobility.

Q9. Explain the role of tribal elites in society.

Q10. What is class conflict? Explain its role in social change.

Q11. Describe the position of child labour in Indian society.

Q12. Explain how the Santhali language movement was as a means of asserting ethnic identity?

SECTION III

Answer any ***two*** *of the following questions in about 100 words each.*

Q13. What do you understand by 'minoritisation'?

Q14. What is meant by 'class consciousness'?

Q15. What is downward mobility?

Q16. What are the main features of capitalist society?

ESO-14: SOCIETY AND STRATIFICATION
December, 2014

Note: This question paper has ***three*** *sections. Attempt the questions as instructed in each section.*

SECTION I

Answer any ***two*** *of the following questions in about 500 words each.*

Q1. Explain how ethnicity serves as a basis of social stratification.

Q2. Discuss Karl Marx's explanation of social stratification.

Q3. What are the basic propositions of Davis and Moore's theory of social stratification?

Q4. What do you understand by 'ethnicity'? Explain the major causes of language movements for assertion of ethnic identity.

SECTION II

Answer any ***four*** *of the following questions in about 250 words each.*

Q5. What are the main features of minority groups outlined by Anthony Giddens?

Q6. How does socialisation contribute to formation of gender identity?

Q7. 'Jajmani system is disintegrating in contemporary Indian society'. Discuss.

Q8. Explain M.N. Srinivas's attributional approach to the understanding of caste.

Q9. Distinguish between 'old middle class' and 'new middle class'.

Q10. Do you think conflict contributes to establishing and maintaining group identities? Critically discuss.

Q11. Describe the position of the aged in society.

Q12. Outline the reasons for declining sex-ratio in India.

SECTION III

Answer any ***two*** *of the following questions in about 100 words each.*

Q13. What were the important objectives of the Women's Liberation Movement in the United States and Europe?

Q14. What is 'embourgeoisement'?

Q15. What is upward mobility? Give examples.

Q16. What are the main features of Socialist societies?

ESO-14: SOCIETY AND STRATIFICATION
June, 2015

Note: This question paper has ***three*** *sections. Attempt the questions as instructed in each section.*

SECTION I

Answer any ***two*** *of the following questions in about 500 words each.*

Q1. In what way does caste operate as a system of social relations?

Q2. Do Marxian concepts and method of social analysis apply to the understanding of class situation in India? Discuss.

Q3. Discuss Tumin's critique of the functionalist analysis of social stratification.

Q4. Are Scheduled Tribes internally differentiated? Discuss with suitable examples.

SECTION II

Answer any ***four*** *of the following questions in about 250 words each.*

Q5. What is ethnicity? Discuss its various features in relation to an ethnic group.

Q6. Explain the objectives and scope of Punjabi Suba Movement.

Q7. How does socialisation process contribute to construction of gender identity.

Q8. What are the core ideas of Dumont's theory of caste?

Q9. Do you agree that the jajmani system is disintegrating? Discuss with suitable examples.

Q10. What are the major ways suggested by Ambedkar to ensure equality and justice for Scheduled Castes in India?

Q11. Explain the concept of 'new middle class'. How does it differ from that of 'old middle class'?

Q12. What are the main features of socialist societies?

SECTION III

Answer any ***two*** *of the following questions in about 100 words each.*

Q13. What do you understand by 'women's empowerment?

Q14. Distinguish between sex and gender.

Q15. Explain Weber's concept of status.

Q16. What is 'class consciousness'?

ESO-14: SOCIETY AND STRATIFICATION
December, 2015

Note: This question paper has ***three*** *sections. Attempt the questions as instructed in each section.*

SECTION I

Answer any ***two*** *of the following questions in about 500 words each.*

Q1. Explain the relationship between caste and class in India.

Q2. How does Gerhard Lenski's notion of class differ from that of Karl Marx?

Q3. Explain Pierre van den Berghe theory of social stratification.

Q4. Discuss the interactional approach to the understanding of caste identity.

SECTION II

Answer any ***four*** *of the following questions in about 250 words each.*

Q5. 'For many years studies on stratification were gender blind.' Critically discuss.

Q6. Explain the functional perspective in understanding social conflict.

Q7. What were the conditions that led to the rise of regional language movements as an expression of ethnicity?

Q8. Outline the important features of capitalist societies.

Q9. Do you agree that Dumont's theory of caste corresponds with the lived reality of caste in India? Discuss.

Q10. What are the major reasons for marginalisation of Indian Tribes? Discuss.

Q11. Is socialist society classless? discuss.

Q12. Explain the theory of 'circulation of elites'.

Q13. What makes religious ethnicity a basis of stratification in society?

SECTION III

Answer any ***two*** *of the following questions in about 100 words each.*

Q14. Outline the concept of gender role stereotyping.

Q15. Bring out the factors that contribute to declining sex-ratio in India.

Q16. What did Weber mean by 'life chances'?

Q17. Explain the concept of peasant society.

ESO-14: SOCIETY AND STRATIFICATION
June, 2016

***Note**: This question paper has **three** sections. Attempt the questions as instructed in each section.*

SECTION I

*Answer any **two** of the following questions in about 500 words each.*

Q1. Discuss the major organising principles of social stratification.
Refer to Chapter-1, Q.No.-5

Q2. Examine the relationship between caste and class.
Refer to Chapter-1, Q.No.-7

Q3. Examine the Marxian approach to the understanding of social stratification.
Refer to Chapter-2, Q.No.-2

Q4. Discuss Coser's theory of social classes.
Refer to Chapter-2, Q.No.-6

SECTION II

*Answer any **four** of the following questions in about 250 words each.*

Q5. Discuss the conditions under which religious ethnicity becomes a basis of stratification.
Refer to Chapter-3, Q.No.-3

Q6. Examine the causes of language movements in India.
Refer to Chapter-3, Q.No.-10

Q7. Explain the role of social institutions in relation to gender and religion.
Refer to Chapter-4, Q.No.-6

Q8. Critically examine the reasons for women's powerlessness in the society.

Ans. One approach to thinking about women's powerlessness focuses on patriarchy as an overarching gender (or kinship) system which determines women's role and relationships, In a male dominated patriarchal society, women are viewed in their traditional social roles which are subordinate to men. If a women wishes to be accepted as a woman she should not be too competent, over ambitious, dominating and devoid of femininity.

Another approach focuses on a single (or primary) domain of women's powerlessness, the most common being the household, giving rise to a focus on women's reproductive or productive roles respectively. (viz. the role of women as child bearers and housewives) In Indian families girls are expected to assume responsibility for housework at a relatively early age. Even in ordinary circumstances the role expectation of girls is that they share the housekeeping chores like cooking and rearing of children along with mothers. Hence such societies assume that women are meant to work in the home and be totally dependent on the menfolk.

A third approach assumes that women experience sub-ordination or powerlessness in multiple domains (either simultaneously or sequentially). These include the home, at work, and all other places. At home a woman is expected to conform to the traditional ideal of a hard working women ready to subjugate her own interests to the happiness of others in the family and demanding nothing in return. At the work place too, she must not be too competent in her job. If she wants to do her job to her satisfaction she faces the prospect of being resented. The reasons for this sub-ordination is that differences between a male and female child are made right from childhood and a girl is socialised to be submissive and passive.

The various approaches though distinct in many regards all assume that women experience powerlessness in (and through interaction of) multiple social political and economic institutions (not just the household).

Q9. Elucidate the main features of caste system.

Refer to Chapter-5, Q.No.-9

Q10. Explain the thesis of 'Embourgeoisement' as a social consequence of social mobility.

Refer to Chapter-8, Q.No.-11

Q11. Discuss the tribal policy of the Indian State.

Refer to Chapter-3, Q.No.-6

Q12. Examine the characteristics of class structure.

Ans. There are specific characteristics of caste. They are:

(i) Vertical order of social classes-there is a hierarchy in terms of privileges and discrimination.

(ii) There is also a permanent idea of class interest.

(iii) Idea of class-consciousness, awareness of class, hierarchy, identity and solidarity is present:

Existence of class implies that there is an idea of social distance. Class distinctions get expressed in the fob of inequalities and class boundaries.

There are two ways of conceiving class structure:

(i) Schemes of gradation

(ii) Schemes based on Relations of dependence:

(a) One-sided dependence

(b) Mutual dependence

As a system of social relations class is understood usually as a subjection of one over the other. Some sociologists view the idea of class as conquest where victors are the upper class and the defeated classes are lower.

With regard to the idea-of development of class, the question usually asked is -Are social classes distinctive of modem contemporary societies, i.e., industrial societies only or does one find them in all known societies? For this Marxist would argue that they exist in all historically recorded societies but other Sociologists argue that social classes exist only in contemporary societies where economic activities pre-dominate and where industrialisation progressively transforms the totality of existence.

People who belong to the same social class have more or less the same "life chances", i.e., the probability of securing the goad things of life. Such a freedom, high standard of living, Leisure or whatever things are highly valued in a given society. Association of different classes is between people of unequal society social class affects the "life-style". Thus, one can conclude by saying that class is implied as an opposition to hereditary privileges, and to an immutable hierarchy of ranks.

SECTION III

Answer any ***two*** *of the following questions in about 100 words each.*

Q13. Define Sanskritisation.

Refer to Chapter-5, Q.No.-10

Q14. Distinguish between conflict and competition.

Ans. The difference between conflict and competition is that

(i) Conflict always included an awareness of an adversary whereas Competition occurs without actual knowledge of other's- existence.

(ii) In competition, two or more parties want something all cannot share, but they do not strive for the purpose of denying or opposing others.

(iii) Competition is always governed by moral norms, fair tactics, while much of Conflict is not.

(iv) Conflict involves discord and disagreement whereas competition can take place without any clash or hard feelings.

(v) Competition is a healthy process that encourages intelligence, innovation and entrepreneurship whereas conflict crushes all such concepts.

(vi) A competition indicates a contest where participants vie for the top spot whereas a conflict indicates a scuffle or a skirmish.

Q15. Define intragenerational mobility.

Refer to Chapter-8, Q.No.-7

ESO-14: SOCIETY AND STRATIFICATION
December, 2016

*Note: This question paper has **three** sections. Attempt the questions as instructed in each section.*

SECTION I

*Answer any **two** of the following questions in about 500 words each.*

Q1. Discuss the functionalist theory of social stratification.

Refer to Chapter-1, Q.No.-5

Q2. Explain the concept social stratification with special reference to gender.

Refer to Chapter-1, Q.No.-10

Q3. Examine the Weberian view on social stratification.

Refer to Chapter-1, Q.No.-2

Q4. Discuss the tribal movements in the North-East with special reference to the Naga movement.

Refer to Chapter-3, Q.No.-6

SECTION II

*Answer any **four** of the following questions in about 250 words each.*

Q5. Discuss the basis of caste hierarchy.

Ans. Sociologists and social anthropologists have carried out large numbers of studies on the system of caste hierarchy. Along with defining the system and identifying its features, they have also offered theories that explain the caste system. Following are the basis of caste hierarchy:

(1) Caste and Race: The connection between caste and race was made by some of the earliest foreign commentators on India. They related it to the so-called Aryan invasion of India. They argued that while upper caste Hindus were of "foreign" or Aryan origin, the lower castes belonged to the "native" or "aboriginal" races. Being the conquerors, the Aryans assigned themselves the status of upper castes and those who were conquered were made subjects by the dominant Aryans and were given the status of lower castes. The fact that members of upper castes had fairer skin than the lower castes was cited as a testimony in support of such a hypothesis. However, this theory has been rejected for being purely speculative in nature. There is very little hard evidence to support such an argument. Further, it has been argued that those from the lower castes had darker skin not because they necessarily belonged to a different racial stock but because they were the ones who did much of the physical work in the fields in the open. Moreover, even if it was true that the Aryans came from outside and subjugated the native population, it does not automatically explain the complex reality of caste distinctions and hierarchy.

(2) Caste and Occupation: Those who look at caste in economic terms generally do so by referring to obvious fact of the relationship between caste and occupation. Caste, they argue, was a kind of division of labour, different groups specialising in different occupations. Some others see it as a specific from of pre-capitalist/feudal separated from each other in certain respects (caste endogamy, restrictions on eating together and on physical contact) but interdependent in other (traditional division of labour). The word 'caste', not only involved hereditary specialisation of occupations but also differential rights. Different occupations were arranged in a hierarchical order that made their occupants socially unequal. Inequality was an essential feature of the caste system. Different groups in a caste society, tend to 'repel each other rather than attract, each retires within itself, isolates itself, makes every effort to prevent its members from contracting alliances or even from entering into relation with neighboring groups'. Thus, Bougle identified three core features of caste system, viz., hereditary occupation, hierarchy and mutual repulsion.

Q6. Explain the theories of sex roles.

Refer to Chapter-4, Q.No.-1

Q7. Describe the concept of 'gender socialisation'.

Refer to Chapter-4, Q.No.-1

Q8. Discuss the concept of 'Purity' and 'Pollution' in understanding caste.

Refer to Chapter-5, Q.No.-3

Q9. Examine the interactional approach to the understanding of caste system.

Refer to Chapter-5, Q.No.-5

Q10. Discuss the constitutional provisions for the upliftment of tribals in India.

Refer to Chapter-6, Q.No.-1

Q11. Examine the process of social mobility among the Scheduled Castes.

Refer to Chapter-6, Q.No.-11

Q12. Discuss the agrarian class structure in India.
Refer to Chapter-17, Q.No.-1

SECTION III

Answer any ***two*** *of the following questions in about 100 words each.*

Q13. Define Scheduled Tribes.
Refer to Chapter.-6, Q.No.-11

Q14. What is horizontal mobility?
Refer to Chapter-8, Q.No.-1

Q15. Define the concept of westernization.
Refer to Chapter-8, Q.No.-6

ESO-14: SOCIETY AND STRATIFICATION
June, 2017

Note: This question paper has ***three*** *sections. Attempt the questions as instructed in each section.*

SECTION I

Answer any ***two*** *of the following questions in about 500 words each.*

Q1. Discuss interactional and attributional approaches to the study of caste.

Refer to Chapter-5, Q.No.-5

Q2. What do you understand by 'social mobility'? Distinguish between horizontal and vertical mobility.

Refer to Chapter-6, Q.No.-4 and Refer to Chapter-8, Q.No.-1

Q3. Critically examine the agrarian class structure in India.

Refer to Chapter-7, Q.No.-1

Q4. Explain the basis of gender inequality in India.

Refer to Chapter-4, Q.No.-7

SECTION II

Answer any ***four*** *of the following questions in about 250 words each.*

Q5. Outline Pierre van den Berghe's theory of social stratification.

Refer to Chapter-2, Q.No.-7

Q6. How has Weber conceptualised social class? Explain.

Refer to Chapter-1, Q.No.-2

Q7. What did Shanin mean by ideal type of a peasant society?

Ans. He defined peasants as "small agricultural producers, who, with the help of simple equipment and the labour of their families, produced mostly for their own consumption, direct or indirect, and for the fulfillment of obligations to holders of political and economic power". He further identified four interdependent facets of peasant societies – (i) Peasant family works as the basic multi-dimensional unit of social organisation. The family farm operates as the major unit of peasant property, production, consumption, welfare, social reproduction, identity, prestige, sociability and welfare. The individual tends to submit to a formalised family role-behaviour and patriarchal authority (ii) Land husbandry works as the main means of livelihood.

Traditionally defined social organisation and a low level of technology. Traditionally defined social organisation and a low level of technology characterise peasant farming. (iii) Peasant societies follow specific cultural patterns linked to the way of life of a small rural community. Peasant culture often confirms to the traditional norms of behaviour and is characterised by face to face relations. (iv) the domination over peasantry by outsiders. The peasants are invariably kept at arm's length from the source of power. Shanin argues that their political subjugation interlinks with their cultural subordination and economic exploitation. In this kind of a framework, though peasants are seen as dominated by outsiders, they are not very different from each other, particularly in terms of their class status. In other words, in this classical notion of the peasant society, there are no internal class differences within the peasantry.

Q8. Discuss the impact of development on empowerment of women.
Refer to Chapter-4, Q.No.-2

Q9. Explain the structure of classes in socialist societies.
Ans. Here the system of stratification is not the result of market economy rather it is a creation of the political elite where in Capitalist society there is plurality of elite's, e.g., C.R. Mills concept of three categories of elites in American Society. However, in Soviet society there was only one elite that is political elite. These elites form an interest group. Stratification is a product of the state imposed by bureaucracy. This uniform elite divides the society into ruling intellectuals vs. peasants. Scholars who have studied classes in socialist societies say that instead of using the word "class" one must use the word "strata". The main stratas being:

(1) Intelligentsia
(i) Ruling elite
(ii) Superior Intelligentsia
(iii) General Intelligentsia

(2) Ruling Class
(i) Aristocracy
(ii) Rank and File
(iii) Disadvantaged worker

(3) Peasants
(i) Well to do
(ii) Average Peasant

According to Milovin Dijilas, a socialist society is not classless. A new ruling class in the East has replaced the Bourgeoisies of the West. This new class is made up of political bureaucrats, many of whom are high-ranking officials of the communist party. They use power to further their own interest. Although in legal terms, the forces of production are communal owned, in practice, they are, controlled by the new class for its own benefit. Political bureaucrats direct and control the economy and monopolise decisions regarding production, consumption, and production. As a result of this wide income differences between this class and masses is observed, associated with this is high privilege and status. According to Dijilas, the ruling class of the late Soviet Union is more exploitative then the bourgeoisie, its power is even greater because it is unchecked by political parties. He claims that in a single party state political bureaucrats monopolise power. He agrees with Marx, in practice their source of power is there because it controls the forces of production. Others reverse this and say that in Soviet societies economic power derives from political power. According to T.B. Bottomore, the new class controls the means of production because of its political power.

Q10. What are 'caste associations'? Explain their role in contemporary Indian society.

Refer to June-2009, Q.No.-9

Q11. Do Other Backward Classes (OBCs) constitute a homogeneous category? Discuss.

Refer to Chapter-6, Q.No.-3

Q12. What are the important reasons for the rise of tribal movements in India?

Refer to Chapter-3, Q.No.-6

SECTION III

*Answer any **two** of the following questions in about 100 words each.*

Q13. What did Srinivas mean by 'social reality of caste'?

Ans. Srinivas insists that the social reality of the caste system in not varna-the ideological categorisation-but jati-the sub-caste that is the actually interacting group. And it is here that he finds evidence to challenge and modify the ideological implications of varna. But just when we might expect the devaluation of varna as a scientific concept we find its inflation as the social ideology of mobility movements. Indeed if varna is not a behavioural concept, it does in fact underlie 'jati', and its reality shaping possibilities cannot be denied. However, varna does underlie jati and is capable of shaping reality, through, for examples, the process of Sanskritisation.

Q14. What is the role of tribal elites in society?

Ans. In the colonial period, most of the struggles for justice were led by the disposed traditional elite with great consequence. Independent India has taken serious note of it and provided several avenues for ameliorating their conditions of living. But as the resources are limited or rather improperly distributed, the spread of benefits are very much limited. Accordingly, the system of granting special facilities has generated as small modem elite among the tribals in terms of education, politics and economics, whereas the large majority of the tribal people have remained where they were before Independence, if not worse. Being a late comer, the tribal elites are not able to compete equal terms with the non-tribal elites and this, tend to be an integral part of their community system.

Q15. Define 'protective discrimination'.

Ans. For years, the backward sections who were oppressed remained submissive and servile. But under British rule they improved their status and tried to legitimise it though Sanskritisation. But simultaneously, the upper castes leaped forward by usurping new opportunities. The gap between the upper and lower castes widened and this they tried to bridge by laying claim to economic and political resources. These under privileged castes consolidated themselves against the upper castes in the form of Caste Sabhas the anti-Brahmin movement date back to 1870's in Maharasthtra and were led by dominant castes such as Kamrnas, Reddis, Nayars etc. The most significant movements were launched by Mahars under the leadership of B.R. Arnbedkar. The other movements include those of "Dalit Panthers" who united all sections of depressed people.

The backward sections have found opportunities for upward mobility on account of 'protective discrimination' policies which involves reservation of seats in educational institutions, freeship and scholarships, Besides, there are reservations in jobs and legislative bodies. These welfare measures have benefited only a small section who have claims to much higher status than their counterparts of the same caste resulting in further divisions in the castes.

Q16. What do you understand by 'ethnic minority'?

Refer to Chapter-1, Q.No.-8

ESO-14: SOCIETY AND STRATIFICATION
December, 2017

Note: This question paper has ***three*** *sections. Answer the questions as instructed in each section.*

SECTION I

Answer any ***two*** *of the following questions in about 500 words each.*

Q1. In what way do ideas about purity and pollution stratify Indian society? Discuss with suitable examples.

Q2. Discuss Dahrendorf's views on social class.

Q3. Highlight the differences and commonalities between caste and class in India.

Q4. Discuss the nature and scope of ethnicity as a basis of social stratification.

SECTION II

Answer any ***four*** *of the following questions in about 250 words each.*

Q5. What are the political consequences of social mobility?

Q6. Outline N. Luhmann's systems' theory of social stratification.

Q7. Discuss the reasons for women's oppression in society.

Q8. In what way does socialisation contribute to the construction of gender-based identity?

Q9. How is mode of production related to class struggle?

Q10. Differentiate between classes in capitalist societies and socialist societies.

Q11. Explain the features of peasant movements in Independence India.

Q12. In caste a closed system? Discuss.

SECTION III

Answer any ***two*** *of the following questions in about 100 words each.*

Q13. What is meant by 'fragmented middle class'?

Q14. What do you understand by 'embourgeoisement'?

Q15. What is 'secularisation'?

Q16. Define ethnicity.

ESO-14: SOCIETY AND STRATIFICATION
June, 2018

***Note**: This question paper has **three** sections. Answer the questions as instructed in each section.*

SECTION I

*Answer any **two** of the following questions in about 500 words each.*

Q1. Discuss the functionalist theory of social stratification.
Refer to Chapter-1, Q.No.-5 (Pg. No.-11)

Q2. Explain class as a form of social stratification.
Refer to Chapter-2, Q.No.-1, 2 (Pg. No.-22, 23)

Q3. What do you understand by ethnicity? Write a brief note on ethnic minorities.
Refer to Chapter-3, Q.No.-1 (Pg. No.-40) and Chapter-1, Q.No.-8 (Pg. No.-16)

Q4. Critically examine the tribal policy in India.
Refer to Chapter-3, Q.No.-6 (Pg. No.-48)

SECTION II

*Answer any **four** of the following questions in about 250 words each.*

Q5. Explain power as an organising principle of social stratification.

Ans. There are three major organising principles of social stratification. These are, status, wealth and power. Sociological observations of many societies over a period of time have revealed some linkages among these principles in any evolutionary process.

(1) Status: The earliest principle of social stratification is that of status. Status in the language of social stratification means ranking of groups in a society on the basis of their relative position in terms of honour or respect. Honour is a qualitative attribute which members in a status group enjoy by birth. Any such attribute which is inherited by birth is ascribed and cannot be acquired by effort. Therefore, status principle of social stratification is also termed as the principle of ascription. In our country, caste is a very appropriate example of status groups. The qualities which go to make a status groups are related more to values and beliefs, to legends and myths perpetuated in societies over a period of time than to principles which are achievable by efforts, whether economic, political or cultural.

(2) Wealth: The second organising principle of social stratification is wealth. Wealth is generated in societies only when technologies advancement takes place and there is a change in the mode of production. Examples are: change from hunting and food gathering economy to settled agriculture, change from agriculture based economy to one based predominantly upon manufacturing and industry. Such changes, not only brought about the institution of social stratification, but in course of time also altered the principles of organization of social stratification. Economic advancement led to generation of more wealth in society, more accumulation of markers of wealth be it in the form of food grains or cattle, or metals and minerals (silver, gold precious stones etc.) or money. At this stage, the groups which had greater control over the economic resources and wealth or which possessed more wealth were ranked higher in society than groups which controlled less of it, or groups which had little or negligible access to wealth (for example, landless workers or industrial workers). The social stratification based on class is its prime example.

(3) Power: The third organising principle of social stratification is power, Unlike status and wealth which can be clearly linked with group characteristics of ranking in societies, the principle of power is a relatively diffused attribute because it is not exclusive in character. It is always possible that a group with higher status in society or that which enjoys greater wealth, also exercises more power in society. Nevertheless, one could make a distinction between say, principle of privileges where as the latter tends to be based on the group's ability to use coercive means for other group's conformity with actions, values and beliefs determined by it. The concept of power as Max Weber has discussed in his treatment of social stratification rests on the fact that it endows the persons or groups which have power to impose their will on other groups by legitimate use of coercive method. In this sense, state offers us a good example of an institution which has maximum power. It has sovereign authority to impose its will on citizens of the society. When legitimacy of exercise of power, is widely accepted by groups, in other words, when it is institutionalized in society, power becomes authority. Authority as a concept could be defined as legitimate power. Power as a principle also enters into the notion of social stratification when its functions or its social ramifications begin to be influenced by the political processes in society, and when state begins to take more active or direct role in influencing the principles of social stratification. A relevant example of this could be found in the policy of positive discrimination or reservation of jobs, political offices and entry into educational institutions in our country by the state in favour of castes and tribes now declared as 'scheduled' or as 'other backward classes'. Max Weber, in his treatment of power as an element in the formation of social stratification has rightly emphasised the significance of politics, political parties and their role in optimizing their access to power.

Q6. Discuss N. Luhmann's systems theory of social stratification.
Refer to Chapter-2, Q.No.-7 (Pg. No.-33)

Q7. Discuss the role of Jyotirao Phule in the Backward Classes Movement.

Ans. The rise of the non-Brahmins under the leadership of crusaders against social injustice mainly from the intermediate castes represents a landmark development. It was reflective of a determined resistance to perpetuation of the traditionally legitimised inequality. Jyoti Rao Govind Rao Phule made the first attempt to form a Bahujan Samaj in Maharashtra to challenge tile supremacy of the Brahmins who constituted the privileged few dominating the socio-economic political contours of the state. Phule himself a Shudra questioned the dominance of Brahmins in the colonial dispensation. His opposition to the caste system found articulation in his efforts to raise a new social order based on truth reason and equality. He initiated a movement to discard the services of Brahmins in the religious ceremonies of the non-Brahmins as he regarded them to be the unwanted middlemen between the people and the God.

The non-brahmanical movement was accorded institutionalisation in the programmes of the Satya Shodhak Samaj founded by Phule. He considered Brahminism as cunning and self-seeking and condemned it as intolerable imposition to ensure the perpetuation of the high in the caste hierarchy. The "dominant agricultural castes' that formed the core and support of this movement subsequently ushered were very pro Congress. Phule's interpretation of lower caste exploitation ignored the economic and political contexts. Exploitation was interpreted in terms of cultural and ethnicity. Phule however stressed the need for return to pre-Brahmin religious tradition. Organisation and education were considered essential for attainment of such goals. He opposed the exploitation of Indian peasants and wage earners. Similar outbursts appeared elsewhere also.

Now, Refer to Chapter-6, Q.No.-3 (Pg. No.-109)

Q8. What are the important features of the caste system?
Refer to Chapter-5, Q.No.-9 (Pg. No.-104)

Q9. Examine Marriott's approach to the understanding of caste hierarchy.
Refer to Chapter-5, Q.No.-6 (Pg. No.-96)

Q10. Explain the concept of 'middle class'.

Ans. For Marx, in the middle classes were the self-employed peasants and the petty bourgeoisie. They were so described because they continued to own the means of production they worked with, without employing wage labour. Marx predicted that these middle classes were destined to disappear as the capitalist system of production developed. Only the two major classes, proletariat or the working class and the bourgeoisie or the capitalist class were significant in the Marxian framework of class relations.

The other theorists of class have assigned much more significance to the 'middle classes'. Foremost of these have been sociologists like Max Weber, Dahrendorf and Lockwood.

A crucial distinction is made in the sociological literature between the "old" middle classes and the "new" middle classes. The term "old" middle class is used in the sense in which Marx had used the term "petty-bourgeoisie" i.e. those who work with their own means of production such as traders, independent professionals and farmers. The term "new" middle class is broadly used to describe the skilled or white-collared workers/salaried employees and the self-employed professionals. Even though they do not own the means of production they work with, they are distinguished from the unskilled blue-collar workers. Their incomes being much higher than that of the blue-collar workers, they can lead a lifestyle that is very different from that of the working class.

Q11. Explain the agrarian class structure in India.

Refer to Chapter-7, Q.No.-1 (Pg. No.-129)

Q12. How are gender identities constructed? Explain with suitable examples.

Refer to Chapter-4, Q.No.-4 (Pg. No.-76)

SECTION III

Answer any ***two*** *of the following questions in about 100 words each.*

Q13. What do you understand by social mobility?

Refer to Chapter-8, Q.No.-4 (Pg. No.-145)

Q14. What is the difference between 'class' and 'status'?

Refer to Chapter-1, Q.No.-7 (Pg. No.-14)

Q15. Explain the concept of 'power elite'.

Refer to June-2009, Q.No.-14 (Pg. No.-185)

ESO-14: SOCIETY AND STRATIFICATION
December, 2018

Note: This question paper has **three** *sections. Attempt the questions as instructed in each section.*

SECTION I

Answer any two of the following questions in about 500 words each.

Q1. Discuss the conflict approach to the understanding of social stratification.

Q2. Discuss the relationship between ethnicity and stratification.

Q3. Explain the constitutional provisions for the upliftment of Scheduled Castes.

Q4. How did the studies of stratification address the gender question? Discuss critically.

SECTION II

Answer any four of the following questions in about 250 words each.

Q5. Outline Berghe's theory of social stratification.

Q6. Discuss the role of tribal elites in society.

Q7. What do you understand by 'embourgeoisement'? What is its relation with social mobility?

Q8. In what way do the notions of purity and pollution determine caste hierarchy?

Q9. Discuss the relationship between caste and class.

Q10. Discuss the role of social institutions in gender construction.

Q11. Explain the notion of undifferentiated peasant societies.

Q12. Discuss the agrarian class structure in India.

SECTION III

Answer any two of the following questions in about 100 words each.

Q13. What do you understand by 'decomposition of labour'?

Q14. What is the difference between 'old middle class' and 'new middle class'?

Q15. Explain Shanin's notion of 'ideal type' of peasant society.

ESO-14: SOCIETY AND STRATIFICATION
June, 2019

Note: This question paper has ***three*** *sections. Attempt the questions as instructed in each section.*

SECTION I

Answer any two of the following questions in about 500 words each.

Q1. Explain the functional approach to the understanding of social stratification.

Q2. Who are the Minorities? Explain the main features of minority group.

Q3. What do you understand by Ethnicity? Elaborate with suitable examples.

Q4. Critically discuss the bases of gender inequality in India.

SECTION II

Answer any four of the following questions in about 250 words each.

Q5. Discuss Karl Marx's perspective on social stratification.

Q6. Is caste an empirical reality? Discuss.

Q7. What did Shanin mean, by ideal type of a peasant society?

Q8. Explain the relationship between class and social mobility.

Q9. How are gender identities formed? Discuss.

Q10. Explain the role of middle class in India's freedom struggle.

Q11. Discuss the features of urban working class in India.

Q12. What are the main features of caste system identified by G. S. Ghurye?

SECTION III

Answer any two of the following questions in about 100 words each.

Q13. What do you understand by 'Life Chances'?

Q14. Explain the concept of dominant caste.

Q15. What do you understand by 'Status'?

Q16. What is 'Class-Conflict'?

www.ingramcontent.com/pod-product-compliance
Ingram Content Group UK Ltd.
Pitfield, Milton Keynes, MK11 3LW, UK
UKHW021703190726
13853UKWH00001B/405

9 789381 690260